Dec

To Lynn and Bill

Bon Appétit!

Your friends,

Susan and Rudolf

Books by Helen Hecht

CUISINE FOR ALL SEASONS   (1983)

COLD CUISINE   (1981)

GIFTS IN GOOD TASTE   (1979)
(with Linda LaBate Mushlin)

CUISINE
FOR
ALL
SEASONS

CUISINE
FOR
ALL
SEASONS

A Menu Cookbook

HELEN HECHT

Atheneum

NEW YORK

1983

Some of the
recipes in this
book appeared
originally in
Vogue and *Cuisine.*

Library of Congress Cataloging in Publication Data

Hecht, Helen.
    Cuisine for all seasons.

    Includes index.
    1. Cookery.   2. Menus.   I. Title.
TX715.H399   1983   641.5'64   82–73033
ISBN 0–689–11351–X

Published simultaneously in Canada by McClelland and Stewart Ltd.
Composition by Maryland Linotype Composition Co., Inc.
Baltimore, Maryland
Printed and bound by Fairfield Graphics, Fairfield, Pennsylvania
Designed by Kathleen Carey
First Edition

With a lifetime of love and gratitude

to my mother,

who has always been there to help

Acknowledgments

I am grateful to many for generous help with this book: my editor, Judith Kern, and designer, Kathleen Carey; and Vee Angle, Miggie Baum, Yvonne Gaudriot, Mark and Mary Bryan Leithauser, Eleanor McQuilkin, Emilie Menguy, Susan Whitbourne O'Brien, U. T. Summers, and Martha Weissberger. And special thanks to my husband, Tony, and my son, Evan, who help me every day.

Contents

FALL

WINTER

SPRING

SUMMER

Introduction

Each time of year has its own unique pleasures, not the least of them the fresh foods that appear and disappear as the months come and go. I find myself measuring the seasons by what is currently in stock on the grocer's shelves. Even if the ground is piled with snow so deep that no groundhog could burrow its way out, I know it's spring when I see asparagus and strawberries in the market. It is summer when roadside stalls, boarded up or carted away for winter, are once more open and bursting with corn, beans, berries, and every kind of fruit. And as suddenly as the supply of tomatoes and peaches diminishes, chestnuts, fat white fennel bulbs, and Caravaggio quince and pears appear to announce the fall. My own way of appreciating each season is to plan meals around whatever fresh foods are currently available, and I find that every month of the year offers new cause for culinary festivity.

This cookbook contains menus for a variety of occasions throughout the year, from informal lunches and suppers for a small group of friends to elaborate dinner parties for twelve. Each menu has a particular seasonal reference, in its use of fresh foods as well as in the nature of the meal. The sort of food we desire in each season often coincides with what is actually available. The variety of fruit, vegetables, and seafood in spring and summer anticipates the light, simple meals appropriate in hot weather. When it is cold and blustery outdoors, we are likely to depend more heavily on the comfort and warmth of a hearty soup or steaming casserole. Substantial main dishes, complemented by root vegetables and fresh-baked breads, are so suitable in winter that we scarcely notice the dearth of fruit and green vegetables.

Several of the recipes included here require a minimum of preparation. Many fresh foods, particularly fish and summer vegetables, are at their best when cooked simply, with little more elaboration than butter, lemon juice, and herbs. Whenever possible, recipes are distinguished by complementary and often unexpected combinations of foods. The flavor of a cold beet soup is enhanced by the addition of fresh gingerroot. A tomato soup borrows interest from a discreet touch of fresh peaches. A dark chocolate roll is filled with a tart lemon mousse. Chicken scaloppine are sautéed with fresh artichoke bottoms; both are delicate in flavor, but they contrast in texture. A simple and novel appetizer consists of alternate slices of avocado and Bosc pears sprinkled with fresh mint and a lime vinaigrette. The menus attempt to balance a variety of factors, including color, flavor, texture, and richness. They are, of course, meant as guidelines from which you may depart at will.

Seasonal dining is more than a matter of taste and economy. Needless to say, most foods taste better fresh than when old, canned, or frozen. (There are certainly exceptions: canned tomatoes are a winter staple; and preserved marrons, ginger, jams, and chutneys are also culinary blessings.) An excessive use of packaged foods, however, has undermined a simple and natural cuisine and disrupted our sense of the cyclical order of nature. The menus in this collection are intended to celebrate the variety, bounty, and virtues of fresh foods in their own good and proper season.

Notes on Ingredients

AMARETTI   Hard Italian macaroons flavored with bitter almonds and available at specialty food shops.

AMARETTO   Almond flavored liqueur imported from Italy.

ARUGOLA   An Italian salad green (also called rucola or rugula), available at special greengrocers. Its English name is garden rocket, and it tastes something like watercress but not as sharp.

CALAMATA OLIVES   Black Greek olives available in delicatessens. They are not as bitter as most imported olives.

CASSIS SYRUP   The syrup is fresher and purer in flavor than crème de cassis (a liqueur) and is usually preferred. A good brand is Cassis Vedrenne, imported from France and available in specialty food shops and some gourmet departments.

CHEVRE CHEESE   A French cheese, made from goat's milk. Varieties with a rind should be used when firm and white; if they are overripe, they have a strong, unpleasant flavor. Rindless chèvre, such as Montrachet, has a milder flavor and a crumbly texture.

CHIVES   When these are not available, the tender green inner tops of scallions may be substituted.

DUCK   Fresh ducks are now widely available in supermarkets. I do not recommend buying frozen ducks, as they are likely to be tough and dry if they have been frozen for a long time.

EGGS   Recipes are based on USDA-graded large eggs.

FENNEL   A plant with edible stalks that, like celery, may be eaten raw or cooked as a vegetable or as a base for a soup. It has a delicate anise flavor. The ferns may be used as an herb, and the seeds are used in flavoring.

FLOUR   Unless otherwise specified, all-purpose flour is intended, preferably unbleached.

GINGER   *Fresh gingerroot* is available in the produce departments of most grocery stores. *Crystallized ginger* is candied ginger, packed dry in tins or boxes or sold loose. *Preserved ginger stem* consists of whole pieces of ginger in syrup. It is packed in jars and sold in gourmet departments. *Ginger preserves* is a jam, packed in jars and available in many supermarkets.

LEMON OR LIME JUICE   Always use fresh.

OLIVE OIL   Use a light, good quality imported oil; those from Lucca, Italy, are very good.

QUINCE   A hard, apple-like fruit but with a distinctive flavor suggestive of pineapple. It is edible only when cooked and used chiefly in jellies, preserves, and pies. Ripe quinces are completely yellow, not green.

SALT   The amount of salt required is rarely specified in a recipe, as this is a matter of individual habit and taste.

TOMATOES   When fresh tomatoes are specified, only ripe, locally grown, vine-ripened tomatoes should be used. When these are not in season, good quality canned tomatoes (usually imported Italian) are good for soups, stews, and sauces.

ZEST   The aromatic rind of a citrus fruit. When grating rind, use only the colored outer part and none of the bitter white pith. Be cautious in selecting oranges for grating as some have a particularly bitter rind. California navel and Florida temple oranges generally have rinds that are less bitter than those of other varieties.

A List of Recipes by Category

APPETIZERS AND HORS D'OEUVRES

Artichoke Salad
Asparagus Vinaigrette
Avocado and Shrimp Cocktail
Baked Fennel and Chèvre
Beef and Orange Consommé
Beet and Claret Soup
Bombay Ice
Celery and Gorgonzola Soup
Cheese and Onion Tart
Chestnut Soup
Chèvre Soufflé
Chilled Beet Soup
Chilled Tomato and Peach Soup
Country Pâté
Deviled Eggs
Fondue Croustades
Gnocchi Verdi
Ham Cornucopias
Insalata Caprese
Insalata di Mare
Istanbul Artichokes
Jellied Beet Soup
Jerusalem Artichoke Soup

Lemon-Parsley Ice
Miggie's Mushroom-Tarragon Soup
Mint Canapés
Minted Pears Vinaigrette
Mushroom Antipasto
Mushroom Caps with Garlic Shrimp
Mushroom Consommé
Mushroom Croustades
Mushroom Timbales
Mussel and Rice Salad
Mussels Rémoulade
Parmesan Toast Strips
Pear and Fennel Soup
Prosciutto and Pears
Roast Peppers with Feta Cheese and Olives
Sautéed Mushrooms
Sorrel and Mint Soup
Tomato and Chèvre Salad
Tomato-Burgundy Soup
Tomato-Ginger Soup
Tomato-Mint Soup

ENTREES

Alsatian Omelet
Beefsteak and Kidney Pie
Carbonnades de Boeuf
Ceylon Coconut Shrimp
Cheese and Onion Tart
Chèvre Soufflé
Chicken and Artichokes in Lemon-Anchovy Sauce
Chicken Cathay
Chicken Curry
Chicken Hadrian
Chicken Malcontenta
Cold Curried Shrimp
Cold Salmon with Scallop Mousse Stuffing

Country Pâté
Curried Lamb
Dolma with Chestnuts and Quince
Duck with Pears
Filets in Filo
Fusilli d'Estate
Game Hens with Celeriac Stuffing
Game Hens with Chicken Liver Sauce
Game Hens with Mushroom Pâté
Greek Shrimp
Greek Tart
Ham Flavored with Port, Apple, and Apricot
Insalata di Pasta Verde
Java Beef Stew
Lake Trout with Sorrel Sauce
Lapin à la Moutarde
Leg of Lamb with Green Peppercorn and Mint Sauce
Leg of Lamb with Mushroom, Spinach, and Prosciutto Stuffing
Lime and Honey Glazed Duck with Mango
Linguine Cornaro
Linguine with Smoked Salmon
Mango Chicken Salad
Mesopotamian Meatballs
Moroccan Lamb with Couscous
Mulligatawny Soup
Mussel and Rice Salad
Paglia e Fieno Barbaro
Pork, Pear, and Fennel Stew
Pork with Fig and Chestnut Stuffing
Ratatouille with Fusilli and Feta Cheese
Roast Beef Salad on French Bread
Roast Beef with Orange-Madeira Sauce
Salmon Fillets with Two Sauces
Sautéed Shrimp and Scallops with Cappelletti
Seafood Risotto
Senegalese Soup
Shad with Roe and Asparagus Mousse Filling
Spareribs with Barbecue Sauce

VEGETABLES, SALADS, AND SIDE DISHES

Potato-Cheese Galette
Potatoes with Hazelnut Stuffing
Puréed Beets
Puréed Parsnips
Puréed Spinach
Rice Salad
Root Vegetable Purée
Sautéed Zucchini
Sliced Beets with Garlic-Crumb Topping
Spinach, Cheese, and Mushroom Casserole
Steamed Fiddleheads
Tomato and Avocado Salad
Tomato, Cucumber, and Onion Salad
Tomatoes Provençale
Tomatoes Stuffed with Spinach
Watercress, Mushroom, and Endive Salad
Wild Rice with Mushrooms

DESSERTS

Apple and Quince Crisp
Apple-Custard Tart
Apricot Florentines
Baked Bananas with Curaçao
Bellini Sorbet
Blueberries and Green Grapes in Lemon Yogurt
Blueberry Sorbet
Bûche de Noel au Citron
Chocolate-Almond Cookies
Chocolate-Amaretti Cake
Chocolate-Lemon Layer Cake
Chocolate-Marron Cake
Coffee-Amaretto Ice Cream
Cranberry-Cassis Ice
Crêpes Aquitaine
Frozen Honey and Almond Torte
Frozen Raspberry Mousse with Nut Crunch

A Word About Salads

A composed salad or a special marinated vegetable such as Asparagus Vinaigrette may be an appropriate appetizer, but a green salad is not. When you are famished, there is nothing more dispiriting than to be confronted with a bowl of iceberg lettuce, which must be taken dutifully like a tonic before the meal. It is my impression that this practice began about ten years ago in "family" restaurants and has been spreading ever since, although many Europeans assume it to be a long-established American custom with obscure origins. Most Americans, however, were brought up with the notion that salads should follow the entrée; or, on informal occasions, accompany it.

The best green salads, in my opinion, are simple and uncluttered, include arugola or watercress, and are dressed in a light vinaigrette. But should you be inclined recklessly to fill the salad bowl with whatever catches your eye, beware of the implications. The following classification of salads according to social rank may restrain and guide you. It is taken from *The Tastemakers*,* Russell Lynes' commentary on American society.

High-Brow: Greens, olive oil, wine vinegar, ground salt, ground pepper, garlic, unwashed salad bowl

Upper Middle-Brow: Same as High-Brow, but with tomatoes, avocado, Roquefort cheese added

Lower Middle-Brow: Quartered iceberg lettuce and store dressing

Low-Brow: Coleslaw

* Russell Lynes, *The Tastemakers: The Development of American Popular Taste.* Dover, 1980.

A Note on the Menus and Advance Preparation

When a dish appears on more than one menu, the page reference for the recipe is given after that item on the menu page.

A dagger after an item on the menu page indicates that no recipe appears in the book. Recipes are not given for basic dishes, requiring little or no preparation, such as green salad, French bread, or fresh fruit.

A rough schedule for each menu indicates when advance preparation is possible. Many of the recipes in this book may be prepared a day before serving. Frozen desserts and appetizer sorbets may be made several days ahead. Homemade pasta, breads, and stock bases for soup may be stored successfully in the freezer, but I do not recommend freezing other foods, such as soups and stews. Such prepared dishes invariably lose quality after freezing.

Please note that the recipes for ice creams, ices, and other frozen desserts in this book do not require an ice cream machine.

FALL

A Farmhouse Lunch

ROAST PEPPERS WITH FETA CHEESE
AND OLIVES (page 9)

ALSATIAN OMELET

BACON†

TOMATOES PROVENÇALE

GREEN SALAD†

APPLE-CUSTARD TART (page 14)

OR

FRESH FRUIT†

T H I S is the sort of earthy, rustic lunch you might serve to week-end guests or to friends who gather at your house after an outing in the country. It is an unpretentious meal, featuring dishes that are pure and robust in flavor without the benefit of kitchen artifice. The meal begins with marinated roasted peppers garnished with black olives and feta cheese. The Alsatian Omelet is composed chiefly of sautéed onions and accompanied by baked tomatoes and bacon. A simple green salad—perhaps Boston lettuce and watercress vinaigrette—should follow, with an Apple-Custard Tart for dessert, or fresh fruit, if you prefer.

Advance Preparation   The Roast Peppers and the Apple-Custard Tart may be made a day before serving. The onions for the omelet and the Tomatoes Provençale may be prepared several hours in advance, but both must be cooked just before serving.

ALSATIAN OMELET

This "omelet" is really a dish of sautéed onions with a light binding of beaten eggs.

4 tablespoons unsalted butter   *4 eggs*
2 tablespoons vegetable oil   *1 teaspoon Dijon mustard*
2 pounds yellow onions,   *¼ teaspoon Worcestershire*
   peeled and sliced   *sauce*
¼ cup fresh-grated Parmesan   *Salt*
   cheese   *Fresh-ground pepper*

FOR THE GARNISH

Watercress

Melt 2 tablespoons of the butter with the oil in a very large skillet. Add the onions and cook over medium heat, stirring occasionally, until they are quite soft but not brown. Lower the heat, cover the pan, and continue cooking until the onions are a light amber color. Uncover and cook over high heat, stirring, for a few seconds to evaporate any moisture. Remove from the heat and stir in the Parmesan cheese.

Beat the eggs lightly, adding the mustard, Worcestershire, and seasoning to taste. Melt the remaining butter in an 8-inch skillet. When it is foaming, add the eggs and cook for a minute. Carefully spoon the onions over the eggs in an even layer. Turn up the heat and cook until the eggs are set and slightly browned on the bottom, but still very moist on top. (The omelet will continue to cook after it is removed from the heat.)

Cut into quarters and serve immediately, garnishing each serving with watercress.

YIELD: 4 SERVINGS

TOMATOES PROVENÇALE

Baked tomatoes with a heady topping of garlic, basil, and Parmesan.

4 large tomatoes
Salt
2 small or 1 large garlic
   clove, peeled and pressed
2 tablespoons minced shallot
½ cup minced fresh basil

6 tablespoons fresh-grated
   Parmesan cheese
½ cup fine, dry bread
   crumbs
1 tablespoon lemon juice
2 tablespoons olive oil

Preheat the oven to 400°.

Core the tomatoes, cut each in half crosswise, and scoop out the seeds with a demitasse spoon. Salt each cut half. Combine the remaining ingredients in a bowl and spread the mixture on top of the tomato halves. Place them close together in a buttered baking dish, and drizzle a little extra olive oil over each tomato. Bake for 15 minutes.

YIELD: 4 SERVINGS

A Fall Picnic

MUSHROOM CONSOMMÉ

OR

TOMATO-BURGUNDY SOUP (page 130)

ROAST BEEF SALAD ON FRENCH BREAD

ROAST PEPPERS WITH FETA CHEESE

AND OLIVES

DEVILED EGGS

FRESH FRUIT AND COOKIES†

I N Rochester, as in New England, the autumn foliage is always a brilliant and spectacular display, meriting a special excursion. We drive into the country through the Bristol Hills west of Lake Canandaigua, hike briefly in the woods if we're feeling energetic, eat a picnic lunch, and stop at an apple farm on the way home to pick up a gallon of cider, a bag of apples, and perhaps a pumpkin. Since early October days are likely to be both sunny and brisk, the picnic begins with a steaming soup, kept hot in a thermos. The roast beef salad is served on small French baguettes. The Roast Peppers, garnished with feta cheese and black olives, are a colorful autumnal accompaniment. I like to include deviled eggs on picnics, and in this case they go particularly well with the roast beef. Conclude the meal with fresh fruit and picnic cookies.

Advance Preparation   Either soup, as well as the Roast Peppers, may be made a day or two before the picnic. The Roast Beef Salad and Deviled Eggs should be made the day of the picnic. Fill the baguettes with the salad just before packing.

MUSHROOM CONSOMMÉ

An invigorating hot soup for chilly weather, subtly flavored with Madeira and chutney.

1 pound mushrooms, cleaned and trimmed
2 tablespoons unsalted butter
2 tablespoons minced shallot
1 garlic clove, peeled and minced
5 cups strong beef stock or broth

2 tablespoons liquid from a jar of Major Grey's chutney, preferably Sun Brand
Fresh-ground pepper
¼ cup Madeira

Chop the mushrooms fine in a food processor, a handful at a time. Melt the butter in a large skillet and sauté the mushrooms, shallot, and garlic over medium heat until the mushrooms render their juices. Stir in the beef stock, chutney juice, and pepper. Cover the pan tightly and simmer for 10 minutes. Add the Madeira and reheat before serving.

YIELD: APPOXIMATELY 6 CUPS

ROAST BEEF SALAD ON FRENCH BREAD

¾ pound rare roast beef,
   sliced thin
⅔ cup minced red onion
½ cup chopped, pitted black
   olives
⅔ cup peeled, seeded, and
   chopped cucumber
¼ cup minced fresh parsley
2 tablespoons capers, well
   drained

1 cup mayonnaise
2 tablespoons plus 2 teaspoons
   Düsseldorf mustard
6 small baguettes, about
   6 inches long, preferably
   Pepperidge Farm Brown
   & Serve or homemade
Watercress

Cut the roast beef into ½-inch squares and combine with the onion, olives, cucumber, parsley, and capers. Mix the mayonnaise and mustard together and combine about ⅔ of it with the salad, reserving the rest to spread on the rolls.

If using Pepperidge Farm rolls, brown according to package directions. Cut along the top depression of each roll, diagonally down toward the bottom without cutting through, to make an opening for the stuffing. Spread the inside of each roll with some of the reserved dressing and fill with the salad. Tuck sprigs of watercress along the length of each roll between the filling and the bread.

YIELD: 6 SERVINGS

ROAST PEPPERS WITH FETA CHEESE AND OLIVES

*2 pounds mixed red and
green sweet peppers
(6 medium)
⅓ cup small pitted black
olives
2 tablespoons capers
2 tablespoons minced fresh
parsley or basil*

*2 tablespoons chopped
scallions
1 garlic clove, peeled and
cut in half
3 tablespoons olive oil
2 teaspoons wine vinegar
½ cup feta cheese, cut into
½-inch cubes*

Place the peppers on a baking tin under the broiler about 2 inches from the heat. Roast, turning the peppers as the skins blacken, until charred on all sides. This will take 10 to 15 minutes. Peel under cold running water. Remove the stems and seeds and cut into 1½-inch wide strips. Leave in a colander to drain.

Combine the drained peppers, the olives, capers, parsley or basil, scallions, and garlic clove with the oil and vinegar and allow to marinate several hours. Remove the garlic clove and add the feta cheese before serving.

YIELD: 6 SERVINGS

DEVILED EGGS

This is a creamy and flavorful formula for deviled eggs. I prefer to use the smaller eggs, classified as "medium," because they are less filling. If you use large eggs, increase the other ingredients slightly and boil the eggs a minute longer.

6 medium-size eggs
3 tablespoons mayonnaise
1 tablespoon plus 2 teaspoons sour cream
1 teaspoon Dijon mustard
¼ teaspoon Worcestershire sauce

A pinch of dried dill weed or ¼ teaspoon fresh
1 tablespoon capers (optional)
Fresh-ground black pepper

Place the eggs in a saucepan, cover with water, bring to a boil, and boil gently for 9 minutes. Remove from the heat, drain, and run ice-cold water over them until they are cool. Gently crack the shell of each egg and peel. Slice in half lengthwise and empty the yolks into a mixing bowl. Mash the yolks thoroughly with a fork until smooth and then mix in the remaining ingredients. Mound this mixture into the egg-white halves, cover with plastic wrap and refrigerate. (Pack them in an egg carton to carry on a picnic.)

YIELD: 12 DEVILED EGG HALVES

A Fireside Supper

PARMESAN TOAST STRIPS

MULLIGATAWNY SOUP

FRENCH BREAD[†]

GREEN SALAD[†]

APPLE-CUSTARD TART

COLD weather has its compensations, although it is sometimes difficult to call them to mind. A veteran of long Rochester winters, where a persistent damp chill and a covering of snow are to be expected by mid-November, I feel I have some advice to pass on. Nothing is more comforting than a bowl of hearty soup and a brisk fire, usually taken together. This is a plain, no-fuss, but satisfying meal to be shared with friends while relaxing by the hearth: Parmesan Toast Strips to serve with drinks; a curried chicken soup; plenty of warm French bread; salad; and an Apple-Custard Tart for dessert.

Advance Preparation The Parmesan Toast Strips may be made several days before serving. The Mulligatawny Soup may be made a day or two ahead, and the Apple-Custard Tart the day before the party.

PARMESAN TOAST STRIPS

These cheese toasts are ideal cocktail fare—simple and not too filling. They can be made in quantity in dry weather and, if stored in airtight tins, will keep fresh and crisp for several days.

> *3 tablespoons unsalted butter*
> *1 garlic clove, peeled and cut in half*
> *12 slices "very-thin" white bread, preferably Pepperidge Farm*
> *¾ cup fresh-grated Parmesan cheese**

Preheat the oven to 350°.

Melt the butter with the garlic clove in a small saucepan or stainless steel measuring cup. Lightly brush a large baking tin with melted butter. Trim the crusts off the bread and cut each slice into 4 long strips. Arrange side by side on the baking sheet without any space between the strips. Using a pastry brush, coat the surface of the bread with melted butter. Sprinkle the cheese evenly over the bread. (There should be a thick layer.) Bake on the middle rack of the oven for 18 to 20 minutes, or until very crisp and well-browned around the edges. (Do not take them out too soon or they will be tough and chewy.) Transfer to a wire rack to cool thoroughly. When cool, separate into individual strips and store in airtight tins. Serve at room temperature.

YIELD: 48 PIECES

* Do not substitute Cheddar or any cheese with a higher moisture content.

MULLIGATAWNY SOUP

A hearty main-course chicken curry soup, flavored with quince, tomato, ginger, and coconut.

One 3-pound chicken, cut up
1 tablespoon vegetable oil
1 tablespoon unsalted butter
2 large carrots, scraped and sliced thin
2 large celery stalks, sliced thin
2 cups chopped onion
3 garlic cloves, peeled and minced
1 pound plum tomatoes, peeled, seeded, and chopped coarse
3 tablespoons flour

1 tablespoon curry powder
7 cups chicken stock or broth
½ cup tomato purée
2 large quinces (1 pound), peeled, cored, and chopped fine
¾ cup grated fresh coconut
Liquid from a fresh coconut
1½ teaspoons grated fresh gingerroot
1 large quince, peeled, cored, and cut into ¼-inch-thick slices*

Sauté the chicken pieces in the oil and butter in a large, deep casserole, until lightly browned. Transfer to a platter and reserve. Add the carrot, celery, onion, and garlic to the pan and sauté for about 5 minutes. Add the tomatoes, flour, and curry powder, stirring to blend. Add 2 cups of the chicken stock and bring to a boil, stirring until thickened. Lower the heat, add the remaining chicken stock, the tomato purée, chopped quince, coconut, coconut liquid, and gingerroot. Return the chicken pieces to the pot. Bring to a simmer and cook uncovered for 20 minutes. Remove the chicken with a slotted spoon and reserve. Skim the fat and any scum off the surface of the soup, and continue cooking for 30 to 40 minutes longer.

Strip the skin and bones off the chicken and discard. Cut the chicken into strips approximately 2 inches long and ½ inch wide.

---

* A tart cooking apple may be substituted if quince is not available.

Add to the soup with the sliced quince and simmer for no longer than 5 minutes. (The fruit should remain crisp. If you are substituting an apple, cook for only 1 or 2 minutes.)

YIELD: 6 ENTRÉE SERVINGS

APPLE-CUSTARD TART

A filling of crisp fall apples baked in a subtly flavored maple custard.

FOR THE TART CRUST

1 ½ cups unsifted flour

2 tablespoons sugar

Grated zest of 1 small lemon

5 tablespoons unsalted butter, chilled and cut into small pieces

3 tablespoons vegetable shortening, chilled

2–3 tablespoons cold water

FOR THE FILLING

1 pound tart apples (3 small to medium)

2 eggs

½ cup pure maple syrup

⅓ cup heavy cream

1 ½ tablespoons brandy

FOR THE GLAZE

2 tablespoons pure maple syrup

To make the tart crust, combine the flour, sugar, and lemon zest in a large mixing bowl. Rub in the butter and shortening with the tips of your fingers, combining until the mixture resembles coarse meal. Add just enough cold water to form into a dough. Knead one or two turns, wrap the dough in wax paper, and refrigerate until firm enough to roll out.

Preheat the oven to 375°. Between 2 sheets of lightly floured wax paper, roll out the dough into a circle large enough to line a 9-inch tart pan. Fit the dough into the pan, doubling it at the sides. Line the inside of the tart shell with aluminum foil and fill with uncooked rice or beans. Bake in the middle of the oven for 20 minutes. Remove the foil and rice and cool on a wire rack before filling. Do not turn off the oven.

To make the filling, peel, quarter, and core the apples, and slice them about ⅛ inch thick. Arrange a circle of closely overlapping apple slices around the outer edge and a small circle in the center of the tart shell. Bake for 20 minutes. While the tart is baking, beat the eggs lightly and stir in the maple syrup, cream, and brandy. After the tart has cooked for 20 minutes, carefully pour the custard into the shell and bake for an additional 20 to 25 minutes, or until the custard is set and the apples are tender. Remove from the oven and transfer to a wire rack.

To glaze the tart, put the maple syrup in a stainless steel measuring cup, bring to a simmer and cook very gently until thickened. Lightly brush the apples and the edge of the crust with the maple glaze. Serve warm. If you are preparing the tart ahead, reheat it for 10 minutes in a 350° oven.

YIELD: 6 TO 8 SERVINGS

A Vegetarian Supper

CHÈVRE SOUFFLÉ

RATATOUILLE WITH FUSILLI AND
FETA CHEESE

OR

GREEK TART

GREEN SALAD†

APPLE AND QUINCE CRISP

A vegetarian meal need not be an occasion for hardship, nor must it involve some nourishing combination of beans and rice. The following menu is for a special vegetarian dinner, beginning with a cheese soufflé, an elegant introduction to any meal. Here the soufflé is made distinctive by the use of chèvre and a mild Graddost. Follow the soufflé with either of two substantial entrées: ratatouille combined with spiral pasta and feta cheese, or a colorful vegetable and feta tart. While the soufflé must be cooked just before serving, it will not be difficult if you have all the ingredients ready. Dessert is an Apple and Quince Crisp for a fine autumnal conclusion.

Advance Preparation The Ratatouille or the Greek Tart, as well as the Apple and Quince Crisp, may be made a day ahead and reheated before serving. The Chèvre Soufflé must be made just before serving.

CHÈVRE SOUFFLÉ

4 tablespoons unsalted butter
4 tablespoons flour
1 ⅓ cups scalded milk
5 egg yolks
2 ounces (½ cup) diced
  French chèvre*

3 ounces (¾ cup) grated
  Danish Graddost
Fresh-ground white pepper
6 egg whites
A pinch of cream of tartar

Preheat the oven to 400°. Adjust the oven shelf to the lowest level. Generously butter an 8-cup soufflé dish.

Melt the butter in a 2-quart saucepan over low heat. Add the flour and stir with a wire whisk. Pour in the scalded milk and whisk until well blended. Turn up the heat and cook for a minute or two, stirring continuously, until the mixture comes to a boil and thickens. Remove from the heat and stir in the egg yolks, one at a time. Add the cheeses and pepper and stir vigorously to blend.

Beat the egg whites until foamy. Add the cream of tartar and continue beating only until the whites hold soft peaks. (Do not allow them to dry out and become too stiff or it will be difficult to fold them into the cheese mixture.) Stir about ¼ of the beaten whites into the cheese base, and then carefully fold in the remaining egg whites. Turn into the prepared soufflé dish and set it on the lowest shelf of the oven. Turn the oven temperature down to 375° and bake for 35 to 40 minutes. When done, the soufflé will have risen about 3 inches above the rim of the dish and shrunk a bit from the sides. A knife inserted through the side of the soufflé and down into the center should test clean. Serve immediately.

YIELD: 6 SERVINGS AS AN APPETIZER; 4 AS AN ENTRÉE

---

* Use the firm French chèvre that has a Brie-like rind, such as Capritarn or Petite Cabrette. It should be firm, white, and not overripe.

RATATOUILLE WITH FUSILLI AND FETA CHEESE

This is a traditional Provençal ratatouille—that is, a Mediterranean vegetable casserole chiefly composed of eggplant, zucchini, and peppers—to which I have added small spiral-shaped pasta and feta cheese.

1 small eggplant (1 pound)
Salt
1 pound zucchini (2 medium)
3 tablespoons olive oil
2 teaspoons lemon juice
1 medium-size sweet green
*   pepper*
2 medium-size sweet red
*   peppers*
¾ pound yellow onions,
*   peeled and sliced thin*
2 large garlic cloves, peeled
*   and minced*
1 pound tomatoes, peeled,
*   seeded, and cut into*
*   ¾-inch strips*

1 cup pitted black olives,
*   preferably Calamata*
1 small jar capers, well-
*   drained*
¼ cup minced fresh parsley
1 ½ tablespoons minced
*   fresh basil or ½ teaspoon*
*   dried*
Fresh-ground pepper
¾ pound feta cheese
3 ounces (1 generous cup)
*   small fusilli (spiral-*
*   shaped pasta)*
¼ cup fresh-grated
*   Parmesan cheese*

Cut off and discard the ends of the eggplant. Slice the eggplant into strips about ½ inch thick and wide and 2½ to 3 inches long. Put into a colander, sprinkle heavily with salt, and toss to distribute. Place a weight on top of the eggplant and set in the sink to drain for a half hour or longer.

Slice the zucchini into strips about ¾ inch wide and thick and 3 inches long. Heat 1 tablespoon olive oil in a very large skillet. Add the zucchini, sprinkle with lemon juice, and stir-fry for about 5 minutes over high heat, or until tender but still firm. Turn into a colander to drain.

Core and seed the peppers and cut into lengthwise strips about

½ inch wide. Add another tablespoon of oil to the skillet and sauté the peppers gently for about 10 minutes. Add the onions and garlic (and more oil if the pan seems dry), and sauté until the onions are soft but not brown. Add the tomatoes and cook, stirring occasionally, for about 5 minutes, or until the moisture evaporates. Turn into an enameled or Pyrex casserole and reserve.

Rinse the eggplant well and dry with paper towels. Add another tablespoon oil to the skillet and cook the eggplant over high heat, stirring, to brown slightly. Lower the heat, cover the pan, and steam until tender. Uncover and cook until the moisture evaporates. Add to the onion and pepper mixture in the casserole. Mix in the zucchini, the olives, capers, parsley, basil, and pepper. Chop the feta cheese into ½ inch cubes and, if salty, put it in a colander and rinse under cold water. Drain well and add to the casserole.

Bring a very large pot of water to a boil. Add salt, a little vegetable oil, and the fusilli. Cook until tender but still firm. Drain well and combine with the vegetables in the casserole. Sprinkle the Parmesan over the top.

Preheat the oven to 350°. Bake the ratatouille, covered, for 15 minutes. Uncover and cook 15 minutes longer.

YIELD: 6 SERVINGS

GREEK TART

Composed of onions, red peppers, black olives, feta cheese, and parsley, this tart is colorful and robust in flavor.

FOR THE CRUST

1 ½ cups all-purpose flour
¼ teaspoon salt
5 tablespoons cold, unsalted butter, cut into small bits
3 tablespoons cold vegetable shortening
Approximately 3 tablespoons cold, dry white wine or water

FOR THE FILLING

2 tablespoons unsalted butter
¾ pound sweet red peppers
(3 small or 2 medium),
cored and cut into narrow
strips
1½ pounds yellow onions,
peeled and chopped
2 large garlic cloves, peeled
and minced

1 tablespoon flour
1 egg, lightly beaten
½ cup halved and pitted
Calamata olives
½ pound feta cheese, cut
into ½-inch dice
(1¾ cups)
3 tablespoons minced fresh
parsley

To make the crust, combine the flour and salt in a large mixing bowl. With the tips of your finger, quickly and lightly rub in the butter and shortening until the mixture resembles coarse meal. Add enough cold wine or water to form the mixture into a dough. Wrap in wax paper and refrigerate until firm enough to roll out.

Preheat the oven to 375°. Roll out the dough between 2 lightly floured sheets of wax paper and fit into a 9-inch tart pan. Line the pan with aluminum foil and fill with uncooked rice or beans. Bake for 15 to 20 minutes, or until dry but not colored. Remove the rice and foil and cool on a wire rack.

To make the filling, melt the butter in a large skillet. Add the peppers and sauté for 10 minutes over medium heat. Add the onions and garlic and continue cooking, stirring occasionally, until the vegetables are soft, but do not let them brown. Stir in the flour. Remove from the heat and cool to room temperature.

Preheat the oven to 375°. In a mixing bowl, combine the beaten egg with the onion-pepper mixture and the olives. Put the diced feta cheese into a sieve and rinse under cold water. Drain well. Stir the cheese and the parsley into the tart mixture. Turn into the tart shell and bake for 45 minutes.

YIELD: 6 SERVINGS

APPLE AND QUINCE CRISP

The combination of apples and quince, punctuated by bits of chopped walnut, give a slightly different character to this traditional apple crisp.

2 pounds Ida Red or other tart, crisp apples (5 medium)
1 tablespoon lemon juice
1 ¼ pounds quinces (3 medium)

2 tablespoons brown sugar, packed
½ teaspoon cinnamon
⅓ cup chopped walnuts

FOR THE TOPPING

6 tablespoons cold, unsalted butter, cut into small pieces
¾ cup flour
¾ cup brown sugar, packed

FOR THE GARNISH

1 cup heavy cream
1 tablespoon brandy
2 teaspoons sugar

Peel, core, and slice the apples ¼ inch thick. Mix in a bowl with the lemon juice. Peel and core the quince and cut out any brown or woody spots. Slice ⅛ inch thick. Mix with the brown sugar and combine with the apples. Sprinkle with the cinnamon and mix well.

In a 10-inch round, 2-quart baking dish, layer the apple-quince mixture alternately with the walnuts.

Preheat the oven to 350°.

Lightly mix all the ingredients for the topping in a large bowl, rubbing in the butter with the tips of your fingers, as for a pie crust. When the mixture is crumbly, spread it over the top of the apple mixture. Bake for about 40 minutes, or until the fruit is tender and the topping lightly browned.

Whip the cream lightly with the brandy and sugar, to the consistency of crème Chantilly.

Serve the dessert warm or at room temperature and pass the whipped cream separately.

YIELD: 6 TO 8 SERVINGS

A Fish Dinner in Early Fall

ARTICHOKE SALAD

SWORDFISH WITH FENNEL SAUCE

SAUTÉED ZUCCHINI

TOMATOES STUFFED WITH SPINACH

PEAR AND LEMON SHERBET

GOOD fish is one of the pleasures of summer and fall, and for most of us, swordfish ranks high among those creatures available in the North Atlantic. Fish steaks or fillets are ideal for entertaining, as they can be prepared with great ease and yet are elegant in their simplicity. Here the swordfish is cloaked in a delicately flavored fennel sauce and cooked briefly in a covered pan so that it does not dry out. Vegetables include stir-fried zucchini julienne and tomatoes stuffed with spinach that has been flavored with basil and pine nuts. The appetizer is a mixture of feta cheese, mozzarella, and artichokes in a vinaigrette. For dessert, a smooth and refreshing Pear and Lemon Sherbet.

Advance Preparation   The Pear and Lemon Sherbet may be made a few days before serving. The Artichoke Salad, the Fennel Sauce for the fish, and the Sautéed Zucchini may be prepared a day ahead. The Tomatoes Stuffed with Spinach may be made early on the day of the party and baked before serving.

ARTICHOKE SALAD

Artichoke hearts are combined with mozzarella and feta cheese, capers, and herbs, and marinated in a light vinaigrette.

FOR THE VINAIGRETTE

⅓ cup olive oil
1 tablespoon plus 2 teaspoons white wine vinegar
2 teaspoons lemon juice
1 large garlic clove, peeled and halved

1½ cups (½ pound) cooked artichoke hearts, fresh or frozen
4 ounces mozzarella cheese
4 ounces feta cheese
½ cup (generous) very thin-sliced celery

¼ cup minced fresh parsley
¼ cup minced fresh mint or basil leaves
2 tablespoons capers
Salt
Fresh-ground pepper

Combine the ingredients for the vinaigrette at least 1 hour before preparing the salad to allow time for the garlic to marinate.

Cut the artichoke hearts into ½-inch wedges. Cut the mozzarella into julienne strips. Rinse the feta cheese under cold water and crumble coarse. In a salad bowl, combine the artichokes, mozzarella, feta, celery, parsley, mint or basil, and capers. Add seasoning to taste. Discard the garlic clove and toss the vinaigrette with the salad. Serve chilled or at room temperature.

YIELD: 4 TO 5 SERVINGS

SWORDFISH WITH FENNEL SAUCE

This is a very delicately flavored sauce that is easy to make. It can be used on other fish such as sole and halibut.

FOR THE SAUCE

2 cups chopped fennel bulb
2 tablespoons minced shallot
1 large garlic clove, peeled
*   and minced*
2 tablespoons unsalted butter
½–⅔ cup fish stock or
*   bottled clam juice*

A large pinch of dried
*   tarragon*
Salt
Fresh-ground pepper
¼ cup heavy cream

FOR THE SWORDFISH

2 pounds swordfish, about 1 inch thick, cut into 4 steaks
2 tablespoons unsalted butter
2 tablespoons lemon juice
1 teaspoon dried tarragon
Fresh-ground pepper

FOR THE GARNISH

Minced fennel ferns

To make the sauce, sauté the fennel, shallot, and garlic in the butter for a few minutes over low heat. Add ½ cup of the fish stock or clam juice, cover the pan tightly, and simmer for 10 to 15 minutes, or until the fennel is tender. Drain, reserving the stock, and purée in a food processor, adding the reserved stock in a thin stream. Turn into a stainless steel or enameled saucepan and add the tarragon and pepper. If preparing the sauce in advance, stop at this point. Just before serving, stir in the cream and heat gently, stirring. If the sauce is too thick, add a little more fish stock.

To cook the fish, preheat the oven to 375°. Oil the bottom of a baking dish, put the fish in, dot with butter, sprinkle with the lemon juice and tarragon, and season with pepper. Cover the pan tightly with aluminum foil and bake for 20 minutes, or just until the fish is cooked through. Do not overcook, or it will be dry. Spoon the fennel sauce over the top of the swordfish and garnish with minced fennel ferns.

YIELD: 4 SERVINGS

SAUTÉED ZUCCHINI

The zucchini is cut into julienne and briefly stir-fried so that it retains its crispness. It may be prepared ahead and reheated before serving.

> *1 pound small, firm zucchini, washed but not peeled*
> *1 tablespoon unsalted butter*
> *Salt*
> *Fresh-ground pepper*
> *1 tablespoon lemon juice*

Sliver the zucchini into julienne strips, about 3 inches long and ¼ inch thick and wide.

Melt the butter to foaming in a large skillet. Add the zucchini; season with salt, plenty of pepper, and lemon juice. Turn up the heat and cook, stirring and tossing constantly, for just a few minutes, until the zucchini is tender but still firm and crisp. Be careful not to overcook it. Transfer to a warm oval serving dish with a slotted spoon.

If you double this recipe, stir-fry it in 2 separate batches, or it will not cook to the proper texture.

YIELD: 4 SERVINGS

TOMATOES STUFFED WITH SPINACH

*Two 10-ounce packages fresh
  spinach
1 tablespoon flour
¼ cup plus 2 tablespoons
  heavy cream
¼ cup sour cream*

*3 tablespoons chopped
  fresh basil or mint leaves
3 tablespoons pine nuts
Salt
4 large tomatoes*

Wash the spinach, discarding the stems and any wilted leaves. Cook in the water clinging to the leaves in a large covered saucepan. Drain well in a colander. When cool, squeeze out as much water as possible, a handful at a time. Chop with a large knife and turn into a bowl. Stir in the flour and then add the cream, sour cream, basil or mint, pine nuts, and salt to taste.

Preheat the oven to 375°.

Cut the stem ends off each tomato and hollow them. Salt the inside of each. Fill with the spinach stuffing. Place in an oiled pan, cover with foil, and bake for 15 minutes, or until the tomatoes are tender.

YIELD: 4 SERVINGS

PEAR AND LEMON SHERBET

A subtle and distinctive blend of flavors in a smooth-textured sherbet that does not require an ice cream machine.

*1 pound ripe Bartlett or
  Anjou pears, peeled, cored,
  and chopped fine
½ cup sugar
½ cup water*

*¼ cup lemon juice
1 cup heavy cream
1 teaspoon grated lemon
  zest*

Put the chopped pears into a heavy saucepan and cook over medium heat, stirring frequently, until they render their juices. Turn up the heat and cook, stirring until the pears are very soft and most of the moisture has evaporated. Purée in a food processor, turn into a mixing bowl, and reserve.

Stir together the sugar and water in a small, heavy saucepan. Bring to a boil and cook until a candy thermometer reaches 234°, or a little of the syrup can be formed into a soft ball when dropped into a glass of cold water. Cool slightly and stir into the pear purée. Add the lemon juice and place in the freezer until firm.

Whip the cream until it holds soft peaks. Remove the frozen pear mixture from the freezer and break into chunks. Purée in a food processor until smooth but not liquefied. Fold the whipped cream and lemon zest into the pear mixture and refreeze immediately.

YIELD: APPROXIMATELY 3½ CUPS OR 4 SERVINGS

A Hearty Stew Dinner

MUSHROOM CROUSTADES (page 151)

PORK, PEAR, AND FENNEL STEW

RICE†

GREEN SALAD†

CRANBERRY-CASSIS ICE

T H E entrée for this dinner is a hearty and aromatic stew in which pork is combined with onions, fennel, and pears. The side dishes include rice and a green salad. It is an informal meal that does not require an appetizer. Mushroom Croustades, an hors d'oeuvre to serve with drinks, is suggested instead. The dessert is a refreshing garnet-colored ice, a product of my Flavor-Color Theory: Foods that are the same color generally go well together. My husband, of course, thinks I am quite mad and is fond of asking why I don't put cherry juice in the red cabbage. Let him scoff; there are many splendid examples to support my theory: honeydew with lime; carrots and orange; cassis with watermelon or any edible red berry; and the Tomato-Burgundy Soup on page 130. The following dessert, combining cranberries with cassis syrup, is a superb example of the validity of my argument.

Advance Preparation The Cranberry-Cassis Ice may be made a few days before serving; the Pork, Pear, and Fennel Stew a day or two ahead. The Mushroom Croustades may be prepared early on the day of the party and heated before serving.

PORK, PEAR, AND FENNEL STEW

The pork is marinated in white wine, rosemary, garlic, and juniper berries and then cooked with onions, fennel, and pears to make an unusual and memorable fall stew.

4½ pounds boneless pork butt, cut into 1½-inch cubes

FOR THE MARINADE

2¼ cups dry white wine
1 teaspoon dried rosemary
3 bay leaves
12 crushed juniper berries

4 large garlic cloves, peeled
  and pressed
3 tablespoons olive oil

FOR THE STEW

Vegetable oil
4½ cups chicken stock or
  broth
⅓ cup dry white wine
Reserved marinade
3 tablespoons brandy
⅓ cup minced fennel ferns
2 garlic cloves, peeled and
  pressed
Fresh-ground pepper

3 medium-large fennel
  bulbs, washed and
  trimmed
2 pounds small white or
  yellow onions
  (¾–1 inch in diameter)
4 tablespoons unsalted
  butter
4 tablespoons flour mixed
  with 3 tablespoons soft
  unsalted butter
2–2½ pounds Bosc pears

Trim any excess fat off the pork and put it in a large ceramic or glass bowl. Combine the ingredients for the marinade and pour over the pork. Marinate in the refrigerator, all day or overnight, stirring occasionally.

Drain the pork. Strain and reserve the marinade. Dry the meat well with paper towels. Heat 2 tablespoons of oil in a large, heavy skillet and brown the pork in batches, adding more oil if necessary. Do not crowd the pan. As the pork is browned, transfer it to a large, heavy casserole or Dutch oven. Pour any excess oil out of the skillet and deglaze the pan with 1 cup of the chicken stock, stirring and scraping any browned bits stuck to the bottom. Stir this into the casserole with the pork and add the remaining chicken stock, the wine, the reserved marinade, brandy, fennel ferns, garlic, and pepper. Salt should not be necessary. Cover and cook on top of the stove at a simmer for 2 hours, or until the pork is tender.

While the pork is cooking, prepare the vegetables: Cut the fennel bulbs in half lengthwise. Then place the cut surface on a cutting board and slice crosswise ¼ inch thick. Cut any long pieces in half. You should have about 9 cups.

Immerse the onions in boiling water for 30 seconds. Drain, cut off the ends, and peel off the skins.

Melt 2 tablespoons of the butter in a large skillet and sauté the fennel, stirring for a few minutes over medium heat. (It should be tender but slightly crisp.) Turn into a bowl and reserve. Melt the remaining butter in the skillet and gently sauté the onions until lightly browned. Add a little water to the pan, cover tightly, and steam over low heat until they are quite tender. Reserve with the fennel.

The stew may be prepared ahead to this point. When the pork is tender, degrease the cooking juices. (Or cool to room temperature, chill, and remove the hardened fat from the surface.)

To serve, return the pork to room temperature if it has been refrigerated. Bring to a simmer on top of the stove and gradually blend in the butter-flour mixture, adding as much as needed to thicken the stew slightly. Add the reserved fennel and onions, cover, and simmer very gently for 15 to 20 minutes, or just until the stew is heated through. (Do not overcook.) Meanwhile, peel, core, and

quarter the pears and slice crosswise into ½-inch-thick pieces. Add the pears to the stew during the last 5 minutes of cooking. (They should be tender, but remain firm in texture.) Serve immediately.
YIELD: 10–12 SERVINGS

CRANBERRY-CASSIS ICE

This is a light and refreshing dessert and would be an unusual way to serve cranberries during the holiday season. The recipe includes pears, which are barely detectable in flavor but have a mellowing effect on the tart berries.

1½ pounds cranberries
2½–2⅔ pounds ripe pears
3 cups water
1⅓ cups sugar
2 envelopes unflavored
  gelatin

½ cup cold water
½ cup cassis syrup,
  preferably Vedrenne

Wash and pick over the cranberries, discarding any that are soft. Peel, core, and chop the pears fine.

Put the cranberries and pears in a large, heavy saucepan with 2 cups water. Bring to a boil and cook for 8 minutes, or until the pears are soft, stirring as the mixture thickens to prevent scorching. Strain through a food mill.

Combine the sugar and 1 cup water in a small saucepan. Heat gradually, stirring until dissolved. Then boil until a candy thermometer reaches 234°, or a little of the syrup can be formed into a soft ball when dropped in a glass of cold water. Cool slightly and stir into the cranberry mixture.

Soften the gelatin in ½ cup cold water and dissolve over low heat, stirring constantly. Remove from the heat and stir for a minute or two to cool, then stir into the cranberry mixture with the cassis syrup. Cover and freeze until firm.

When frozen, break the ice into chunks and purée, in several batches, in a food processor until smooth but not liquefied. As each batch is puréed, return immediately to the freezer.

YIELD: APPROXIMATELY 9 CUPS OR 12 SERVINGS

A Bachelor's Dinner

DOLMA WITH CHESTNUTS AND QUINCE

TOMATO, CUCUMBER, AND

ONION SALAD

OR

TOMATO AND BASIL SALAD†

FRENCH BREAD†

FRESH FRUIT AND CHEESE†

OR

HONEYDEW ICE (page 244)

THE recipe for dolma is one my husband learned years ago when cooking for himself in a cold water "palazzo" on the island of Ischia. It was taught to him by a Turkish friend residing in a neighboring villa, and it became one of his favorite company recipes. Men who cook for a hobby often draw from exotic and unfamiliar cuisines, and so I think of this as a typical bachelor's meal. It is a hearty, no-fuss dinner, and all the preparation can be done in advance. The main course requires only French bread and a salad for accompaniment. For the salad, serve either sliced tomatoes sprinkled with fresh basil and vinaigrette or prepare the recipe given for

Tomato, Cucumber, and Onion Salad. For dessert, a cooling Honey-dew Ice or fresh fruit and cheese.

Advance Preparation   The Honeydew Ice may be made several days ahead. The Dolma may be made a day in advance, but do not add the chestnuts, quince, raisins, and pine nuts until 10 minutes before serving. The salad should be made shortly before serving.

DOLMA WITH CHESTNUTS AND QUINCE

This is a Turkish dish, composed of ground meat, onions, and rice wrapped in vine leaves and cooked in a broth with quince, chestnuts, raisins, and pine nuts.

28 chestnuts
1 ¼ pounds ground chuck or
  ground beef (not too lean)
1 cup (generous) chopped
  yellow onion
½ teaspoon salt
1 cup uncooked rice
1 teaspoon allspice
A large pinch of hot red
  pepper flakes

¼ cup minced fresh parsley
1 jar vine leaves preserved
  in brine
12 cups beef stock or broth
4 medium quinces
1 cup dark raisins
⅓ cup pine nuts

FOR THE GARNISH

2 large lemons, cut into wedges

Preheat the oven to 375°.

With a sharp knife, cut an X into the flat side of each chestnut. Place them on a baking sheet in the oven and bake for 15 minutes. Remove the shells and skins while the chestnuts are still warm. Reserve.

In a large mixing bowl, thoroughly combine the ground beef with the onions, salt, rice, allspice, pepper flakes, and parsley. Shape into meatballs 1½ inches in diameter. You should have about 21. Rinse enough vine leaves to cover the meatballs. Tightly wrap each meatball in a leaf, and tie with kitchen string. Place the dolma in the bottom of a large, heavy Dutch oven or casserole. Pour in the beef stock, bring to a simmer, cover tightly, and cook very gently for about 35 minutes.

Meanwhile, peel, quarter, and core the quince and cut into slices ⅜ inch thick. As they are sliced, drop them into a bowl of cold water to prevent discoloring.

When the dolma have cooked for 35 minutes, skim the fat from the broth. Drain the quince well and add them to the pot along with the chestnuts, raisins, and pine nuts. Cover and simmer 5 to 8 minutes longer. The quince and chestnuts should be tender but not soft.

Serve the dolma in large soup plates with the fruit and nuts and some of the broth. Serve with a lemon wedge, which should be squeezed over each portion.

YIELD: 6 TO 8 SERVINGS

TOMATO, CUCUMBER, AND ONION SALAD

Prepare this dish no longer than an hour or two in advance and do not add salt until just before serving, or the vegetables will be watery.

FOR THE VINAIGRETTE

½ cup olive oil
2 tablespoons white wine vinegar
1 garlic clove, peeled and cut in half

FOR THE SALAD

*8 large tomatoes, peeled
and sliced or chopped
coarse*
*4 very small, young
cucumbers, washed and
sliced**

*2 medium-size red onions,
peeled and sliced thin*
*½ cup chopped fresh mint
leaves*
Salt
Fresh-ground pepper

Combine the ingredients for the vinaigrette at least an hour before serving to allow time for the garlic to marinate.

Combine the tomatoes, cucumbers, onions, and mint in a salad bowl. Just before serving, add seasoning. Discard the garlic clove and toss with the vinaigrette.

YIELD: 8 SERVINGS

* If young cucumbers are not available, use 2 medium-size and peel them.

A Curry Buffet Dinner

MINTED PEARS VINAIGRETTE

CURRIED LAMB WITH ASSORTED
CONDIMENTS

ORANGE AND COCONUT RICE

ORANGE AND ALMOND MOUSSE

CURRY dinners are ideal for buffets. With the addition of rice, the main course is complete in one dish; and the accompanying condiments are most easily served from the buffet table where guests can choose among them. The Curried Lamb on this menu is a festive prepare-ahead party entrée flavored with mint, ginger, lime, and quince. The appetizer is a light and simple combination of sliced avocados alternating with crisp Bosc or Anjou pears, sprinkled with fresh mint and a lime vinaigrette. A satisfactory conclusion to a curry meal is a refreshing citrus dessert, such as the Orange and Almond Mousse given below or a lemon sherbet.

Advance Preparation　The Curried Lamb may be made a day or two before the party, and the Orange and Almond Mousse one day ahead. The Orange and Coconut Rice should be cooked just before serving, or a few hours before the party and steamed to reheat. The Minted Pears Vinaigrette may be prepared two hours before serving.

MINTED PEARS VINAIGRETTE

A light and unusual appetizer contrasting crisp Bosc or Anjou pears with avocados.

3 tablespoons lemon juice
1 cup water
3 medium-size firm, ripe
 Bosc or Anjou pears
3 medium-size avocados
1 tablespoon lime juice
1 tablespoon white wine
 vinegar

¼ cup olive oil
Salt
¼ cup minced fresh mint
 leaves
1 ½ tablespoons minced
 fresh chives or tender
 green scallion ends

Combine the lemon juice and water in a small bowl. Peel the pears, cut in half, core, and slice lengthwise ¼ inch thick. As they are cut, dip in the lemon juice and water to prevent discoloring. Prepare the avocados in the same way. Alternate overlapping slices of pears and avocados on a large serving platter or, in a crescent pattern, on 10 individual plates. Cover each plate airtight with plastic wrap and refrigerate until serving. Thoroughly combine the lime juice, vinegar, and olive oil and, just before serving, drizzle over the pears. Salt lightly. Sprinkle with the mint and chives.

YIELD: 10 SERVINGS

CURRIED LAMB

5 ½ pounds lean lamb
   shoulder,* cut into
   1 ½-inch cubes
Vegetable oil
3 ¼ cups chopped onion
1 tablespoon minced garlic
6 tablespoons flour
1 tablespoon curry powder
6 cups beef stock or broth
¼ cup sieved Major Grey's
   chutney, preferably Sun
   Brand
6 tablespoons dried currants

6 tablespoons minced fresh
   mint leaves
½ cup tomato purée
1 teaspoon grated fresh
   gingerroot
⅓ cup minced fresh parsley
1 tablespoon plus 1
   teaspoon lime juice
¼ teaspoon allspice
1 ¼ pounds quinces, peeled,
   cored, and sliced ¼ inch
   thick†

FOR THE CONDIMENTS

Sliced almonds, lightly toasted
Minced crystallized ginger
Minced chives or scallions
Minced fresh mint leaves
Major Grey's chutney, preferably Sun Brand

Trim any visible fat from the lamb. In a large, heavy skillet, brown
the lamb in batches in vegetable oil. As it is browned, transfer it to
a platter. Wash the skillet, add more oil, and sauté the onions and
garlic until soft but not brown. Blend in the flour and curry powder.
Add 2 cups of the beef stock and bring to a simmer, stirring until
thickened. Add the remaining stock, the chutney, currants, mint
leaves, tomato purée, ginger, parsley, lime juice, and allspice. Trans-

---

* The amount of fat in a lamb shoulder will vary with different lambs and also
with the part of the shoulder used. If your butcher cannot supply lean shoulder
meat, use 5 pounds from the leg.
† Substitute tart, crisp apples if quinces are not available, and cook for only 1 or
2 minutes.

fer the mixture to a heavy, lidded casserole and add the lamb and any accumulated juices. Cover tightly, and simmer gently for 2 hours or until the lamb is tender. Skim the fat from the surface of the stew. Add the quince and cook for an additional 5 minutes, or just until the fruit is tender but not soft. (If you are preparing this a day or two ahead of time, degrease after the stew has cooled and the fat hardened on the surface. Reheat in a 375° oven for 20 to 30 minutes, adding the quince during the last 5 minutes.) Serve the condiments on the side.

YIELD: 10 SERVINGS

ORANGE AND COCONUT RICE

Salt
2 cups uncooked rice
2 cups grated, unsweetened coconut*
3 tablespoons unsalted butter
Grated zest of 3 medium oranges

Bring a very large pot of water to a boil. Add salt and the rice and cook for about 15 minutes, or until tender but still firm. Drain in a colander and rinse under hot water. Stir in the coconut. Toss with the butter and orange zest and serve immediately. (If preparing ahead, the cooked rice may be reheated in a covered colander over boiling water. Toss with the butter and orange zest just before serving.)

YIELD: 10 SERVINGS

* If using packaged, sweetened coconut, soak it in water to cover for 30 minutes or longer, drain well, and pat dry.

ORANGE AND ALMOND MOUSSE

½ cup milk
*¼ cup almond paste (not
  "marzipan")*
4 eggs, separated
*¾ cup plus 1 tablespoon
  sugar*
*1 envelope plus ½ teaspoon
  unflavored gelatin*

*1 ¾ cups strained, fresh
  Valencia or navel orange
  juice*
1 cup heavy cream
3 tablespoons curaçao

FOR THE GARNISH

Zest of 1 orange
½ cup sugar
½ cup water

Heat the milk with the almond paste, stirring until the paste is dissolved. With a wire whisk, beat the egg yolks with ¼ cup sugar. Stir in the almond-milk mixture and cook in a heavy saucepan over medium-low heat for 15 to 20 minutes, or until very thick. Cool on a wire rack.

In a stainless steel measuring cup or small saucepan, soften the gelatin in ¼ cup of the orange juice. Dissolve over low heat, stirring constantly. Add the dissolved gelatin and the rest of the orange juice to the almond custard. Stir over a bowl of ice cubes or refrigerate until thickened but not set.

Beat the egg whites until they hold soft peaks. Continue beating as you gradually add ½ cup sugar. Whip the cream with the remaining tablespoon sugar and the curaçao. Fold together the egg whites and custard and then fold in the whipped cream. Turn into a serving bowl and chill until set.

To prepare the garnish, pare the zest from an orange in long strips without cutting off any white pith. Cut each strip into thin slivers. Combine the sugar and water in a saucepan, add the orange zest, and bring to a boil. Simmer for 10 to 15 minutes, or until the zest is transparent. Keep the zest and syrup in a covered glass jar until shortly before serving. To serve, drain well, and scatter the candied zest over the mousse.

YIELD: 10 SERVINGS

A Fancy Dinner Party for Ten

TOMATO-BURGUNDY SOUP (page 130)

VEAL ST. ANDRÉ

JULIENNE CARROTS

GREEN SALAD[†]

MARRONS FAVORITE

T H I S is a dinner party for special occasions. The highlight is veal scaloppine, topped with mushroom duxelles and St. André cheese and encased in filo pastry. While the preparation for this is elaborate, it can be done the day before the party; it is then baked briefly before serving. The meal begins with a spicy, deep red Tomato-Burgundy Soup, a warming brew that is likely to appeal on brisk fall or winter evenings. A very simple but colorful vegetable dish of steamed julienne-cut carrots accompanies the veal, followed by a green salad.

The dessert is a sumptuous and smooth soft-frozen concoction laced with marrons.

Advance Preparation   The Marrons Favorite may be made several days before serving, and the Tomato-Burgundy Soup a day or two ahead. The Veal St. André and the Julienne Carrots may be prepared a day ahead and baked just before serving.

VEAL ST. ANDRÉ

FOR THE MUSHROOM DUXELLES

5 tablespoons unsalted butter
3 anchovy fillets, boned
3 tablespoons minced shallot
2 ¼ pounds fresh mushrooms, cleaned, trimmed, and minced

FOR THE VEAL SCALOPPINE

3 pounds large veal scallops, pounded very thin (each about 5 ½ by 4 inches)
Flour
Salt
Fresh-ground pepper
Approximately 3 tablespoons unsalted butter
Approximately 2 tablespoons olive oil

¾ pound St. André cheese, firm and slightly underripe
Reserved mushroom duxelles
Approximately 12 tablespoons unsalted butter, melted
1 package frozen filo pastry, defrosted
Fine, dry bread crumbs
1 egg, lightly beaten

Prepare the mushrooms in 2 batches: Melt 2½ tablespoons butter in a very large skillet, add half the anchovies, and stir until dissolved. Add half the shallots and half the mushrooms and cook over moderately high heat, stirring often, until all the moisture has evaporated and the mushrooms are dry but not scorched. Turn into a bowl and cook the remaining mushrooms in the same way. Reserve.

Lightly dredge the veal in flour seasoned with salt and pepper. Melt 2 tablespoons of the butter and 1 tablespoon olive oil in a large skillet. Add as many scallops as will fit in 1 layer without crowding. Sauté over moderate heat for about 1 minute on each side. As they are cooked, transfer to a platter to cool. Add more butter and oil to the pan as necessary. When the veal has cooled to room temperature, cover one side of each scallop with a thin slice of St. André cheese. Press about 2 tablespoons of the mushroom duxelles over the cheese and reserve.

Put the melted butter in the top of a double boiler over hot water and put it near your work area. Brush 3 large baking sheets with a little of the butter. Dampen 2 clean cotton or linen dish towels and wring out. Lay one towel over your work area. Unfold the stack of filo sheets and lay them flat over 2 sheets of wax paper. Remove one sheet of filo and place it on top of the damp towel. Cover the remaining filo with additional wax paper and with the other wet towel.

Brush half of the sheet of filo with melted butter and sprinkle lightly with bread crumbs. Fold over the unbuttered half so that you have a rectangle about 8 by 14 inches. Butter the top layer and dust with bread crumbs. Fold the edges of each side of the rectangle in about 1 inch. (The amount folded in will vary with the size of each scallop.) Brush the edges with beaten egg. Lay a veal scallop (topped with cheese and mushrooms) in the center of the rectangle. Fold the bottom flap over the veal and then the top, as you would a letter, and lightly press the edges to seal. Brush the top and sides of the pastry with melted butter and transfer to a baking sheet. Continue assembling the filo packages in this way. If some scallops look rather small, you may lay 2 side by side on one sheet of filo. As you work, always remember to keep the filo that is not in use covered with wax paper and a damp towel or it will dry out and become too brittle to use. (The dish can be prepared in advance to this point. Cover the baking sheets with plastic wrap and refrigerate. Remove from the refrigerator several hours before baking to return to room temperature.)

To serve, preheat the oven to 375°. Bake, uncovered, for 15 minutes, or just until the pastry is golden brown. Be careful not to over-cook or the veal will be dry.

YIELD: APPROXIMATELY 15 TO 17 VEAL PACKAGES, OR ENOUGH TO SERVE 10 OR 12, WITH SOME SECOND HELPINGS

JULIENNE CARROTS

This is a colorful, simple, and delicious accompaniment for the veal. The carrots are steamed al dente (and this can be done the day before serving), and then reheated with butter and orange juice.

2 ½ pounds carrots, trimmed and scraped
3 tablespoons unsalted butter, melted
½ cup fresh orange juice
Minced parsley

Cut the carrots into strips, ¼ inch wide and thick and 3 inches long. Put them in a colander and set over a large pot with a little boiling water in it. (The carrots should not rest in the water.) Cover and steam for 30 to 35 minutes, or until the carrots are tender but still quite firm. Stir frequently so that they cook evenly and replenish the water in the pot if necessary. Remove from the heat when cooked, rinse under cold water, and cool.

To serve, preheat the oven to 375°. Gently toss the carrots with the melted butter. Arrange neatly in a baking dish and pour the orange juice over them. Cover the pan with foil and heat for 10 to 15 minutes, or just until heated through. Be careful not to overcook them. Sprinkle with the minced parsley and serve.

YIELD: 10 TO 12 SERVINGS

MARRONS FAVORITE

A soft-textured frozen dessert composed of crumbled meringues, cream, and candied chestnuts.

FOR THE MERINGUES

> *4 egg whites, at room temperature*
> *⅛ teaspoon cream of tartar*
> *1 teaspoon vanilla extract*
> *1 cup sugar*

FOR THE MARRON MIXTURE

> *2½ cups heavy cream*
> *2½ tablespoons brandy*
> *1 teaspoon vanilla extract*
> *One 10-ounce jar Raffetto vanilla-flavored marron pieces,*
>   *well-drained*

Preheat the oven to 250°. Line 2 large baking sheets with brown paper.

To make the meringues, beat the egg whites until frothy. Add the cream of tartar and continue beating until they hold soft peaks. Add the vanilla and gradually add the sugar, beating until stiff. Shape into 8 large meringues on the prepared baking sheets. Bake for 1¼ to 1½ hours, or until dry in the center. (If the baking sheets are on 2 separate shelves, switch them halfway through cooking.) Leave the meringues to cool in the turned-off oven with the door ajar.

When the meringues have cooled, break them up into inch-size pieces. Whip the cream with the brandy and vanilla until it holds very soft peaks. Do not overbeat; it should have the consistency of crème Chantilly. Fold the broken meringues and marron pieces into the cream. Turn into a serving dish, cover with plastic wrap, and freeze until firm.

YIELD: 10 SERVINGS

A Salmon Dinner for Special Guests

TOMATO-GINGER SOUP

SALMON FILLETS WITH TWO SAUCES

SAUTÉED ZUCCHINI (page 26)

FENNEL, CELERY ROOT, AND
CHÈVRE SALAD
OR
FUSILLI D'ESTATE (page 286)

BELLINI SORBET

I served this dinner at a party in honor of two literary friends, James Merrill and David Kalstone, when they visited us in Rochester en route home from a lecture engagement in Canada. The last dinner we'd all had together was at Harry's Bar in Venice. With this rather daunting comparison in mind, I quickly determined that simplicity was the safest approach, and fortunately salmon was at the peak of its season.

While this is, without question, a very simple menu, it has some innovative touches. The light, noncreamy tomato soup acquires an interesting new character when flavored with fresh ginger. The salmon could not be easier to prepare, but it is important to buy the flat fillet cuts rather than the thicker steaks, as they cook quickly and retain their moisture. Served with two cold sauces, Lime and Mint Mayonnaise and Salsa Verde, the entrée becomes quite special. The salad—crisp, julienne-cut celery root and fennel with crumbled chèvre cheese—is a monochromatic blend of contrasting flavors and textures, generously sprinkled with fresh parsley and doused in a light vinaigrette. (Fusilli d'Estate on page 286 would be an appropriate and colorful alternative.) The peach and spumante sorbet for dessert is an adaptation of the famous Bellini cocktail served at Harry's Bar.

Advance Preparation   The Bellini Sorbet may be made two days before serving. The Tomato-Ginger Soup, the sauces for the salmon, the zucchini, and the salad may be prepared the day before the party.

TOMATO-GINGER SOUP

A simple tomato soup recipe that is given character by the addition of fresh ginger. Do not substitute dried, ground ginger. This soup is good served hot or cold.

> 3½ pounds ripe tomatoes,   1 tablespoon grated fresh
>   cored and chopped coarse   gingerroot
> 2 garlic cloves, peeled and   2 cups chicken stock or
>   halved   broth
> 2 tablespoons unsalted butter   Salt

Sauté the tomatoes gently with the garlic and butter for a few minutes. Add the grated ginger and chicken stock, cover the pan, and simmer for 20 minutes. Strain through a food mill, pressing through as much pulp as possible. Taste, and add a little salt if necessary. Serve chilled or hot.

YIELD: APPROXIMATELY 7 CUPS OR 8 SERVINGS

SALMON FILLETS WITH TWO SAUCES

These fish fillets are cooked very simply, with a sprinkling of fresh herbs and wine. Covering the pan so that they steam in their juices keeps the fish moist. Buy the fillet-cut rather than the thicker fish steaks. Served with two sauces, this entrée is suitable for a special dinner party.

Olive oil
2 tablespoons minced shallot
3 pounds salmon fillets
¼ cup dry white wine
1 ½ tablespoons minced fresh basil

1 ½ teaspoons minced fresh rosemary
½ teaspoon minced fresh thyme
Salt
Fresh-ground pepper

FOR THE GARNISH

Watercress or parsley

Salsa Verde (recipe follows)
Lime and Mint Mayonnaise (recipe follows)

Preheat the oven to 375°. Oil the bottom of a large baking pan and sprinkle with half the shallots. Put in the fish, skin side down, and rub a little oil into the flesh of each fillet. Sprinkle with the wine, the remaining shallots, the herbs and seasonings. Cover the pan tightly with aluminum foil and bake for about 20 minutes, or just until the fish flakes and is cooked through. Transfer to a heated serving platter, spoon on some of the pan juices, and surround with watercress or parsley. Serve the sauces on the side, chilled or at room temperature.

YIELD: 8 SERVINGS

SALSA VERDE

This is a very versatile sauce, equally good with meat, fish, or fowl.

1 small garlic clove, peeled
1 cup parsley sprigs, packed
¼ cup basil leaves, loosely
*   packed*
3 thick slices plain white
*   bread (not "Toasting*
*   White"), crumbled*

2 anchovy fillets, rinsed and
*   patted dry*
1 tablespoon lemon juice
Approximately ½ cup olive
*   oil*

Mince the garlic, parsley, and basil in a food processor. Add the bread, anchovies, and lemon juice and process. With the motor running, add as much olive oil as necessary in a thin stream. The consistency of the sauce should be fairly thick. Serve cool or at room temperature.

YIELD: ABOUT 1 CUP

LIME AND MINT MAYONNAISE

This is good also with seafood such as shrimp and boiled lobster.

1 extra-large egg yolk
1 tablespoon plus ½
*   teaspoon lime juice*
1 ¾ teaspoons Dijon mustard
½ cup light olive oil

½ cup vegetable oil
Grated zest of 1 lime
1 ½ tablespoons fine-minced
*   fresh mint leaves*
Salt

Beat the egg yolk, lime juice, and mustard together in a small mixing bowl. Put the olive oil and vegetable oil into a 2-cup Pyrex measure. Beating the egg mixture continuously with a wire whisk, add the oil drop by drop. After the mayonnaise becomes thick, the oil may be added in a thin stream. (Should the mayonnaise separate, begin again with another egg yolk; whisk in the curdled sauce drop by drop and then slowly add any remaining oil.) Stir in the lime zest and mint leaves, and add salt to taste.

YIELD: ABOUT 1 CUP

SAUTÉED ZUCCHINI. Prepare double the recipe on page 26.

FENNEL, CELERY ROOT, AND CHÈVRE SALAD

This salad is an unusual medley of delicate flavors and contrasting textures that can be served as an appetizer as well as a salad course. It looks particularly attractive presented in a glass bowl.

FOR THE VINAIGRETTE

> *½ cup olive oil*
> *2 tablespoons white wine vinegar*
> *1 garlic clove, peeled and cut in half*

FOR THE SALAD

> *1 pound celery root (1 very large or 2 medium roots)*
> *3 tablespoons lemon juice*
> *2 small fennel bulbs (3 cups sliced)*
>
> *12 ounces French chèvre cheese**
> *Fresh-ground white pepper*
> *⅔ cup minced fresh parsley*

---

* Use a firm, underripe chèvre that has a Brie-like rind, such as Capritarn or Petite Cabrette.

Combine the ingredients for the vinaigrette at least an hour before using, to allow time for the garlic to marinate.

Peel the celery root and slice into julienne strips about ⅛ inch wide and thick. Bring a large saucepan of water to a boil and add the lemon juice and the celery root. Cook for 1 or 2 minutes, until softened but still crisp. Drain, rinse with cold water, and dry on paper towels.

Trim the green stalks off the fennel and remove any tough outer pieces. Slice crosswise ⅛ inch thick. You should have about 3 cups.

Peel the rind off the chèvre. Cut the cheese into inch-long sticks, combine it with the celery root and fennel, and add pepper to taste.

Just before serving, remove the garlic clove from the vinaigrette. Toss the salad with the dressing and sprinkle minced parsley over the top. Serve at room temperature.

YIELD: 8 SERVINGS

BELLINI SORBET

Harry's Bar, the Cipriani, and other fine restaurants and hotels in Venice are famous for, among other things, their Bellini cocktails, a delicious concoction of puréed fresh peaches and sparkling white Italian wine. I had only to drink a few of these before realizing that they might do well translated into a frozen dessert. The following recipe can be made easily and does not require a special ice cream machine. Be sure to use an Italian spumante, such as Prosecco, and not a grapey-tasting wine.

2 pounds ripe peaches
2 tablespoons water
4–8 tablespoons sugar
1 ½ cups Italian spumante

Peel the peaches by immersing in boiling water for about 20 seconds. Cut each in half, discard the pits, and purée in a food processor or blender. You should have about 3 ½ cups purée.

Stir 2 tablespoons water into 4 tablespoons sugar. Heat to boiling. Remove and stir into the peach purée. Stir in the spumante and freeze until firm. Break into chunks and purée in a food processor, in batches, until smooth but not liquefied. Taste and add more sugar if necessary. Refreeze immediately.

YIELD: APPROXIMATELY 5 CUPS OR 6 TO 8 SERVINGS

A Game Dinner
for Nonhunters
in Hunting Season

BEET AND CLARET SOUP

LAPIN À LA MOUTARDE

STEAMED BROCCOLI†

CRÊPES AQUITAINE

FALL is hunting season, and I feel I should take note of that fact. But the truth is, I come from a family of nonhunters, and my husband's only contact with the animal world is to feed the birds. This, therefore, is the sort of meal you can serve when you want to enter the spirit of fall and the mysteries of the outdoors without picking up a rifle. The "game" entrée is, in fact, domestic, grocery-store rabbit. Wild rabbit, which is tough and stringy and requires long cooking, should not be substituted. In this variation of the traditional French recipe, the rabbit is marinated in mustard before cooking, producing a more succulent meat. The appetizer is a steaming, jewel-colored Beet and Claret Soup. Serve steamed broccoli or spinach with the rabbit and warm crêpes with pear sauce for dessert.

Advance Preparation The Beet and Claret Soup, the Lapin à la Moutarde, and the Crêpes Aquitaine may be made a day or two in advance and reheated before serving.

BEET AND CLARET SOUP

In combining ingredients for this soup, I was guided as much by color as flavor. The result is a ruby-red consommé, an impressive beginning to any dinner party. It tastes as good as it looks.

10 medium-size beets, peeled and sliced thin (10 cups)
2 pounds fresh or canned, drained tomatoes
6½ cups chicken stock or broth

2⅓ cups dry red wine (Bordeaux or Beaujolais)
2 teaspoons peeled and sliced fresh gingerroot
¾ cup strained fresh orange juice

FOR THE GARNISH

Paper-thin orange slices

Put the beets in a large saucepan with the tomatoes, which should be left whole. Add the chicken stock, wine, and gingerroot. Cover tightly and simmer until the beets are very tender—about 1 to 2 hours. Strain the mixture carefully; do not press down on the tomatoes or the soup will be cloudy. Stir the orange juice into the strained soup and reheat before serving. Garnish each serving with an orange slice.

YIELD: 9 CUPS OR 10 SERVINGS

LAPIN À LA MOUTARDE

After marinating in mustard, the rabbit is sautéed and served in a light mustard-cream sauce, spiked with a little bourbon. It can be made ahead and reheated before serving.

3 fresh, young domestic rabbits, each about 2½ pounds
⅓ cup plus 3 tablespoons Dijon mustard
2–3 tablespoons bacon fat or vegetable oil

5–6 tablespoons unsalted butter
1½ pounds firm, white mushrooms, cleaned and trimmed
2 tablespoons flour
2 cups sour cream
1½ tablespoons bourbon

FOR THE STOCK

4 cups water
1 bay leaf
1 small onion, peeled and quartered
1 garlic clove, cut in half
Several sprigs of fresh parsley

FOR THE GARNISH

Minced fresh parsley

Cut the rabbit into serving pieces: Separate the forelegs at the shoulder and the hind legs at the knee and hip, and cut the body section into four pieces. Trim off the lower part of the rib cages where there is very little flesh and reserve for the stock, along with any odd scraps.

Rinse and dry the rabbit pieces and coat them with ⅓ cup of the mustard. Place in a large glass, ceramic, or enamel pan or bowl, cover loosely, and refrigerate overnight.

Put the ribs and scraps from disjointing the rabbit in a large sauce-pan. Add the water, bring to a boil, and skim off the scum. Add the bay leaf, onion, garlic, and parsley; partially cover and simmer for about 2 hours or until reduced to ¾ cup liquid. Strain and reserve the broth.

Melt a little bacon fat or oil and about 1 tablespoon butter in a large skillet. Add as many rabbit pieces as will fit without crowding. (Do not wipe off the mustard marinade.) Sauté on both sides over moderate heat to brown lightly. Transfer to a dish as the pieces are browned, and continue cooking the remaining rabbit, adding more fat and butter to the skillet as necessary. After all the pieces have been browned, pour off any excess fat from the skillet, return the rabbit and all accumulated cooking juices to the pan, cover tightly, and cook over low heat until tender. This will take about 50 minutes for the smaller pieces and 1 hour or longer for the large pieces. Remove the cooked rabbit and degrease the pan juices. You should have about ½ cup after degreasing. Reserve.

Melt 2 tablespoons butter in the skillet and sauté the mushrooms until tender but still firm. Transfer to a bowl and reserve. Add another tablespoon of butter to the pan and blend in the flour. Add the reserved stock and cooking juices, and cook, stirring with a whisk, until slightly thickened. Add to this sauce all the accumulated juices from the mushrooms. Whisk in the sour cream, 3 tablespoons mustard, and the bourbon.

If you are not serving the rabbit at this time, cover the rabbit and the sauce and refrigerate separately. Before serving, return the rabbit to room temperature. Put the rabbit and sauce in a large skillet, cover tightly, and reheat very gently. Add the mushrooms to the pan and continue cooking for 1 or 2 minutes longer. Sprinkle with minced parsley and serve.

YIELD: 10 TO 12 SERVINGS (18 MEATY PIECES, 12 LEAN PIECES)

CRÊPES AQUITAINE

These dessert crêpes are filled with a mixture of cream cheese and minced crystallized ginger and served with a warm pear sauce. They can be assembled ahead of time and heated before serving.

FOR THE CRÊPES

1 cup milk
3 eggs
½ cup water
1½ tablespoons sugar

1 cup flour
2 tablespoons unsalted butter, melted
1 teaspoon vanilla extract

FOR THE FILLING

12 ounces cream cheese, softened
¼ cup light cream
½ teaspoon vanilla extract
6 tablespoons finely minced crystallized ginger
2 teaspoons sugar

FOR THE PEAR SAUCE

2½ pounds Bartlett or Anjou pears
3 tablespoons fresh lemon juice
½ cup sugar
⅓ cup water
1 teaspoon vanilla extract

To make the crêpes, thoroughly blend all the ingredients for the crêpes in a food processor or blender. Allow the batter to rest, covered and refrigerated, for 2 hours or longer. Lightly oil the bottom of a 5- or 6-inch skillet. Place it over moderately high heat, and when the skillet is hot, lift it off the burner. Pour in approximately 1½ tablespoons batter, swirl it around quickly to coat the pan, and place the pan back over the heat. Cook the crêpe until it is lightly browned on the underside, then turn it over and brown the other side. The crêpe should be paper-thin and lacey. Continue cooking the remaining batter in the same way, separating the crêpes with sheets of waxed paper. You should have 2 dozen crêpes.

To make the filling, beat the cream cheese with the cream and vanilla until light. Stir in the ginger and sugar. Place a heaping teaspoon of filling at one end of each crêpe and roll up. Place them, seam side down, in a lightly buttered baking dish, preferably one that can be used for serving. Cover and refrigerate until serving time.

To make the pear sauce, peel and core the pears. Put the lemon juice in a large, heavy saucepan and finely chop the pears into the pan. Add the sugar and water and bring to a simmer. Cook over moderate heat for 35 to 45 minutes, stirring as the mixture becomes thick. When done, the pears will be soft and the juice almost as thick as applesauce. You should have approximately 2⅔ cups. Stir in the vanilla extract.

To serve, heat the crêpes, uncovered, in a 350° oven for about 5 minutes, or until heated through but not browned. Reheat the pear sauce and spoon some of the sauce over each crêpe.

YIELD: 24 CRÊPES OR 8 TO 12 SERVINGS

An Autumnal Dinner

CHESTNUT SOUP (page 111)

GAME HENS WITH
CELERIAC STUFFING

GLAZED ACORN SQUASH

FENNEL, ENDIVE, AND
MUSHROOM SALAD

PEAR AND QUINCE TART

HERE is a menu with which you can savor the bounty of autumn, as it includes many of the foods special to that season. The first course is a creamy chestnut soup flavored with Madeira. For the entrée, small Cornish hens are prepared with an unusual stuffing of puréed celery root. Fresh Cornish hens are now generally available; do not buy the frozen, which tend to be tough. They should be small—no larger than 1¼ pounds each—so that one hen can be used per serving. Glazed Acorn Squash and a salad complete the entrée, with Pear and Quince Tart for dessert.

Advance Preparation The Chestnut Soup, the stuffing for the hens, and the Pear and Quince Tart may be made a day before serving. But do not stuff the hens until you are ready to cook them.

CHESTNUT SOUP. Prepare half the recipe on page 111.

GAME HENS WITH CELERIAC STUFFING

Puréed celery root with sautéed celery and scallions makes a unique savory stuffing for small hens.

FOR THE STUFFING

1 large celery root, peeled and sliced
1 medium potato, peeled and sliced
1 tablespoon lemon juice
3 tablespoons unsalted butter
1 ⅓ cups chopped celery
⅓ cup chopped scallion

2 garlic cloves, peeled and minced
1 tablespoon heavy cream
2 tablespoons minced fresh parsley
Salt
Fresh-ground white pepper

FOR THE HENS

4 game hens, 1 ¼ pounds each
3 tablespoons unsalted butter, softened
Salt
Fresh-ground pepper

FOR THE GARNISH

Several sprigs parsley

To make the stuffing, put the sliced celery root and potato in a saucepan, cover with water, and add the lemon juice. Boil until tender.

Drain well and purée in a food mill or food processor, adding 1 tablespoon of the butter.

Melt the remaining butter in a skillet and gently sauté the celery for 5 minutes. Add the scallions and garlic and cook until slightly softened, but do not brown. The celery should remain crisp. Stir the sautéed vegetables, cream, parsley, and seasoning into the puréed celery root mixture.

Preheat the oven to 350°. Remove the necks and giblets from the cavities of the hens. Wash the birds and dry them with paper towels. Stuff the hens, rub them with softened butter, and sprinkle with salt and pepper. Roast for 50 minutes to an hour, or until the juices from the thigh run clear, basting occasionally with the pan juices. To serve, degrease the pan juices and spoon over the hens. Garnish with parsley.

YIELD: 4 SERVINGS

GLAZED ACORN SQUASH

1 large acorn squash
1 tablespoon unsalted butter, melted
Cinnamon
Salt
Approximately 1 ½ tablespoons light brown sugar

Preheat the oven to 350°. Cut the squash into quarters and discard the seeds and fibers. Place in a baking dish and pour a little water into the bottom of the dish. Brush the cut surfaces of the squash with the melted butter and sprinkle with cinnamon and a little salt. Bake, uncovered, for 50 to 60 minutes, or until tender. Sprinkle the sugar on top, place under the broiler, and broil for 1 or 2 minutes, watching closely so the sugar doesn't burn.

YIELD: 4 SERVINGS

FENNEL, ENDIVE, AND MUSHROOM SALAD

1 ¼ cups sliced fennel
  (1 small bulb)
2 Belgian endive, sliced
  crosswise
1 cup sliced mushrooms
2 tablespoons minced fresh
  parsley

2 tablespoons crumbled
  Rondolé or Roquefort
  cheese
Fresh-ground pepper

FOR THE VINAIGRETTE

3 tablespoons olive oil
2 teaspoons lemon juice
1 teaspoon white wine vinegar

Combine the ingredients for the salad. Toss with the vinaigrette just before serving.

YIELD: 4 SERVINGS

PEAR AND QUINCE TART

This combination works particularly well. The flavor is lovely, and since quince is a comparatively dry fruit, the pears contribute necessary moisture to the filling.

4 cups peeled, cored and
  chopped, ripe quinces
2 tablespoons water
1 cup plus 2 tablespoons
  sugar
3 cups peeled, cored and
  fine-chopped Bartlett pears

1 tablespoon lemon juice
½ teaspoon cinnamon
2 tablespoons brandy
1 partially baked 9-inch tart
  crust (page14)

FOR THE TOPPING

¼ teaspoon cinnamon
1 tablespoon sugar
½ cup chopped walnuts

Put the quinces, water, and 1 cup sugar in a large, heavy saucepan. Cook over low heat, stirring frequently, until the quinces render their moisture. Then simmer until the fruit is soft and transparent, but not mushy. This should take 20 to 30 minutes, depending on the ripeness of the fruit. Stir often to prevent sticking. When the quinces are cooked, most of the moisture will have evaporated. Turn into a mixing bowl and reserve.

Put the pears, lemon juice, and remaining 2 tablespoons sugar in the saucepan and slowly bring to a simmer. Cook, stirring often, for 15 to 25 minutes, or until the pears are soft and most of the juice has evaporated or is as thick as applesauce. Combine with the quince and add ½ teaspoon cinnamon and the brandy. (If the mixture looks particularly juicy, stir in 1 or 2 teaspoons arrowroot. This will not be necessary if the juice appears to be no more than a few tablespoons.) Allow the tart shell to cool completely before putting the filling in.

Preheat the oven to 375°. Fill the tart with the fruit mixture. Combine the cinnamon, sugar, and walnuts for the topping and sprinkle evenly over the tart. Bake for 20 minutes, or until the crust is lightly browned. Cool on a wire rack.

YIELD: 6 TO 8 SERVINGS

A Harvest Dinner Party

PEAR AND FENNEL SOUP

PORK WITH FIG AND
CHESTNUT STUFFING
AND APPLE CONSERVE

STEAMED SPINACH[†]

OR

BROCCOLI[†]

WILD RICE WITH MUSHROOMS

PUMPKIN-PRALINE MOUSSE

OR

CRANBERRY-CASSIS ICE (page 32)

I always feel a certain pleasure and excitement when certain seasonal foods reappear in the market, and I find this particularly true in the fall. It is not simply the reassuring knowledge that the seasons are progressing according to schedule, nothing having gone drastically wrong in the natural world. Perhaps it is because so many of the foods special to this season have become associated with the holidays, and when they reappear, they bring a sense of festivity and anticipation. I have tried in this menu to include as many of the traditional fall foods as possible, sometimes with new variations. The menu begins with a soup that combines the subtle flavors of pear and fennel. The pork roast is stuffed with figs and chestnuts and served with a ginger and brandy flavored applesauce. For dessert, serve either a fluffy pumpkin mousse laced with bits of praline or a cool and tart Cranberry-Cassis Ice.

Advance Preparation   If you are serving the Cranberry-Cassis Ice for dessert, it can be made several days ahead. The Pear and Fennel Soup and the Apple Conserve may be made a day in advance. The pork should be marinated the day before cooking, and it can be stuffed early on the day of the party. The Wild Rice with Mushrooms may also be prepared that morning and reheated before serving. The Pumpkin-Praline Mousse can be made several days ahead if frozen; if chilled, it should be made about six hours before it is served or the praline will melt.

PEAR AND FENNEL SOUP

This is a puréed soup made without milk or cream. It is therefore both lighter and more intensely flavored than a creamed soup would be.

3 medium-large fennel bulbs (about 3 pounds untrimmed)
1 large potato (½ pound), peeled and sliced
1 medium onion, peeled and chopped coarse
Several sprigs parsley
3½ cups chicken stock or broth

1 cup peeled, cored, and chopped Bosc pear
2 teaspoons minced fresh tarragon or ½ teaspoon dried
1 scant tablespoon Pernod
Salt
Fresh-ground white pepper

FOR THE GARNISH

Minced fennel ferns

Trim the stalks off the fennel bulbs and discard. Slice the bulbs crosswise about 1 inch thick. Put the fennel in a large saucepan with the potato, onion, parsley, and chicken stock. Cover tightly, bring to a simmer, and cook for 15 minutes. Add the pears and cook for 10 minutes longer, or until the vegetables and pears are soft.

Purée the solids in a food processor or blender, adding the stock in a thin stream. Return the soup to the saucepan and stir in the tarragon, Pernod, and seasoning to taste. Reheat before serving. Garnish each portion with minced fennel ferns.

YIELD: APPROXIMATELY 8 CUPS OR 10 SERVINGS

PORK WITH FIG AND CHESTNUT STUFFING

This dish combines many of the flavors evocative of fall—it is stuffed with chestnuts and Madeira-soaked dried figs and served with an applesauce mixture that combines gingerroot, brandy, and thyme. To keep the pork moist, it is cooked in its marinade in a cooking bag. An alternative method would be to braise it in the marinating liquid in a covered roasting pan or casserole.

On 5 ½- to 6-pound boneless pork loin, including tenderloin
Salt
Fresh-ground pepper

FOR THE MARINADE

1 *cup dry white wine*   One 14-by-20-inch plastic
2 *tablespoons brandy*   Brown-in-Bag cooking
2 *tablespoons olive oil*   bag
2 *teaspoons grated fresh*   1 *tablespoon flour*
   gingerroot   1 *tablespoon cornstarch*
½ *teaspoon dried thyme*
2 *large garlic cloves, peeled*
   and pressed

FOR THE STUFFING

6 *ounces dried light figs*
½ *cup Madeira*
1½ *cups peeled, parboiled chestnuts (see page 111)*

FOR THE APPLE CONSERVE

4 *cups chunky applesauce*   3 *tablespoons brandy*
1 *tablespoon grated fresh*   ⅓ *teaspoon dried thyme*
   gingerroot

FOR THE GARNISH

Fresh parsley

Combine the wine, brandy, and olive oil in a large, shallow glass or
ceramic pan or bowl. Make a paste of the gingerroot, thyme, and
garlic and rub it into the flesh of the pork. Sprinkle with salt and
pepper and put the pork in the bowl with the marinade. Cover loosely
with wax paper and refrigerate overnight, turning once or twice.

While the pork is marinating, combine the figs and Madeira in a
small saucepan and simmer very gently for 10 to 15 minutes. Remove from the heat and let the figs stand in the Madeira until you
are ready to stuff the pork.

To make the Apple Conserve, combine the applesauce, gingerroot,
brandy, and thyme, turn into a serving bowl, cover, and reserve.

To prepare the pork for stuffing, remove it from the marinating liquid and reserve the marinade. Either cut a lengthwise slit along the inside of the loin to make room for the stuffing, or cut the loin in half crosswise so that you have 2 shorter pieces. Trim the stems off the figs, cut each into quarters, and combine with the chestnuts. Fill the slit with the stuffing. Or if you have cut the loin in half, cover the inside surface of one half with the stuffing and place the other half on top, sandwiching the stuffing between. Tie the loin securely at 2-inch intervals with kitchen string.

Preheat the oven to 325°. Proceed according to the directions on the cooking bag package: Put 1 tablespoon flour in the bag and shake to coat the inside. Place the bag in a large, shallow roasting pan, put the pork and the marinade in the bag, and tie securely. With the point of a knife, make 6 half-inch slits along the top of the bag to allow steam to escape. Place in the center of the oven, allowing plenty of room around the sides so that as the bag inflates, it will not touch the oven walls. The cooking time will vary according to the thickness of the pork. If you have tied the loin in one long, sausage-like piece, it will require 20 minutes per pound, or about 1¾ to 2 hours. If the loin has been cut in half and sandwiched together to make one short, thick roll, it will require 30 minutes per pound, or about 2¾ to 3 hours. The pork is done when a meat thermometer registers 165°.

When the pork is cooked, transfer it to a warm serving platter and keep warm. Place the roasting pan on top of the stove and discard the cooking bag, leaving all the juices in the pan. Degrease the pan juices. Blend 1 tablespoon cornstarch into a little of the juice, then return to the pan, whisking over moderate heat until the sauce thickens slightly. Carve the roast and spoon the pan juices over each slice. Garnish the edges of the platter with parsley and serve the Apple Conserve on the side.

YIELD: 10 TO 12 SERVINGS

WILD RICE WITH MUSHROOMS

3–4 tablespoons unsalted butter
1 tablespoon olive oil
12 ounces mushrooms, cleaned, trimmed, and sliced
½ pound wild rice
1 tablespoon salt

Heat 1 tablespoon butter and the olive oil in a large skillet and sauté the mushrooms until slightly wilted, but still plump and firm. Remove from the heat and reserve.

Rinse the rice well under cold running water. Bring a very large pot of water to a boil. Add the rice and salt, and stir until the water returns to a boil. Boil for 35 minutes, or until the rice is tender but still firm. Drain in a colander. Turn into a covered casserole dish and add 2 to 3 tablespoons butter and the sautéed mushrooms. (The rice may be prepared ahead to this point.)

To serve, preheat the oven to 350°. Cover the casserole and re-heat the rice for about 15 minutes. Do not overcook, or it will dry out.

YIELD: 8 TO 10 SERVINGS

PUMPKIN-PRALINE MOUSSE

If you like, you may substitute chopped pecans or walnuts for the praline. The mousse may be served chilled or frozen.

5 eggs, separated
½ cup light cream, scalded
¾ cup plus 2 tablespoons sugar
1 envelope plus ½ teaspoon unflavored gelatin
¼ cup cold water
2½ cups cooked and puréed pumpkin, fresh or canned

1½ teaspoons vanilla extract
¾ teaspoon cinnamon
A pinch of nutmeg
3 tablespoons brandy
1¼ cups heavy cream
¾ cup coarse-chopped Praline (page 311)

In a small, heavy saucepan, whisk together the egg yolks, scalded cream, and ¼ cup sugar. Cook over medium heat, stirring until thick. Remove from the heat and cool to room temperature.

Soften the gelatin in the cold water and dissolve over low heat, stirring constantly. Stir into the custard.

Combine the pumpkin with the vanilla, cinnamon, nutmeg, and brandy. Add to the custard mixture.

Beat the egg whites until almost stiff. Continue beating as you gradually add the remaining sugar. Beat the cream until it holds soft peaks. Fold the beaten egg whites and the cream into the pumpkin-custard mixture. Fold in the praline and turn into a serving bowl. Chill until firm or freeze.

If chilled, the dessert should be served from the bowl and not unmolded. Do not let it stand in the refrigerator for longer than 6 hours, or the praline will melt. If frozen, remove it from the freezer about ½ hour before serving to soften slightly at room temperature.
YIELD: 10 SERVINGS

WINTER

A Savory Lunch

CHEESE AND ONION TART

SENEGALESE SOUP

TOASTED SYRIAN BREAD WITH
SESAME SEEDS (page 312)

GREEN SALAD[†]

FRESH FRUIT[†]

OR

PEAR AND LEMON SHERBET (page 27)

THIS is a good menu for a winter lunch party, as the food is substantial enough to stand up to cold-weather appetites, and yet it is not so filling as to make you lethargic for the rest of the day. Because the entire meal can be prepared ahead, it can be served with ease after a morning spent out of doors, skiing or walking in the snow. When you return home in the company of cold and hungry friends, you need only warm things up. The first course is a dense, flavorful tart that is not a custardy quiche, but is composed almost entirely of sautéed onions and cheese. The entrée is a thick curried chicken soup, a subtle blend of a variety of flavors. Serve fresh fruit for dessert or Pear and Lemon Sherbet.

Advance Preparation   The Pear and Lemon Sherbet may be made several days before serving. The Cheese and Onion Tart and the Senegalese Soup may be made a day in advance.

CHEESE AND ONION TART

Unlike a quiche, this tart does not have a custard base. It is dense with sautéed onions, streaked with mozzarella and Jarlsberg cheese, and lightly crusted with Parmesan. It can be made in either a tart pan or a 9-inch pie plate.

2 tablespoons unsalted butter	*1 egg, lightly beaten*
2 pounds yellow onions,	*One 9-inch tart crust,*
peeled and chopped	*partially baked*
6 ounces mozzarella cheese,	*(page 19)*
cut into small dice	*5 tablespoons fresh-grated*
4 ounces grated Jarlsberg	*Parmesan cheese*
cheese	
1 teaspoon Worcestershire	
sauce	

Melt the butter in a large, heavy skillet, add the onions, and cook over moderate heat, stirring occasionally, until very soft and pale yellow. Do not allow to brown. (You should have about 2½ cups after cooking.)

Preheat the oven to 375°. In a large mixing bowl, combine the onions with the mozzarella, Jarlsberg, Worcestershire sauce, and beaten egg. Turn into the prepared tart crust and sprinkle with the Parmesan cheese. Bake for 35 to 40 minutes, or until browned on top.

YIELD: 8 SERVINGS AS AN APPETIZER, 4 TO 6 AS AN ENTREE

SENEGALESE SOUP

A thick chicken curry soup, with a suggestion of apple and banana.

One 3½-pound chicken,
including neck and giblets
1 large carrot, sliced
1 large yellow onion, peeled
and quartered
1 large celery stalk, trimmed
and sliced
2 garlic cloves, peeled
A few sprigs of fresh parsley
½ teaspoon salt
2 cups chicken broth
4 cups water
1 medium-size tart apple,
peeled, cored, and chopped
coarse

2 tablespoons unsalted
butter
2 tablespoons flour
1¼ teaspoons curry powder
1 small banana, puréed
(scant ⅓ cup)
2 tablespoons tomato purée
2 teaspoons sieved or
minced Major Grey's
chutney
⅔ cup heavy cream
¾ cup fine-diced tart apple

FOR THE GARNISH

Minced fresh mint leaves or minced parsley

Rinse the chicken and giblets and put them in a large pot with the carrot, onion, celery, garlic, parsley, salt, chicken broth, and water. Partially cover, bring to a simmer, and cook for 30 minutes, or just until the chicken is done. Remove from the heat and skim any scum from the surface of the broth. Take out the chicken and, when it is cool enough to handle, strip off the meat, discarding the skin. Cut the chicken into julienne pieces, and reserve. Return the carcass to the pot with any juice from the chicken. Add the coarse-chopped apple and continue to cook the soup, partially covered, until the vegetables are very soft and the liquid has reduced to 4 to 4½ cups. Discard the carcass, giblets, and neck. Skim off as much fat as possible. Remove the solids with a slotted spoon and purée through a food mill. Stir the purée into the broth.

Melt the butter in a small enameled or stainless steel skillet. Blend in the flour and curry powder. Add the mashed banana, tomato purée and chutney and gradually whisk in the cream. Heat the mixture, stirring, until it simmers and thickens. Add to the soup. (The soup may be prepared ahead to this point.)

To serve, add the diced apple and the reserved julienne chicken, cook for 1 minute, and remove from the heat. Garnish each serving with minced mint leaves or parsley.

YIELD: APPROXIMATELY 7 CUPS OR 6 ENTREE SERVINGS

PEAR AND LEMON SHERBET. Make double the quantity on page 27.

A Tea Party After Holiday Shopping

PARMESAN TOAST STRIPS (page 12)

HAM CORNUCOPIAS

ROAST BEEF WITH HORSERADISH-
SOUR CREAM DRESSING†

CHICKEN OR TURKEY WITH
RUSSIAN DRESSING†

CUCUMBER AND WATERCRESS†

EGG SALAD WITH DILL AND CAPERS†

VEE ANGLE'S GINGERBREAD

APRICOT-ALMOND TEA BREAD

PEAR-PECAN TEA BREAD

APRICOT FLORENTINES

MINIATURE LEMON TARTS

GINGER AND KUMQUAT CAKE (page 128)

CHOCOLATE-ALMOND
COOKIES (page 108)

VIN CHAUD

A N invitation to tea in some cozy sitting room warmed by a fire is an appealing prospect on a damp and gray winter afternoon, particularly if your guests have spent the earlier part of the day shopping for the holidays. The restrained and quiet atmosphere of a tea party is one of the pleasures of civilized society. It can be a festive and relaxing way to entertain a group of friends without the time-consuming demands of a dinner party. Several appropriate tea-time recipes follow; prepare as many as you like, depending on how large or elaborate a party you are planning. Be sure to include a selection of small sandwiches along with the sweets. Sandwich suggestions are given on the menu page. A recipe for Vin Chaud is included should you want to supplement the tea with a hot spiked beverage.

Advance Preparation   The cakes, cookies, and tea breads may be prepared at least a day before serving. The Parmesan Toast Strips may be made a few days ahead. Prepare the Ham Cornucopias and sandwiches on the day of the party.

HAM CORNUCOPIAS

---

6 large, round, thin slices of baked ham (approximately
  ½ pound)
Approximately ½ cup Boursin or Rondolé cheese

Cut each round of ham into quarters. Spread each quarter with a thin layer of cheese and roll up into a cone shape. Place seam side down on a platter, cover, and refrigerate until serving.

YIELD: 24 CORNUCOPIAS

VEE ANGLE'S GINGERBREAD

An old-fashioned recipe for a moist gingerbread.

¼ pound unsalted butter,
  softened
1 cup light brown sugar,
  packed
1 egg
1½ cups flour
1 teaspoon baking soda

1 teaspoon ground ginger
1 teaspoon cinnamon
½ teaspoon ground cloves
A pinch of salt
½ cup unsulfured molasses
⅓ cup boiling water

Preheat the oven to 350°. Generously butter a 13-by-9-inch baking pan.

Cream the butter with an electric mixer and beat in the sugar. Add the egg and beat well. Sift the flour with the baking soda, ginger, cinnamon, cloves, and salt. Combine the molasses and boiling water. Stir the flour mixture into the batter alternately with the molasses mixture, beginning and ending with the flour. Turn into the prepared pan and bake for 30 minutes. The gingerbread is done when it has sunk slightly in the middle. Cool in the pan on a wire rack and cut into squares when cool.

YIELD: 24 PIECES, APPROXIMATELY 2 INCHES SQUARE

APRICOT-ALMOND TEA BREAD

This is a very moist loaf, made with ground almonds, apricots, and orange juice.

¾ cup blanched, slivered almonds	⅔ cup chopped dried apricots
6 tablespoons unsalted butter, softened	1½ cups flour
1 cup sugar	¼ teaspoon baking soda
2 eggs, separated	1½ teaspoons baking powder
Grated zest of 1 orange, preferably California navel or Florida temple	¼ teaspoon salt
	⅔ cup fresh orange juice
	½ cup sliced almonds

Preheat the oven to 350°. Spread the blanched, slivered almonds in a single layer on a baking sheet. Toast for 5 or 6 minutes, or just until they begin to color. Do not let them brown. Leave the oven on. Cool the almonds and grind them in a food processor.

Generously butter and lightly flour one 9-by-5-inch loaf pan. (Use a pure aluminum, stainless steel, or Pyrex pan, not an alloyed metal. If using Pyrex, lower the oven temperature to 325°.) Cream the butter with an electric mixer and gradually add ¾ cup of the sugar. Beat in the egg yolks and orange zest.

Combine the apricots with 2 tablespoons of the flour in a small bowl and stir to coat them thoroughly. Sift the remaining flour with the baking soda, baking powder, and salt into a separate bowl and stir in the ground almonds. Fold the flour mixture into the batter alternately with the orange juice, beginning and ending with the flour. Fold in the apricots and sliced almonds.

Beat the egg whites until they hold firm peaks. Continue beating as you gradually add the remaining ¼ cup sugar. Carefully fold the egg whites into the batter. Turn into the prepared pan and bake for about 1 hour, or until a toothpick tests clean. Partially cool in the pan on a wire rack. Loosen the edges with a knife, unmold, and complete cooling.

YIELD: I LOAF

PEAR-PECAN TEA BREAD

An unusual quick bread, studded with chopped pears and flavored with ground pecans and a pear and lemon glaze.

1 cup pecans
4 ounces cream cheese,
  softened
1 tablespoon vegetable oil
¾ cup plus 2 tablespoons
  sugar
2 eggs
Grated zest of 1 medium
  lemon

1 cup peeled, chopped Bosc
  pears
½ cup coarse-chopped
  pecans (optional)
1 cup flour
2 teaspoons baking powder
¼ teaspoon salt

FOR THE GLAZE

3 tablespoons pear nectar
1 tablespoon lemon juice
3 tablespoons sugar

Preheat the oven to 350°. Spread 1 cup pecans in a baking pan and toast for about 8 minutes. Do not brown. Cool and grind in a food processor. Leave the oven on.

Butter and lightly flour an 8½-by-4½-inch loaf pan. Using an electric mixer, whip the cream cheese with the vegetable oil. Gradually add the sugar. Beat in the eggs, one at a time, and continue beating until the mixture is light and fluffy. Stir in the lemon zest, pears, and, if desired, the chopped pecans.

Sift the flour, baking powder, and salt into a separate mixing bowl and stir in the ground pecans. Fold the dry ingredients into the batter, mixing only until combined. Turn the mixture into the prepared pan and bake for 55 to 60 minutes, or until a toothpick tests clean.

While the bread is baking, combine the ingredients for the glaze in a small saucepan. Stir over medium heat until the sugar is melted. When the bread is done, pour the glaze over the hot loaf and cool in the pan on a wire rack.

YIELD: 1 LOAF

APRICOT FLORENTINES

A crisp, lacy cookie, studded with apricots and almonds and coated on one side with dark chocolate.

⅔ cup dried apricots	*1 cup sliced or blanched,*
½ cup plus 2 tablespoons	*slivered almonds*
sugar	*¼ pound unsalted butter*
1 cup all-purpose flour	*2 tablespoons light honey*
Grated zest of 1 Florida	*2 tablespoons heavy cream*
orange	*2 tablespoons curaçao*

FOR THE CHOCOLATE COATING

8 ounces Baker's German's Sweet Chocolate
1½ tablespoons unsalted butter

Preheat the oven to 350°. Butter a large cookie sheet.

With kitchen shears, cut the apricots into small dice and dredge in 2 tablespoons sugar. Combine the sugared apricots, the flour, orange zest, and almonds in a small bowl.

In a heavy, 1-quart saucepan, melt the butter with the remaining sugar, the honey, and the cream over low heat. Do not let the mixture boil.

As soon as the butter has melted, stir in the flour mixture and remove immediately from the heat, or the batter will cook and will
fail to spread properly. Stir in the curaçao.

Drop by teaspoonfuls onto the cookie sheet, about 2 inches apart,
and flatten each cookie slightly with the back of a spoon. Bake for 8
minutes, or until lightly browned around the edges. Let stand for
half a minute and then remove with a spatula to a wire rack to cool.

To make the chocolate coating, break up the chocolate into very
small pieces and put it in the top of a double boiler with the butter.
Stir continuously over hot, not simmering, water until melted. Continue stirring for a minute off the heat until the chocolate is glossy.
Spread the flat underside of each cookie with a thin coating of
chocolate and dry on a wire rack.

YIELD: APPROXIMATELY 3½ DOZEN COOKIES

MINIATURE LEMON TARTS

Cookie dough shells with a lemon custard filling.

FOR THE DOUGH

*½ cup blanched, slivered
    almonds*
¼ pound unsalted butter
*6 tablespoons confectioners'
    sugar*

1 egg yolk
*1 teaspoon grated lemon
    zest*
1 cup flour

FOR THE LEMON FILLING

6 egg yolks
½ cup sugar
6 tablespoons unsalted butter, cut up
6 tablespoons lemon juice
Grated zest of 1 large lemon

Preheat the oven to 350°.

To make the dough, spread the almonds on a baking sheet and bake for 5 or 6 minutes, or until very lightly toasted but not brown. Cool and grind in a food processor. Leave the oven on.

Cream the butter and beat in the sugar. Add the egg yolk and lemon rind and then stir in the flour and ground almonds. Form the dough into a ball. Pinch off small pieces and press into the bottom and halfway up the sides of ungreased miniature muffin tins (1¼ inches diameter at base). Bake the shells for about 10 minutes or until very lightly browned. Let them cool for a few minutes and then carefully lift them out of the pan to a wire rack to cool completely.

To make the lemon filling, combine the egg yolks, sugar, butter, and lemon juice in a heavy saucepan. Stir continuously over low heat until thick. Do not let the mixture boil. Stir in the lemon zest and cool to room temperature. When cool put a spoonful of filling into each tart shell.

YIELD: APPROXIMATELY 2½ DOZEN

VIN CHAUD

A hot, spiced wine to warm the body and lift the spirits. The wine reduces in cooking, strengthening and mellowing in flavor.

1 bottle dry red Burgundy or Bordeaux
2 cinnamon sticks
6 whole cloves
1 teaspoon whole mace
A 2-inch piece of vanilla bean

2 tablespoons sugar
Zest of ½ lemon
Zest of 1 California navel or Florida temple orange

Empty the wine into a large saucepan and add all the remaining ingredients. Heat and cook for 15 minutes at just below the simmering point, stirring occasionally.

Remove from the heat and let stand until cool. Strain into a clean container and cork tightly. If it is not to be used within 2 days, store in the refrigerator. Reheat, but do not boil, before serving and serve in mugs with a slice of orange or lemon.

YIELD: ABOUT 2¼ CUPS

A Storybook Supper

MESOPOTAMIAN MEATBALLS

ORANGE RICE

GREEN SALAD[†]

FROZEN HONEY AND ALMOND TORTE

T H I S is not an authentic Mesopotamian recipe. There is, however, some connection. In *The Story of the Amulet* by E. Nesbit, five children journey back through time to the ancient land of Mesopotamia and venture into the royal palace of Babylon, as it happens, just in time for supper. They dine with the queen on an exotic dish of meat and raisins in a rich broth. It was, as one of the children observed, "the kind of dinner you hardly ever get in Fitzroy Street." Here it is the inspiration for an informal fireside supper. Small meatballs are flavored with mint, pine nuts, and onions, and served in a sweet and sour broth with orange-flavored rice on the side. The dessert is Middle Eastern in flavor—a frozen confection of honey ice cream and almonds.

Advance Preparation The Frozen Honey and Almond Torte may be made a day or two before serving. The Mesopotamian Meatballs may be prepared a day in advance and reheated, but do not add the orange juice until just before serving.

MESOPOTAMIAN MEATBALLS

Little meatballs, with mint, pine nuts, and other flavorings, are served in a sweet and sour broth containing raisins or dried currants.

FOR THE MEATBALLS

3/4 cup minced onions
1 tablespoon minced garlic
4 tablespoons vegetable oil
2 eggs
1/2 pound ground beef
1/2 pound ground veal
1/2 pound ground pork
1/3 cup pine nuts

1/3 cup minced fresh parsley
2 tablespoons minced fresh
mint leaves or 1 teaspoon
dried
3 slices white bread, stale
or dried in the oven
1/2 teaspoon salt
Fresh-ground pepper

FOR THE BROTH

4 cups beef broth or stock
2/3 cup dark raisins or dried
currants
1/4 cup red wine vinegar
1/4 cup lemon juice

1/4 cup sugar
A large pinch of allspice
2 tablespoons cornstarch
1/4 cup orange juice

To make the meatballs, sauté the onions and garlic in 2 tablespoons of the oil, but do not brown. Beat the eggs lightly in a large mixing bowl and add the beef, veal, pork, pine nuts, parsley, mint leaves, and sautéed onions and garlic. Moisten the bread with cold water, squeeze dry, and crumble into the mixing bowl. Season with salt and pepper and mix thoroughly. Shape firmly into about 30 meatballs, each about 1 1/2 inches in diameter.

Heat the remaining oil in a large Dutch oven and brown the meatballs on all sides, in two batches. Transfer them to a platter as they are browned.

To make the broth, wipe out the Dutch oven, and put in the beef broth, raisins, vinegar, lemon juice, sugar, and allspice. Add the meatballs, cover the pot, and simmer for 20 minutes. Dissolve the cornstarch in a little cold water, stir into the broth, and simmer for a minute to thicken. Stir in the orange juice and serve.

YIELD: 6 SERVINGS

ORANGE RICE

1 ½ cups uncooked rice
2 tablespoons unsalted butter
Grated zest of 2 medium oranges

Bring a very large pot of water to a boil. Add salt and the rice and cook for about 15 minutes, or until cooked but still firm, Drain in a colander and rinse under hot water. Toss with the butter and orange zest and serve.

YIELD: 6 SERVINGS

FROZEN HONEY AND ALMOND TORTE

This is a mellow and creamy honey and almond flavored ice cream on a crust of chopped almonds.

FOR THE CRUST

4 tablespoons unsalted butter, softened
1 tablespoon flour
¼ cup sugar
1 cup blanched, slivered almonds, chopped coarse

FOR THE ICE CREAM

4 egg yolks	*1 ½ teaspoons vanilla extract*
⅓ cup light, mild honey	*1 cup heavy cream*
⅛ teaspoon almond extract	*3 egg whites*

To make the crust, preheat the oven to 300°. Cream the butter and blend in the flour, sugar, and chopped almonds. Press into the bottom of a 9-inch pie plate. Bake for 20 minutes, or until lightly browned around the edges. Cool on a wire rack.

To make the ice cream, combine the egg yolks and honey in a small, heavy saucepan or the top of a double boiler. Stir with a wire whisk over low heat or simmering water until thick. Do not let the mixture boil. Stir in the almond and vanilla extracts and cool to room temperature.

Whip the cream until it holds soft peaks. Wash the beaters and beat the egg whites until stiff but not dry. Fold the whipped cream and then the egg whites into the custard. Turn onto the almond crust and freeze until firm, and then cover tightly with plastic wrap.

To serve, remove the torte from the freezer. Fill a pan, 9 or more inches in diameter, with hot tap water. Dip the bottom of the pie plate in the hot water. (This will loosen the crust from the pie plate.) Cut into wedges and serve.

YIELD: 8 SERVINGS

A Variation on Roast Duck

LEMON-PARSLEY ICE

DUCK WITH PEARS

PURÉED PARSNIPS

GREEN SALAD[†]

GINGER BOMBE FAVORITE

On a recent visit to Montreal, I was told about a splendid French restaurant with an innovative cuisine, serving, among other things, Duck with Pears. It sounded intriguing, but we never made it to that restaurant, electing instead a pizzeria that caught my son's eye. Nevertheless, I thought about that recipe for some time and eventually tried out a version of my own. It is an exceedingly simple dish and, I believe, a very successful combination of flavors. The first course is a tart and refreshing Lemon-Parsley Ice to offset the richness of duck. The creamy, soft-frozen dessert is flavored with ginger preserves and is covered with a shell of chocolate glaze.

Advance Preparation The Lemon-Parsley Ice and the Ginger Bombe Favorite may be made several days before serving. The Puréed Parsnips may be made a day ahead and reheated before serving. The duck must be cooked just before serving.

LEMON-PARSLEY ICE

Serve this ice as an appetizer or, if you're in a Victorian mood, as a refresher between fowl and meat. Many variations can be worked on this recipe. You may substitute lime for the lemon, or basil or mint for the parsley.

1 ½ cups strained, fresh lemon juice
½ cup strained, fresh orange juice
1 ½ cups sugar
4 cups water

2 teaspoons unflavored gelatin
¼ cup cold water
2 tablespoons minced fresh parsley

FOR THE GARNISH

Fresh parsley sprigs

Combine the lemon and orange juice in a bowl or freezer container. Put the sugar and 4 cups water in a saucepan and boil until a candy thermometer reaches 220°. Add to the juice mixture. Soften the gelatin in the cold water and dissolve over low heat, stirring constantly. Combine with the juice mixture and freeze until firm.

Break the ice into chunks and purée in a food processor, in batches, until smooth but not liquefied. Stir in the minced parsley and refreeze immediately.

Garnish each serving with a sprig of parsley.

YIELD: 1 QUART OR 8 SERVINGS

DUCK WITH PEARS

Roast quartered duck flavored with pear liqueur and served with sautéed pears. A distinctive combination that is elegant in its simplicity.

Two fresh 5-pound ducks,	*⅓ cup sugar*
* quartered*	*⅓ cup water*
Half a lemon	*4 Anjou pears*
Salt	*1 tablespoon unsalted butter*
Fresh-ground pepper	*½ teaspoon cinnamon*
Zest of 1 large lemon	*½ cup pear liqueur*

FOR THE GARNISH

Watercress

Preheat the oven to 375°.

Rinse and dry the ducks, removing as much fat as possible. Rub the flesh with the half-lemon and sprinkle with salt and pepper. Arrange skin side up on a rack in a roasting pan and roast for 1¾ to 2 hours, pricking the skin occasionally with a fork to release the fat. The duck is done when the flesh feels tender and the thigh juices run clear when pierced with a fork.

While the ducks are roasting, prepare the garnish. Cut the lemon zest into the thinnest possible slivers. Combine the sugar and water in a small, heavy saucepan, add the lemon zest, bring to a simmer, and simmer for 10 to 15 minutes, or until the rind is transparent. Drain and reserve.

Shortly before the ducks are done, peel and core the pears and slice lengthwise into ¼-inch-thick wedges. Melt the butter in a large skillet, add the pears, and sprinkle with the cinnamon. Stir to blend and sauté gently for a couple of minutes, just until the pears are tender but not soft. Remove from the heat and reserve in a warm place.

Transfer the roasted duck to a large heated serving platter. Heat the pear liqueur in a small saucepan, pour over the duck, and ignite. Spoon the pears and pear juices on top and around the duck. Garnish with the lemon zest and decorate the edges of the platter with watercress.

YIELD: 8 SERVINGS

PURÉED PARSNIPS

3 pounds parsnips, peeled, trimmed, and sliced thin
1½ tablespoons unsalted butter
¼ cup Madeira
½ cup heavy cream
Fresh-ground white pepper

FOR THE GARNISH

Minced fresh parsley

Put the parsnips in a steamer basket over boiling water, cover tightly, and cook about 20 minutes, or just until tender. (You will probably have to cook them in 2 batches.) Do not overcook. Purée in a food processor in batches, and turn into an ovenproof casserole. Add the butter and stir until it melts. Stir in the Madeira, cream and white pepper to taste.

To serve, preheat the oven to 375°. Cover the casserole and reheat for 15 minutes. Sprinkle with minced fresh parsley just before serving.

YIELD: 8 SERVINGS

GINGER BOMBE FAVORITE

This is a frozen dessert made with crumbled meringues and whipped cream. It is flavored with ginger preserves and brandy, and the top is coated with melted dark chocolate.

FOR THE MERINGUES

> *4 egg whites*
> *A pinch of cream of tartar*
> *1 teaspoon vanilla extract*
> *1 cup sugar*

FOR THE CREAM MIXTURE

> *2 cups heavy cream*
> *2 tablespoons brandy*
> *¼ cup plus 2 tablespoons ginger preserve, such as Keiller's*

FOR THE CHOCOLATE COATING

> *4 ounces Baker's German's Sweet Chocolate*
> *1½ tablespoons unsalted butter*

Preheat the oven to 250°. Line 2 large baking sheets with brown paper.

To make the meringues, beat the egg whites until frothy. Add the cream of tartar and continue beating until they hold definite peaks. Add the vanilla and continue beating while gradually adding the sugar. Shape into 8 large meringues on the prepared baking sheets. Bake for 1¼ to 1½ hours, or until they are dry in the center. (If the baking sheets are on 2 separate shelves, switch them halfway through baking.) Leave the meringues to cool in the turned-off oven with the door ajar.

When the meringues are cool, break them into inch-size pieces.

Whip the cream with the brandy until it holds soft peaks. Be careful not to overbeat; it should have the consistency of crème Chantilly. Fold in the crumbled meringues and the ginger preserve. Turn into an 8-cup serving or soufflé dish and freeze until firm.

When the dessert is frozen, make the chocolate coating. Break the chocolate into very small bits and put it in the top of a double boiler with the butter. Stir constantly over hot, not simmering, water until melted. Stir off the heat to cool. Remove the dessert from the freezer and pour the melted chocolate over the top. Spread evenly with a knife. Return to the freezer until serving. (It is not necessary to remove this dessert from the freezer before serving time as the meringues prevent it from becoming too hard.)

YIELD: 10 SERVINGS

A Gala of Game Hens

BEEF AND ORANGE CONSOMMÉ

GAME HENS WITH MUSHROOM PÂTÉ

POTATO-CHEESE GALETTE

GREEN SALAD[†]

COFFEE-AMARETTO ICE CREAM

SMALL hens are an easy entrée to serve at a dinner party as each bird is an individual portion requiring no last-minute carving. They vary in size, however, and it is important to select very small ones, no larger than 1¼ pounds, to avoid overtaxing anyone's capacity. A pâté seemed a likely stuffing for these hens, but after experimenting, I found most meat preparations too rich and heavy. Mushrooms, flavored with bits of prosciutto and the sautéed hen livers, produced an equally savory filling that was lighter and more moist. Crisp brown wedges of a shredded potato and cheese mixture go with the hens. Dessert is a coffee ice cream flavored with amaretto liqueur.

Advance Preparation The Coffee-Amaretto Ice Cream may be made several days ahead. The Beef and Orange Consommé may be made a day or two ahead and reheated, but do not add the orange juice until just before serving. The Mushroom Pâté stuffing for the hens may be made a day ahead and kept tightly covered in the refrigerator. Do not stuff the hens, however, until you are ready to cook them. Some advance work may be done in the morning for the Potato-Cheese Galette, but it should be baked shortly before serving. Because the hens and Galette are cooked at different temperatures, they cannot be baked simultaneously unless you have a double oven. Bake the Galette first and keep it warm while the hens are roasting. Reheat the Galette by returning it to the oven during the last 5 to 8 minutes of cooking the hens.

BEEF AND ORANGE CONSOMMÉ

This is a simple, delicious, and warming soup for a cold winter evening. Because it is so light, it is a suitable prelude to a wide variety of entrées. Use homemade beef stock if you have it; if not, a good canned bouillon will do nicely.

5 cups strong beef stock or broth
¼ cup Madeira
1 cinnamon stick
1 cup fresh orange juice

FOR THE GARNISH

Paper-thin orange slices, seeded

In a large saucepan, combine the beef stock, Madeira, and cinnamon stick and bring to a simmer. Cover tightly and cook gently for 6 or 7 minutes. Add the orange juice and cook for half a minute, or just long enough to heat. (Do not boil after adding the juice.) Remove from the heat, discard the cinnamon stick, and ladle into bouillon cups. Garnish each serving with an orange slice.
YIELD: APPROXIMATELY 6 CUPS OR 6 TO 8 SERVINGS

GAME HENS WITH MUSHROOM PÂTÉ

Small hens are stuffed with a mushroom duxelles mixture flavored with bits of prosciutto and the chopped, sautéed hen livers.

Six 1- to 1 ¼-pound game hens
2 tablespoons unsalted butter, melted
Salt
Fresh-ground pepper

FOR THE STUFFING

1 ½ pounds mushrooms,
* cleaned and trimmed*
3 tablespoons plus 1 teaspoon
* unsalted butter*
⅓ cup minced shallot
2 garlic cloves, peeled and
* minced*
½ cup minced fresh parsley
¼ cup dry white wine
Fresh-ground pepper

2 tablespoons flour
¾ cup milk
Reserved hen livers
3 ounces prosciutto, sliced
* thin*
1 ½ slices fresh white bread,
* trimmed and crumbed*
* by hand*
1 egg, lightly beaten

FOR THE GARNISH

Watercress

Rinse the hens, removing any visible fat. Discard the neck and gizzards and reserve the livers. Dry the hens with paper towels.

To make the stuffing, chop the mushrooms fine. This can be done, a handful at a time, in a food processor. Melt the 3 tablespoons butter in a large skillet, add the mushrooms, shallot, and garlic, and sauté until the mushrooms begin to render their juices. Add the parsley, wine, and pepper (no salt), turn up the heat, and cook, stirring occasionally, until the moisture has evaporated and the mixture is fairly dry. Sprinkle with the flour, stir to blend, and gradually add the milk, stirring and cooking over moderate heat until the mixture comes to a simmer and thickens. Continue cooking for a minute or two until quite thick and then remove from the heat and let cool. Sauté the reserved hen livers in 1 teaspoon butter until cooked but slightly pink inside. Remove from the heat and chop into small pieces. Trim away all fat from the prosciutto and chop into small squares. In a mixing bowl, combine the mushrooms with the liver, prosciutto, bread crumbs, and egg. Refrigerate until the mixture is firm.

Preheat the oven to 350°. Just before cooking, stuff each hen with a couple of heaping tablespoons of the mushroom mixture. Skewer closed and truss, if desired. Place the hens in a roasting pan and brush with the melted butter. Sprinkle with salt and pepper. Roast for about 50 to 60 minutes, basting occasionally with the pan juices. When done, the juices from the thigh should run clear. Place on a heated serving platter and surround with the watercress. Skim the fat from the pan juices and spoon the juices over the hens.

YIELD: 6 SERVINGS

POTATO-CHEESE GALETTE

This is a delicious side dish, made simply of coarse-shredded potatoes and grated Parmesan and Jarlsberg and baked in a hot oven until crisp and golden brown on both sides.

> *1 pound red-skinned potatoes (approximately 4 cups, shredded)*
> *½ cup fresh-grated Parmesan cheese*
> *¾ cup grated Jarlsberg cheese*
> *Salt*
> *1 tablespoon unsalted butter*

Peel and rinse the potatoes. Pat them dry and shred coarse. (This is most easily done by processing them twice with the slicing blade of a food processor, as most shredding blades will shred them too fine.) With the slicing blade in place, run the potatoes through the feed tube. Take the slices out of the work bowl and push them through the feed tube again. You should have coarse shreds. As the potatoes are shredded, put them into a large bowl of cold water to prevent discoloring. (The recipe may be prepared ahead to this point.) Drain them well in a colander and pat dry with paper towels. In a mixing bowl, combine the potatoes, Parmesan, and Jarlsberg, and salt to taste. Melt the butter in the bottom of a 9-inch round aluminum cake pan.

Preheat the oven to 425°. Turn the potato mixture into the buttered pan, pressing it down firmly. Bake on the bottom shelf of the oven (2½ inches above the heating element) for 35 to 45 minutes, or until well browned and crusty on the top and bottom. Cut in wedges to serve.

YIELD: 6 SERVINGS

COFFEE-AMARETTO ICE CREAM

This is a soft-textured ice cream with a slight almond flavor. The recipe can be varied by substituting brandy or crème de cacao for the amaretto.

> *2 egg whites*
> *½ cup sugar (scant)*
> *1 teaspoon vanilla extract*
> *2 teaspoons instant coffee*
>   *dissolved in 2 teaspoons*
>   *hot water*
>
> *1 teaspoon unsweetened*
>   *cocoa*
> *2 tablespoons amaretto*
> *1 cup heavy cream*

Beat the egg whites until they hold soft peaks. Continue beating until stiff while gradually adding the sugar. Beat in the vanilla, dissolved coffee, and cocoa.

Whip the cream with the amaretto and fold into the meringue mixture. Turn into a serving bowl or freezer container and freeze until firm. Serve with amaretti (Italian macaroons) on the side, or, if desired, dust the top of each serving with amaretti crumbs.

YIELD: APPROXIMATELY 1 QUART OR 6 SERVINGS

A Mediterranean Dinner

PROSCIUTTO AND PEARS

GREEK SHRIMP

RICE†

GREEN SALAD†

SLICED ORANGES WITH CURAÇAO†
AND CHOCOLATE-ALMOND COOKIES

IN the middle of winter it is tempting to dream of a warmer climate, and here is a Mediterranean-style dinner to encourage fantasies of sun and warm beaches. The appetizer is a winter variation of prosciutto and melon, substituting pears; the entrée a Greek seafood dish combining shrimp, tomatoes, and feta cheese. It is a simple but hearty and flavorful meal, and practical for entertaining, as the entrée can be made ahead. Serve a light dessert of sliced oranges and cookies.

Advance Preparation The Greek Shrimp can be made a day ahead and reheated before serving. The cookies may also be made a day in advance. Prepare the Prosciutto and Pears about 2 hours before serving.

PROSCIUTTO AND PEARS

3 tablespoons lemon juice
1 cup water
4 Bosc or Anjou pears
6–8 ounces prosciutto, sliced very thin

Combine the lemon juice and water in a small bowl. Peel, quarter, and core the pears and slice lengthwise ¼ inch thick. As they are sliced dip in the water and lemon juice to prevent discoloring. Arrange the pears on 8 appetizer plates and drape 1 or 2 slices of prosciutto on top. Cover tightly with plastic wrap and refrigerate until serving.

YIELD: 8 SERVINGS

GREEK SHRIMP

Sautéed shrimp combined with tomatoes, onions, and chunks of feta cheese, as well as fennel and ouzo, which give the dish a faint anise flavor. It can be made ahead and reheated before serving.

2 tablespoons unsalted butter
1⅓ cups chopped fennel bulb
1 cup chopped yellow onion
2 teaspoons minced garlic
Two 28-ounce cans Italian plum tomatoes, well-drained and chopped coarse
¼ cup minced fennel ferns
Grated zest of ½ a large lemon
A strip of orange zest
Fresh-ground pepper
2 pounds large or medium-size, unshelled shrimp
¼ cup ouzo*
10 ounces feta cheese, cut into ¾-inch chunks and rinsed

* Ouzo is an anise-flavored Greek liqueur. You may substitute Pernod, but since it is stronger in flavor, use less. Start with 2 tablespoons, adding more to taste if necessary after the casserole is assembled. The Italian anisette is not a satisfactory substitute as it is too sweet.

FOR THE GARNISH

¼ cup minced fresh parsley

Melt 1 tablespoon of the butter in a very large skillet and sauté the fennel for a few minutes; then cover the pan and cook over low heat until softened. Add the onion and garlic to the pan and cook, uncovered, until the vegetables are soft. Do not brown. Add the chopped tomatoes, fennel ferns, lemon zest, orange zest, and pepper. Do not add salt. Turn up the heat and cook, stirring frequently, until most of the liquid has evaporated. Turn the mixture into a casserole, and discard the orange zest.

Peel and devein the shrimp. Melt the remaining tablespoon butter in the skillet and sauté the shrimp, stirring, for 1 or 2 minutes, or just until they turn pink. Add the ouzo, ignite, and shake the pan until the flames die down. Add the mixture to the casserole. Stir in the feta cheese. (The dish may be prepared ahead to this point. Cover and refrigerate.)

To serve, return the casserole to room temperature. Preheat the oven to 400°, and bake the casserole, uncovered, for 15 to 20 minutes, or just until heated through. The cheese should be quite soft, but not completely melted. Garnish with minced parsley and serve over plain cooked rice.

YIELD: 6 TO 8 SERVINGS

CHOCOLATE-ALMOND COOKIES

These drop cookies are dark, moist, and intensely flavored.

½ cup blanched, slivered almonds
2½ ounces unsweetened baking chocolate
4 tablespoons unsalted butter
1 egg

¾ cup plus 1 tablespoon sugar
¼ teaspoon almond extract
¼ teaspoon vanilla extract
⅓ cup flour

Preheat the oven to 350°.

Spread the almonds on a baking sheet and bake for 5 minutes. They should be very faintly colored, but not browned. Grind them in a food processor and reserve.

Lightly butter a large cookie sheet.

Break the chocolate into small pieces and melt it with the butter in the top of a double boiler over hot, not simmering, water, stirring constantly. Beat the egg with an electric mixer, adding the sugar gradually. Stir in the almond and vanilla extracts, the melted chocolate mixture, the ground almonds, and the flour. Drop by teaspoonfuls, about 1 inch apart, on the prepared cookie sheet. Bake for 8 to 10 minutes, or until dry on the outside but slightly moist in the center. Cool for a minute before transferring to a wire rack.

YIELD: APPROXIMATELY 2½ DOZEN

A Holiday Dinner Party

CHESTNUT SOUP OR
BAKED FENNEL AND CHÈVRE

BEEFSTEAK AND KIDNEY PIE

ROOT VEGETABLE PURÉE OR
MUSHROOM TIMBALE

GREEN SALAD†

BÛCHE DE NOËL AU CITRON

T HERE are plenty of recipes for roast turkey, and I am not inclined to add to them. (Nor would I feel entirely confident about it. One year, attempting novelty, I made turkey with oyster stuffing, and my son, then five, ate nothing. When I asked why he didn't like the turkey, he replied, "It tasted like walrus.") The entrée for this holiday menu is Beefsteak and Kidney Pie, one of the many gifts of traditional English cookery. Because it is not so commonly served in the United States, it can be the basis for a festive and unusual holiday meal. Begin the meal with a creamy chestnut soup flavored with Madeira or with Baked Fennel and Chèvre. Serve Mushroom Timbale or Root Vegetable Purée with the entrée, then a green salad, and a Bûche de Noël for dessert. In this variation of the traditional

Christmas "log," the chocolate sponge cake is filled with an unexpected, tart lemon mousse.

Advance Preparation The Chestnut Soup, the Baked Fennel and Chèvre, the Root Vegetable Purée, and the Bûche de Noël may be made a day in advance. Most of the work for the Beefsteak and Kidney Pie may be done the day before serving, as indicated in the recipe. The Mushroom Timbale mixture may be prepared on the morning of the party and cooked before serving.

CHESTNUT SOUP

A smooth, thick purée of chestnuts, delicately flavored with Madeira.

2½ pounds unshelled chestnuts (5 cups shelled)	*4¼ cups chicken stock or broth*
3 tablespoons unsalted butter	*1 cup heavy cream*
2½ tablespoons minced shallot	*¼ cup Madeira*
3 tablespoons flour	*A pinch of nutmeg*

Cut an X into the flat side of each chestnut shell. Cover them with water, bring to a boil, and boil for 5 minutes. Drain and, while they are still warm, peel off the shells and skins. Put the chestnuts in a large saucepan with the butter and shallots and cook gently for a few minutes. Blend in the flour. Add the chicken stock gradually, blending with a whisk, and bring to a simmer. Cover and cook gently for 30 to 40 minutes, or until the chestnuts are soft.

Purée the chestnuts in a food processor or blender, in batches, adding the stock in a thin stream. Stir in the cream and Madeira and a little nutmeg. Reheat before serving.

YIELD: 7½ TO 8 CUPS OR 8 SERVINGS

BAKED FENNEL AND CHÈVRE

These may be served as a first course or as an hors d'oeuvre with drinks.

FOR EACH SERVING

> *3–4 inner stalks from a fennel bulb*
> *1 ½–2 ounces rindless chèvre**
> *Minced fennel ferns*

Cut the green part off the fennel stalks so that only the triangular white part remains. Bring a pot of water to a boil and blanche the fennel for 2 minutes. Drain and rinse under cold water. Dry the leaves and spread the inside with the chèvre. Arrange in a shallow baking dish and cover tightly with plastic wrap until you are ready to serve.

To serve, preheat the oven to 375°. Bake the fennel for 10 minutes. Remove from the oven and garnish each leaf with minced fennel ferns.

* Use a mild chèvre, such as Montrachet, or an herb-flavored Lezay.

BEEFSTEAK AND KIDNEY PIE

*Ingredients for single-crust
  pie (page 19)*
1 pound veal kidneys
1 tablespoon unsalted butter
5 slices bacon
*3 pounds beef chuck, cut
  into 1-inch cubes*
*1 pound small white pearl
  onions*
¼ cup flour
3 cups beef stock or broth
½ cup Madeira

3 tablespoons tomato paste
*1 ½ teaspoons minced
  garlic*
¼ teaspoon dried thyme
*3 tablespoons minced fresh
  parsley*
Fresh-ground pepper
Salt, if necessary
*1 tablespoon flour blended
  with 1 tablespoon soft
  butter (optional)*

FOR THE GLAZE

1 egg beaten with 1 teaspoon water

Mix the ingredients for the pie crust according to the directions on page 20. Wrap the dough in wax paper and refrigerate.

Remove the outer white membrane from the kidneys. Melt the butter in a large skillet and cook the kidneys over moderate heat for about 10 minutes, turning to brown both sides. When done, they should be slightly pink inside. Remove from the pan and reserve.

Fry the bacon until crisp, reserving the fat. Drain on paper towels, crumble, and reserve.

Heat a little of the bacon fat in the skillet. Dry the beef with paper towels and brown a handful at a time on all sides, adding more fat to the pan as necessary. As it is browned, transfer to a platter and reserve.

Bring a pot of water to a boil and boil the onions for 1 minute to facilitate peeling. Drain, run under cold water, and peel. Add the onions to the skillet in which the beef was browned and cook, stirring occasionally, until golden. Cover the pan, lower the heat, and cook until they are tender. Reserve.

Put the beef into a heavy, flame-proof casserole. Sprinkle with the flour and stir to blend. Add the bacon, beef stock, Madeira, tomato paste, garlic, thyme, parsley, pepper, and salt if needed. Cover tightly and simmer for about 2 hours, or until the meat is tender. After the meat has cooked, check the consistency of the gravy. If it is not thick enough, stir in 1 tablespoon of flour that has been thoroughly blended with 1 tablespoon of soft butter. Remove from the heat. (The recipe may be prepared in advance to this point. Cool to room temperature and refrigerate.)

To complete cooking, preheat the oven to 375°. Remove the fat from the top of the stew. Return to room temperature. Slice the kidneys ⅛ inch thick and trim off any fat. Add the kidneys and reserved onions to the stew and transfer to a deep, 2-quart baking dish or soufflé dish. Roll out the pastry between lightly floured sheets of wax paper to fit the top of the dish. Place it on top, doubling the crust at the rim. Decorate with leaves cut from scraps of pastry and cut air vents in the crust. Brush with the egg glaze. Bake for about 30 minutes, or until the crust has browned.

YIELD: 6 TO 8 SERVINGS

ROOT VEGETABLE PURÉE

4 tablespoons unsalted butter
1 large garlic clove, peeled
  and minced
1 pound yellow onions,
  peeled and chopped fine
  (3 cups)
1 pound parsnips, peeled
  and sliced thin

½ pound turnips, peeled
  and sliced thin
1 pound new potatoes
2 tablespoons heavy cream
Salt

FOR THE GARNISH

2 tablespoons minced fresh parsley

Melt 2 tablespoons butter in a skillet and sauté the garlic and onions until very soft, but do not brown.

Place the parsnips and turnips in a steamer basket and cook, covered, over boiling water until tender.

Boil the potatoes in water to cover until tender. Peel and chop coarse.

In a large mixing bowl, combine the parsnips, turnips, potatoes, and a little more than half the sautéed onion mixture. Purée, in batches, in a food processor. Turn into an oven-proof serving dish and stir in the remaining onions, the remaining 2 tablespoons butter, the cream, and salt to taste.

To serve, preheat the oven to 375°. Cover the vegetable dish and bake for 15 to 20 minutes, or until heated through. Sprinkle with minced parsley and serve.

YIELD: 4 CUPS OR 6 TO 8 SERVINGS

MUSHROOM TIMBALE

This is a soufflé-like mixture of sautéed mushrooms delicately flavored with sour cream, St. André cheese, and mozzarella. It can be made either in a large terrine or in individual custard cups that can be unmolded.

1½ pounds firm, white
  mushrooms, cleaned and
  trimmed
4 tablespoons unsalted butter
⅓ cup minced shallot
¼ cup dry white wine
Salt
Fresh-ground pepper
¼ pound St. André cheese,
  firm and slightly underripe

½ cup sour cream
¼ cup milk
⅓ cup minced fresh parsley
8 eggs
4 ounces mozzarella cheese,
  diced fine

FOR THE GARNISH

Minced fresh parsley

Reserve 2 cups of the mushrooms and chop the rest fine. (This may be done in a food processor, a handful at a time.) Melt 3 tablespoons of the butter in a large skillet. Sauté the shallots gently for 1 or 2 minutes. Add the minced mushrooms, sprinkle with the wine, and season lightly with salt and pepper. Turn up the heat and cook, stirring occasionally, until the moisture evaporates. Turn into a heatproof bowl.

Slice the reserved 2 cups mushrooms and sauté until tender in the remaining tablespoon butter. Add to the minced mushrooms. Cream the St. André cheese and combine with the sour cream, milk, and parsley. Stir into the mushroom mixture, along with 6 of the eggs, lightly beaten. Place the mixing bowl over a pan of barely simmering water and cook, stirring constantly, until the mixture thickens (about 5 minutes). Remove from the heat. (The dish may be prepared ahead to this point.)

Preheat the oven to 375°. Generously butter a 6-cup charlotte mold or soufflé dish; and if the dish is to be unmolded, fit the bottom with a buttered piece of wax paper. Beat the 2 remaining eggs and fold into the mushroom mixture along with the mozzarella. Turn into the prepared baking dish and place inside a large baking pan. Pour enough boiling water into the pan to reach about halfway up the mold. Bake for 40 to 45 minutes. Serve from the dish or unmolded, and garnish with minced parsley.

To make individual timbales, generously butter 8 small ramekins or custard cups and fill each about ⅔ full. Place them in a large pan, add an inch of boiling water, and bake at 375° for 15 minutes, or until a knife inserted in the center tests clean. Run a knife around the sides of each to loosen and unmold onto serving plates. Garnish each serving with minced parsley.

YIELD: 8 SERVINGS

BÛCHE DE NOËL AU CITRON

This is a variation on the classic chocolate sponge roll. Instead of using whipped cream, it is filled with a tart lemon mousse, for an interesting contrast of flavors. The chocolate roll itself has a rich, chocolaty flavor, using 1½ times as much chocolate as most recipes. Because the lemon mousse is held firm with gelatin, the dessert can be made and assembled the day before serving without becoming soggy.

FOR THE CHOCOLATE SPONGE

6 eggs, separated
¾ cup plus 1 tablespoon sugar
1 teaspoon vanilla extract
3 tablespoons unsweetened cocoa, sifted
6 ounces Baker's German's Sweet Chocolate

FOR THE LEMON MOUSSE FILLING

4 egg yolks
½ cup strained lemon juice
¾ cup sugar
2 teaspoons unflavored
gelatin

2 tablespoons cold water
Grated zest of 1 large lemon
2 egg whites
1 cup heavy cream

FOR THE GARNISH

Confectioners' sugar

Preheat the oven to 375°. Line a 15-by-10-inch jelly roll pan with wax paper and butter and flour the paper.

To make the chocolate sponge, beat the egg yolks, gradually adding all but 3 tablespoons of the sugar, until the mixture is light. Fold in the vanilla and sifted cocoa.

Break the chocolate into small pieces and melt it in the top of a double boiler over hot, not simmering, water, stirring constantly. Remove from the heat, stir to cool slightly, and fold into the egg yolk mixture.

Beat the egg whites until they hold peaks. Continue beating while gradually adding the remaining 3 tablespoons sugar. Carefully, but thoroughly, fold the egg whites into the chocolate mixture. Spread evenly in the prepared pan and bake for 15 minutes, or until a toothpick tests clean. While the cake is baking, wring out a clean cotton or linen dish towel in cold water. Place the cake, in the pan, on a wire rack and cover with the damp towel. When the cake is cool, place in the refrigerator to chill.

While the cake is baking and cooling, prepare the lemon mousse. Lightly beat the egg yolks in a small, heavy saucepan. Stir in the lemon juice and ½ cup of the sugar. Cook over low heat, stirring constantly, for 10 to 15 minutes, or until thick. Cool to room temperature. Soften the gelatin in the cold water and dissolve over low heat, stirring constantly. Stir the dissolved gelatin and the grated zest into the lemon custard. Beat the egg whites until almost stiff. Gradually add 2 tablespoons sugar, and beat until stiff. Whip the cream with the remaining 2 tablespoons sugar until it holds soft peaks. Fold together the whipped cream, egg whites, and lemon custard. Refrigerate for 20 to 30 minutes, or until slightly firm.

Place 2 long, overlapping sheets of wax paper on the counter and dust lightly with confectioners' sugar or cocoa. When the cake is cold, take it out of the refrigerator and loosen the edges with a knife. Unmold onto the wax paper and peel the paper off the bottom of the cake. Spread with the lemon mousse. Carefully roll up the cake from the long side by lifting the wax paper and turning the cake onto itself. It will crack a bit at the sides. Lift the roll onto a serving platter and cover loosely with wax paper. Refrigerate until serving. Sift confectioners' sugar over the top of the cake just before serving.

YIELD: 10 TO 12 SERVINGS

A Roast Lamb Dinner for
Ten or Twelve

CELERY AND GORGONZOLA SOUP

LEG OF LAMB WITH GREEN
PEPPERCORN AND MINT SAUCE

SPINACH, CHEESE, AND
MUSHROOM CASSEROLE

BRAISED FENNEL

GREEN SALAD†

MOCHA MOUSSE WITH CHOCOLATE-
ALMOND BRITTLE (page 147)

A roast leg of lamb is a popular entrée for a dinner party, and the house smells wonderful as it is cooking. For this recipe, the lamb is accompanied by an equally aromatic pan gravy flavored with green peppercorns and mint. Opinions vary about whether to shave off the fell—the fiberlike layer covering the leg. My butcher maintains that it gives the meat a strong, muttony flavor that many people object to, and so I always let him remove it. The recipe for the soup, a discreet blend of celery and Gorgonzola, is one I created when

Leo Lerman asked me to develop some cheese recipes for *Vogue*. Braised Fennel, as well as a mixture of spinach, cheese, and mushrooms, is served with the lamb. Such a meal seems to require a dessert with its own assertive character, and so the menu concludes with a Mocha Mousse punctuated with bits of chocolate brittle.

Advance Preparation   The Mocha Mousse may be made one day before serving. The Celery and Gorgonzola Soup, the Spinach, Cheese, and Mushroom Casserole and the Braised Fennel may be made a day ahead and reheated before serving. The lamb should be marinated the day before cooking. Except for the addition of pan juices, the gravy for the lamb can be prepared on the morning of the party.

CELERY AND GORGONZOLA SOUP

For many years, celery sticks filled with blue cheese have been a favorite cocktail party hors d'oeuvre. Here, the same flavors, in delicate balance, are translated into a smooth and thick soup. The Gorgonzola sold in Italy is as creamy as a ripe Brie. While it is difficult to find one so mellow here, try to select an imported Gorgonzola that is soft and cream-colored and not overripe. Avoid the hard, white variety.

2 extra-large heads celery (4–4½ pounds total), washed, trimmed, and cut into 1 inch lengths
2 large potatoes, peeled and sliced
1 medium yellow onion, peeled and quartered
4 large garlic cloves, peeled
A few sprigs of parsley
3½–4 cups chicken stock or broth
4 ounces mild Gorgonzola (use 1 ounce less if not mild)
Fresh-ground white pepper

Put the celery, potato, onion, garlic, parsley, and 3½ cups chicken stock into a large, heavy saucepan. Cover tightly and simmer for 30 to 40 minutes, or until the celery is soft. In a food processor, purée the vegetables with the Gorgonzola and a few tablespoons of the cooking broth, in several batches. Turn into a bowl and stir in the rest of the cooking broth. If the mixture is too thick, add a little extra chicken stock. Season with pepper. Reheat before serving.

If you prefer a richer soup, prepare the recipe above using 1 cup less chicken stock and add 1 cup heavy cream to the soup just before reheating.

YIELD: APPROXIMATELY 10 CUPS OR 10 TO 12 SERVINGS

LEG OF LAMB WITH GREEN PEPPERCORN AND MINT SAUCE

The lamb is marinated in red wine flavored with mint and garlic and served with green peppercorn and mint sauce to which cooking juices have been added. If you prefer to use a boned leg of lamb, roast for 25 to 30 minutes per pound or until a meat thermometer registers 145° to 150°.

One 7-pound leg of lamb with bone in
4 garlic cloves, peeled and slivered

FOR THE MARINADE

1½ cups dry red wine
3 tablespoons olive oil
1 teaspoon dried mint leaves
Fresh-ground pepper

FOR THE GRAVY

1 teaspoon green peppercorns
3 tablespoons unsalted butter
2 tablespoons minced shallot
2 tablespoons minced fresh
mint leaves or ¼ teaspoon
dried

2 tablespoons flour
2 teaspoons Düsseldorf or
Dijon mustard
1 cup beef stock or broth
Degreased pan juices

FOR THE GARNISH

2 bunches watercress

Wipe the lamb with damp paper towels. Make small incisions here and there on the surface of the lamb and stud with slivers of garlic. Combine the ingredients for the marinade in a large glass, ceramic, or enamel pan. Put in the lamb, cover loosely, and marinate in the refrigerator for 24 hours, turning a few times.

Except for the addition of pan juices, the gravy for the lamb can be prepared well in advance of roasting. Crush the peppercorns in a garlic press or with the back of a spoon. Melt the butter in a heavy saucepan. Add the peppercorns, shallot, and mint leaves and sauté very gently until the shallot is soft, but do not brown. Blend in the flour and mustard. Slowly add the beef stock, stirring to blend. Bring to a simmer and cook for a few minutes, stirring. Remove from the heat and reserve.

Several hours before roasting, remove the lamb from the refrigerator and marinate at room temperature. To roast, preheat the oven to 500°. Take the lamb out of the marinade, dry thoroughly with paper towels, and put it on a rack in a roasting pan. Reserve the marinade for basting. Roast for 15 minutes at 500°. Lower the oven temperature to 350° and cook for 1 to 1¼ hours longer, or a total cooking time of 11 to 13 minutes per pound. When done, a meat thermometer should register 145° to 150°. (If your lamb weighs more or less than 7 pounds, adjust the cooking time accordingly, and if it is boned, it will take about a half hour longer to cook.) While the lamb is cooking, baste it with all the reserved marinade, as the pan juices will be used in the gravy.

When done, remove the lamb from the oven, transfer to a warm platter, and allow it to rest in a warm place for about 20 minutes. Meanwhile, degrease the pan juices and stir into the gravy. Heat the gravy to simmering before pouring into a warm sauceboat. Carve the lamb, garnish the platter with watercress, and serve immediately.
YIELD: 12 SERVINGS

SPINACH, CHEESE, AND MUSHROOM CASSEROLE

Six 10-ounce packages fresh spinach
1 1/4 pounds mushrooms
2 1/2 tablespoons unsalted butter
12 ounces Jarlsberg cheese, grated
1/4 cup fresh-grated Parmesan cheese

Wash the spinach, discarding the stems and any wilted leaves. Cook in a covered enamel or stainless steel pot in the water clinging to the leaves. Drain well in a colander, pressing out the moisture with a large wooden spoon. Chop coarse.

Clean and trim the mushrooms, reserving 10 to 12 medium-size caps for garnish. Slice the remainder and sauté in 2 tablespoons of the butter until tender. Remove from the skillet and gently sauté the reserved caps in the remaining 1/2 tablespoon butter.

Combine the spinach with the sliced mushrooms and any accumulated juices and the Jarlsberg cheese and turn into a buttered 2-quart casserole. Arrange the mushroom caps in a border around the top. Sprinkle with the grated Parmesan.

To serve, preheat the oven to 350°. Bake, uncovered, for 20 minutes, or until heated through.
YIELD: 10 TO 12 SERVINGS

BRAISED FENNEL

6 medium-large fennel bulbs (¾ pound each)
2 tablespoons butter
2½ cups chicken broth
½ cup fresh-grated Parmesan cheese

Trim the green stalks and ferns and any tough outer stalks from the fennel bulbs and discard. Cut each bulb lengthwise into quarters or sixths and wash well under running water, being careful not to separate the stalks. Melt the butter in a large, heavy skillet and brown the fennel, cut side down. When the fennel is browned, pour the chicken broth into the pan, bring to a simmer, cover, and cook gently for about 20 minutes, or until the fennel is tender, turning over once so that it cooks evenly. Drain and arrange the fennel quarters in one layer in a large, shallow baking dish, cut sides up. Sprinkle with the Parmesan.

To serve, preheat the oven to 350°. Bake the fennel for 20 minutes, or until heated through.

YIELD: 10 TO 12 SERVINGS

A Holiday Buffet

CHICKEN CURRY WITH

ASSORTED CONDIMENTS

RICE[†]

BAKED BANANAS WITH CURAÇAO OR

SLICED ORANGES WITH CURAÇAO[†]

GINGER AND KUMQUAT CAKE

HAM and turkey are served too often at holiday parties, both because they are considered seasonal and because they are easy entrées to make for a crowd. But by the time your friends arrive at your house, they are likely to be surfeited with holiday foods. Treat them to something different and equally festive. A creamy and spicy chicken curry, served with an impressive array of condiments and rice, is a delicious and easy alternative for a buffet dinner. A fruit dessert should follow the curry, with slices of Ginger and Kumquat Cake, an unusual holiday fruitcake. The recipes on this menu can be doubled to serve twelve.

Advance Preparation   The Chicken Curry and the Ginger and Kumquat Cake may be made the day before the party. If you are making the Baked Bananas for dessert, they must be cooked just before serving.

CHICKEN CURRY

This is a good party dish because it can be made ahead and reheated before serving. The curry sauce is mild and creamy, flavored with lime and chutney as well as spices.

One 4-pound chicken, cut up
2 carrots, scraped and chopped
2 ribs of celery, chopped
1 large yellow onion, peeled and quartered
Several sprigs of parsley

FOR THE CURRY SAUCE

4 tablespoons unsalted butter
3 medium yellow onions,
  peeled and chopped
  (2 cups)
3 garlic cloves, peeled and
  minced
2 tart apples, peeled, cored,
  and chopped (3 cups)
½ cup flour
2 cups reserved chicken broth
2 tablespoons curry powder

1 teaspoon cumin
1 teaspoon soy sauce
Grated zest of 1 lime
1½ tablespoons lime juice
1 pint sour cream
½ cup yellow raisins
2 tablespoons Major Grey's
  chutney, preferably Sun
  Brand, sieved (or use
  liquid only)
Salt

FOR THE CONDIMENTS

Chopped, salted peanuts
Toasted, flaked coconut
Dark raisins
Cucumber sticks
Major Grey's chutney, preferably Sun Brand

Wash the chicken and put it in a pot with the chopped carrots, celery, onion, parsley, and just enough water to cover. Place the lid, slightly ajar, on the pot and bring the water to a simmer. Cook gently for 20 minutes, or just until done. Do not overcook. Remove the chicken pieces and, when cool enough to handle, strip the meat from the skin and bones and cut into strips or bite-size pieces. Boil the cooking broth in the pot until it is reduced to 2 cups. Skim the fat off the top and reserve the broth.

To make the sauce, melt the butter in a large skillet and sauté the onions, garlic, and apples until softened, but do not brown. Sprinkle with the flour, stir to blend, and gradually add the 2 cups reserved broth, stirring constantly until the broth comes to a simmer and thickens. Stir in the remaining ingredients for the sauce, adding salt to taste. (The curry may be prepared ahead to this point.)

Before serving, gradually bring the sauce to a simmer and cook, stirring occasionally, for a few minutes. Add the chicken and heat it briefly, being careful not to overcook it. Serve with boiled rice and set out the condiments separately.

YIELD: 6 SERVINGS

BAKED BANANAS WITH CURAÇAO

A quick and simple fruit dessert. Serve with a scoop of vanilla ice cream if you like.

FOR EACH SERVING

1 large banana, peeled and cut in half lengthwise
1 tablespoon brown sugar
Cinnamon
1 tablespoon unsalted butter
2 tablespoons curaçao

Preheat the oven to 375°.

Put the bananas, cut side up, in a buttered baking and serving dish. Spread the brown sugar over the top, dust lightly with cinnamon, and dot with the butter. Bake for 20 minutes and remove from the oven. Heat the curaçao in a small saucepan and pour over the bananas. Ignite and serve.

The bananas can be baked in the same way, flaming them with rum instead of curaçao and sweetening with brown sugar, honey, or maple syrup.

GINGER AND KUMQUAT CAKE

This is a very different kind of holiday fruitcake—light cake squares studded with preserved kumquats and ginger stem and flavored with curaçao or brandy.

6 tablespoons unsalted butter
½ cup sugar
1 egg
½ teaspoon grated lemon zest
1½ tablespoons curaçao or brandy
½ cup blanched, slivered almonds, ground

¾ cup flour
1 teaspoon baking powder
¼ cup thin-sliced preserved ginger stem
¼ cup chopped and seeded preserved kumquats

Preheat the oven to 325°. Butter an 8-inch-square baking pan.

Cream the butter, gradually adding the sugar. Add the egg and beat well. Stir in the lemon zest, curaçao or brandy, and ground almonds. Sift together the flour and baking powder and fold into the batter. Mix in the preserved ginger and kumquats. Turn into the prepared pan and bake for about 30 minutes, or until a toothpick tests clean. Cool in the pan on a wire rack and cut into 16 squares.

YIELD: 16 PIECES

A Birthday Dinner for Tony

TOMATO-BURGUNDY SOUP

FILETS IN FILO

MOUSSELINE SAUCE (page 179)

PURÉED SPINACH

GREEN SALAD WITH ARUGOLA[†]

GORGONZOLA AND ST. ANDRÉ CHEESE[†]

CHOCOLATE-MARRON CAKE

My husband loves to celebrate his birthday, and I love giving him parties. For a few years, these were surprise parties, but he caught on to that rather quickly. Now they are likely to be large cocktail-buffets for about sixty guests. There is almost always a blizzard on that evening, but in Rochester it is considered poor form to be deterred by a little bad weather. Everyone always shows up in high spirits, having successfully defied the elements. On Tony's most recent birthday, we were in Washington and elected to celebrate with a small dinner party. The entrée was my own version of Beef Wellington, made up in individual filo-wrapped portions of filet mignon. With this method, most of the cooking can be done in advance. Each year I feel challenged to create yet another special birthday cake. The present one is .a four-layered composition of génoise, chestnut cream, and chocolate mousse with marrons, and is modestly offered as my third contribution to a spectacular series of birthday cakes for Tony.

Advance Preparation   The Tomato-Burgundy Soup, the Filets, the Puréed Spinach, and the Chocolate-Marron Cake may be made a day before serving. If you are preparing the filets in advance, they must be returned to room temperature before the final baking.

TOMATO-BURGUNDY SOUP

A good cold-weather appetizer; it is warming and invigorating without being filling.

1 tablespoon unsalted butter
2 medium garlic cloves,
    peeled and minced
2 tablespoons minced shallot
Three 28-ounce cans Italian
    tomatoes, well-drained
2½ cups chicken stock or
    broth
A 3-inch strip of lemon zest
    without white pith

A 2-inch piece of cinnamon
    stick
A small piece of whole
    nutmeg
5 peppercorns
1 cup Burgundy or dry red
    wine
1 cup orange juice

FOR THE GARNISH

Paper-thin orange slices, seeded

Melt the butter in a large skillet and gently sauté the garlic and shallot for a few minutes without browning. Add the tomatoes and break them up with a metal spoon. Add the chicken stock, lemon, zest, and spices, cover tightly, and simmer gently for 45 minutes.

Strain through a food mill, pressing through as much pulp as possible. To serve, put in a large saucepan with the Burgundy and reheat. Stir in the orange juice and heat for a few seconds but do not boil. Garnish each serving with an orange slice.

YIELD: 10 SERVINGS

FILETS IN FILO

This is a beef Wellington made in individual portions, using a separate filet mignon for each serving and wrapping it, with the mushroom and foie gras stuffing, in flaky filo pastry. The dish can be prepared a day ahead; it is then baked for 15 minutes before serving to reheat the beef and brown the pastry.

1–2 tablespoons unsalted butter

8 small filets of beef, each 1¼–1⅜ inches thick*

Approximately 8 tablespoons unsalted butter, melted

1 package frozen filo pastry, defrosted

Fine, dry bread crumbs

1 egg, lightly beaten

Mousseline Sauce (page 179)

FOR THE STUFFING

2 tablespoons unsalted butter

3 tablespoons minced shallots

1 pound mushrooms, cleaned, trimmed, and minced

Fresh-ground pepper

3 tablespoons Madeira

4½ ounces tinned foie gras or smoked goose pâté

To make the stuffing, melt the butter in a large skillet. Add the shallots, mushrooms, and a generous amount of pepper. Cook over moderately high heat until the mushrooms begin to render their juices. Sprinkle with the Madeira and continue to cook, stirring

---

* If the filets are cut thicker, the serving size will be too large, and if they are thinner, they will not remain rare after baking.

frequently, until all the moisture has evaporated and the mushrooms are completely dry. Remove from the heat and cool to room temperature. Stir in the foie gras, taste, and add 1 or 2 more teaspoons Madeira, if desired. Cover, and chill.

To cook the filets, melt 1 tablespoon butter in a large skillet and add half the filets. Sauté over high heat for no more than 2 minutes on each side. The outside should be browned and the inside quite undercooked. Remove from the heat and cook the remaining filets in the same way, adding more butter if necessary. Cool to room temperature. Dry the filets thoroughly with paper towels. Press equal amounts of the chilled mushroom mixture on top of each filet.

To wrap in filo, put the melted butter in the top of a double boiler over hot water and place it near your work area. Brush a shallow baking pan large enough to hold the filets with a little of the butter. Dampen 2 clean cotton or linen dish towels and wring out. Lay one towel over your work area. Unfold the stack of filo sheets and lay them flat over 2 sheets of wax paper. Remove one sheet of filo and place it on top of the damp towel. Cover the remaining filo with additional wax paper and with the other wet towel.

Brush half the sheet of filo with melted butter and sprinkle lightly with bread crumbs. Fold over the unbuttered half so that you have a rectangle about 8 by 14 inches. Butter the top layer and dust with bread crumbs. Fold the edges of each side of the rectangle in about 1 inch and brush the edges with beaten egg. Place a filet in the center of the rectangle, mushroom side down. Fold the bottom flap over the beef and then the top, as you would a letter, and lightly press the edges to seal. Invert the wrapped filet onto the baking pan so that the stuffing is uppermost and brush the top and sides with melted butter. Continue assembling the remaining filets in this way. As you work, remember to keep the filo that is not in use covered with wax paper and a damp towel or it will dry out and become brittle. The dish can be prepared in advance to this point. Cover the baking sheet with plastic wrap and refrigerate.

To make the Mousseline Sauce, prepare the Mint and Chive Mousseline Sauce on page 179, substituting ¼ teaspoon dried tarragon for the mint and chives.

To serve, remove from the refrigerator 3 hours before serving to return the beef to room temperature. Preheat the oven to 375°.

Bake, uncovered, for 12 to 15 minutes, or just until the pastry is lightly browned and the beef reheated. Serve the sauce on the side.
YIELD: 8 SERVINGS

PURÉED SPINACH

Four 10-ounce packages fresh spinach
1½ tablespoons flour
⅓ cup heavy cream
1 cup plus 2 tablespoons sour cream

1¼ teaspoons Worcestershire sauce
Salt
Fresh-ground pepper
A pinch of nutmeg

Wash the spinach, discarding the stems and any wilted leaves. Drain and cook in a large stainless steel or enameled saucepan in the water clinging to the leaves. Drain well in a colander. When the spinach is cool enough to handle, squeeze out as much water as possible, a handful at a time. Purée, with the flour, in a food processor or blender, gradually adding the cream and sour cream. Add the Worcestershire sauce and seasonings and blend. Transfer to an oven-proof casserole or vegetable dish. (The dish may be prepared ahead to this point.)

To serve, preheat the oven to 375°. Heat the spinach, covered, for 15 minutes. Do not overcook or it will discolor.
YIELD: 8 SERVINGS

CHOCOLATE-MARRON CAKE

Four thin génoise—or butter sponge—layers are filled alternately with a chocolate-marron mousse (containing pieces of candied chestnuts) and a chestnut-cream filling. The top layer is glazed with chocolate icing.

FOR THE CAKE LAYERS

6 eggs, at room temperature
¾ cup sugar
1 ½ teaspoons vanilla extract
1 cup plus 2 tablespoons flour
8 tablespoons unsalted butter, melted

FOR THE CHOCOLATE MOUSSE FILLING

6 ounces Baker's semi-sweet
   chocolate
4 tablespoons unsalted butter
3 egg yolks
2 egg whites
2 ½ tablespoons sugar
¾ cup heavy cream

1 ½ teaspoons vanilla
   extract
One 10-ounce jar Raffetto
   vanilla-flavored marron
   pieces, very well drained
   (¾ cup)

FOR THE CHESTNUT FILLING

⅔ cup heavy cream
2 teaspoons brandy
½ cup Clément Faugier chestnut spread

FOR THE ICING

4 ounces Baker's semi-sweet chocolate
2 ½ tablespoons unsalted butter

To make the cake layers, preheat the oven to 350°. Butter and lightly flour 2 pieces of wax paper to fit the bottom of two 9-inch round cake pans. Combine the eggs and sugar in a large mixing bowl and place over a pan of simmering water. Stir continuously until the eggs are quite warm, but do not let them cook. Remove the bowl from the heat and beat with an electric mixer for 7 or 8 minutes, or until the mixture has the consistency of lightly whipped cream and has tripled in volume. Blend in the vanilla. Sift the flour on top and gently fold it in with a rubber spatula. Drizzle the melted butter over the batter and fold it in gently but thoroughly. Turn the batter into the prepared pans and bake for about 17 to 20 minutes, or until a toothpick tests clean and the cake springs back when pressed lightly. Cool in the pans on a wire rack.

To make the chocolate mousse filling, cut the chocolate into small pieces and put it in the top of a double boiler with the butter. Melt over hot, not simmering, water, stirring constantly. Off the heat, stir in the egg yolks, one at a time. Cook, stirring, over simmering water for 5 minutes. Remove from the heat and cool to room temperature.

Beat the egg whites until they hold firm peaks. Continue beating while gradually adding the sugar. Whip the cream with the vanilla. Fold the egg whites and cream into the cooled chocolate mixture. Break up any large marron pieces into ½-inch size and fold into the chocolate mousse. Refrigerate until firm.

To make the chestnut filling, whip the cream with the brandy until it is stiff. Fold into the chestnut spread.

Holding the blade of a long, serrated knife parallel to the cake, carefully cut each layer in half horizontally to make 4 thin layers. The cake should be at room temperature when you do this.

To assemble the cake, place one cake layer on a plate. Spread with half the chocolate mousse filling. Set another cake layer on top of the chocolate filling and spread with all of the chestnut filling. Place a third cake layer on top and spread with the rest of the chocolate filling. Top with the fourth cake layer.

To make the icing, cut the chocolate into small pieces and put it in the top of a double boiler with the butter. Stir continuously over hot water until it has melted. Remove from the heat and continue stirring until the chocolate is smooth and shiny. Pour it over the top of the cake all at once and spread evenly with a knife, allowing some to drip over the sides. Refrigerate the cake until shortly before serving.

YIELD: ONE 4-LAYER CAKE OR 8 TO 12 SERVINGS

A Special Dinner for Four

MUSHROOM CAPS WITH
GARLIC SHRIMP

SWEETBREADS WITH
CAPER-BÉARNAISE SAUCE

SAUTÉED SNOW PEAS†

WATERCRESS, MUSHROOM, AND
ENDIVE SALAD (page 146)

PEAR AND LEMON SOUFFLÉ PIE

HERE is a menu for special occasions, as each course is a delicacy. While the entrée does not take long to prepare, most of the cooking must be done at the last minute, and the dinner should therefore be limited to just a few friends. The meal starts with shrimp (posing as snails), nested in mushroom caps and immersed in garlic butter. The recipe calls for very large shrimp in very large mushroom caps, as they look quite splendid on a serving plate. But if these are difficult to find, the recipe can easily be adapted to accommodate more modest sizes of each. To offset this assertive beginning, there follows a delicate entrée of sautéed sweetbreads in a smooth and tart Caper-Béarnaise Sauce. To add a little color and texture, sautéed snow peas accompany the sweetbreads. Dessert is a warm Pear and Lemon Soufflé Pie.

Advance Preparation   The Mushroom Caps with Garlic Shrimp may be prepared the morning of the party and heated before serving. Most of the preparation for the Pear and Lemon Soufflé Pie may also be done that morning, as indicated in the recipe. The sweetbreads may be poached several hours ahead, but the final cooking is a last-minute job.

MUSHROOM CAPS WITH GARLIC SHRIMP

8 extra-large raw unshelled shrimp (½ pound)

8 large mushroom caps (2–2½ inches in diameter)

6 tablespoons unsalted butter, softened

2 small or 1 medium garlic clove, peeled and crushed

1½ teaspoons minced fresh chives

1½ teaspoons minced fresh tarragon

2 tablespoons dry vermouth

FOR THE GARNISH

Minced fresh parsley

Shell and devein the shrimp. Clean the mushroom caps with a damp towel.

Melt 2 tablespoons butter in a large skillet with half the garlic. Sauté the mushrooms very gently until softened. Transfer to a shallow baking dish. Add another tablespoon of butter to the skillet and sauté the shrimp just until pink—about 1 minute. Remove from the heat.

Cream the remaining 3 tablespoons butter with the remaining garlic, the chives, and the tarragon. Spread equal amounts of the mixture inside each mushroom cap and top with a shrimp. Add the vermouth to the liquid remaining in the pan and simmer, stirring, for a minute to reduce. Drizzle over the shrimp.

To serve, preheat the oven to 350°. Bake for 8 minutes, or until heated through. Place 2 stuffed mushrooms on each of 4 serving plates and garnish them with minced parsley.

YIELD: 4 SERVINGS

SWEETBREADS WITH CAPER-BÉARNAISE SAUCE

The delicate flavor and texture of sweetbreads is enhanced by this variation on a béarnaise sauce, subtly flavored with tarragon, capers, and mustard.

> *1 ½ pounds calves' sweetbreads*
> *2 tablespoons lemon juice*
> *Flour for dredging*
> *3 tablespoons unsalted butter*
> *2 tablespoons minced shallot*

FOR THE CAPER-BÉARNAISE SAUCE

> *3 egg yolks*
> *6 tablespoons unsalted butter*
> *⅓ teaspoon dried tarragon*
> *2 teaspoons white wine vinegar*
> *1 ½ teaspoons dry white wine*
>
> *1 ½ teaspoons Düsseldorf mustard*
> *Fresh-ground white pepper*
> *1 ½ tablespoons well-drained capers*

FOR THE GARNISH

> *Minced fresh parsley*
> *Watercress*

Rinse the sweetbreads, cover with cold water, and soak for 1 to 2 hours. Drain. Bring a saucepan of water to a boil. Add 2 tablespoons lemon juice and the sweetbreads and simmer gently for 10 minutes. Drain, rinse under cold water, and peel off the membranes and any connective tissues. Separate the sweetbreads into 2- or 3-inch medallions, cut each in half horizontally, and dredge lightly in flour. Melt 3 tablespoons butter in a large skillet and sauté the sweetbreads over high heat for a few minutes on both sides to brown. Remove from the heat and keep warm.

Add the shallots to the pan and sauté gently until soft. Do not brown. Turn the heat to very low to make the béarnaise. Add the egg yolks, butter, tarragon, vinegar, and wine to the pan and stir constantly with a wire whisk until the sauce becomes very thick. (If it becomes too hot and separates, add about a tablespoon of hot water, remove from the heat, and stir vigorously until homogenized.) Add the mustard, pepper, and capers to the sauce and remove from the heat. Put the sweetbreads on a serving dish, spoon the sauce over them, and sprinkle with minced parsley. Garnish the plate with watercress.

YIELD: 4 SERVINGS

WATERCRESS, MUSHROOM, AND ENDIVE SALAD. Prepare half the recipe on page 146.

PEAR AND LEMON SOUFFLÉ PIE

A winter fruit pie containing sliced pears topped with a tart lemon soufflé. It should be served while still warm.

FOR THE PIE CRUST

1½ cups flour
3 tablespoons sugar
Grated zest of 1 small lemon
4 tablespoons unsalted butter,
  chilled and cut up

4 tablespoons chilled
  vegetable shortening
Approximately 3
  tablespoons cold water

FOR THE FILLING

> *3 eggs, separated*
> *¼ cup plus ⅓ cup sugar*
> *½ cup lemon juice*
> *1 large Anjou pear*

To make the pie crust, combine the flour, sugar, and lemon zest in a large mixing bowl. Rub in the butter and shortening with the tips of your fingers until the mixture resembles coarse meal. Add enough cold water to form into a dough. Knead one or two turns, wrap in wax paper, and refrigerate until firm enough to roll out.

Preheat the oven to 375°. Between 2 lightly floured sheets of wax paper, roll the dough into a circle to fit a 9-inch pie plate. Fit the dough into the plate, crimping the edges. Prick the bottom with a fork, line the inside of the pie shell with aluminum foil and fill with uncooked rice or beans. Bake in the middle of the oven for 20 minutes. Remove the foil and rice and bake a few minutes longer. Cool on a wire rack.

To make the filling, whisk the egg yolks and ¼ cup sugar together in a small, heavy saucepan or the top of a double boiler. Stir in the lemon juice. Cook over low heat or simmering water, stirring constantly, until thick. (This will take about 20 minutes.) Remove from the heat, stir for a few seconds to stop the cooking, and then cool on a rack to room temperature. (The pie may be made ahead to this point.)

Peel, core, and quarter the pear and slice into ¼-inch-thick wedges. Arrange in a circular pattern inside the baked pie shell. Beat the egg whites until they hold soft peaks. Continue beating while gradually adding the remaining sugar. Fold into the lemon custard and pour into the pie shell. Bake for 35 to 40 minutes. A knife, inserted in the center of the pie, will be slightly moist. Cool on a rack for 10 or 15 minutes and serve warm.

YIELD: 8 SERVINGS

A Formal Dinner Party
for Twelve

MIGGIE'S MUSHROOM-TARRAGON SOUP

VEAL EN CROÛTE WITH
SPINACH-CHÈVRE FILLING

JULIENNE CARROTS (page 47)

WATERCRESS, MUSHROOM, AND
ENDIVE SALAD

MOCHA MOUSSE WITH
CHOCOLATE-ALMOND BRITTLE

HERE is an elegant menu for special parties. The first course is a steaming, aromatic consommé, warming without being filling. For the entrée, a loin of veal is covered with a spinach mixture and the whole encased in pastry. This method of cooking is particularly successful with veal because it is a meat that tends to dry out if roasted uncovered. Here the veal is browned and braised in its wine marinade, and this can be done the day before the dinner. It is then wrapped with the spinach in pastry, and the veal reheats as the pastry browns in the oven. It is a glamorous dish, each slice of veal encircled with spinach and a crisp golden crust, and most of the cooking can be done in advance. Julienne carrots, steamed al dente and reheated with orange juice and a little butter, are a colorful accompaniment. The dessert is a fluffy mocha mousse containing pieces of chocolate brittle.

Advance Preparation   The Mushroom-Tarragon Soup, Julienne Carrots, and Mocha Mousse may be made a day before serving. Marinate the veal a day before cooking it; the rest of the dish can be prepared several hours or even the day before serving, as indicated in the recipe. It should then be returned to room temperature before the final baking. After the veal has baked, lower the oven temperature to 375° and reheat the carrots.

MIGGIE'S MUSHROOM-TARRAGON SOUP

This is not a creamy mushroom soup but a lovely wine and tarragon flavored broth thick with chopped mushrooms.

1 ½ pounds mushrooms, cleaned and trimmed
3 tablespoons unsalted butter
⅓ cup minced Bermuda onion
6 cups chicken stock or broth
1 ½ tablespoons minced fresh tarragon or 1 ½ teaspoons dried

6 tablespoons minced fresh parsley
Salt
Fresh-ground pepper
¾ cup dry white wine

Cut the mushrooms in halves or quarters and mince them, a handful at a time, in a food processor, using an off-on motion. Do not overprocess.

Melt the butter in a large, heavy saucepan. Add the onion and sauté gently until softened, but do not brown. Add the mushrooms and continue to cook over medium-low heat until they render their juices. Add the stock, tarragon, parsley, and seasoning to taste. Cover tightly and simmer for 5 to 10 minutes. (The soup may be prepared ahead to this point.) If serving immediately, add the wine, simmer briefly, and serve in bouillon cups. If serving later, add the wine before reheating the soup.

YIELD: 10 TO 12 SERVINGS

VEAL EN CROÛTE WITH SPINACH-CHÈVRE FILLING

This is an elaborate dish for special occasions: a marinated, braised loin of veal is coated with a spinach-cheese mixture, encased in a rough puff pastry, and served with a mushroom gravy. While it takes some time in preparation, the veal can be cooked and almost all the work done ahead of time, leaving only the final baking in pastry for after your guests arrive.

> *One 5 ½-pound loin of veal, boned but not tied*
> *(weighed after boning)*
> *2 tablespoons olive oil*

FOR THE MARINADE

> *1 ½ cups dry white wine*
> *3 tablespoons olive oil*
> *1 large garlic clove, minced*
> *Several sprigs parsley*

FOR THE PASTRY

> *3 cups flour*
> *¾ teaspoon salt*
> *2 ½ sticks unsalted butter*
> *Approximately ½ cup cold, dry white wine or cold water*

FOR THE FILLING

1½ pounds fresh spinach
1½ tablespoons flour
¼ cup fresh parsley sprigs,
    packed
⅓ cup sour cream

½ cup mild chèvre cheese
¼ cup grated Graddost
    cheese
¼-pound slice baked ham,
    cut into ⅓-inch dice

FOR THE GRAVY

6 ounces mushrooms,
    cleaned, trimmed, and
    sliced
1½ tablespoons unsalted
    butter
½ teaspoon dried tarragon

1 tablespoon minced fresh
    parsley
1 tablespoon cornstarch
1⅔ cups reserved veal
    cooking juices

FOR THE GLAZE

1 egg yolk lightly beaten with 1 tablespoon water

FOR THE GARNISH

1 bunch fresh parsley

Combine the ingredients for the marinade in a large ceramic or glass pan. Put in the veal and marinate in the refrigerator for 12 to 24 hours, turning occasionally.

While the veal is marinating, the pastry and spinach filling can be prepared. To make the pastry, combine the flour and salt in a large mixing bowl. Cut the butter into small bits and rub it into the flour with the tips of your fingers, until the mixture resembles coarse meal. Add enough cold wine or water to form a dough. Wrap in wax paper and refrigerate until firm. Roll out the dough between lightly floured sheets of wax paper into a rectangle approximately 9 by 15 inches. Fold the dough into thirds, like a business letter. (This is a "turn.") Turn the dough 90° so that you will be rolling in the opposite direction, and roll again into a rectangle. Fold again into thirds and wrap in wax paper. Refrigerate ½ hour or longer. Roll out as before to make two more turns and refrigerate again until firm. Roll out again to make a fifth and sixth turn and refrigerate again before forming the crust.

To make the spinach filling, wash the spinach, discarding the stems and any wilted leaves, cover, and simmer for a few minutes. Drain well in a colander. When the spinach is cool enough to handle, pick up handfuls and squeeze out as much water as possible. Purée in a food processor or blender with the flour and parsley. Add the sour cream, chèvre, and Graddost, and blend. Turn into a bowl and mix in the diced ham.

To braise the veal, preheat the oven to 325°. Remove the veal from the marinade and tie it with kitchen string at 2-inch intervals to form a compact roll. Dry the veal with paper towels. Reserve the marinade. Heat 2 tablespoons olive oil in a large skillet and brown the veal on all sides. Transfer to a heavy, flame-proof casserole, pour in the reserved marinade, and cover tightly. Cook in the oven for 1½ hours, or until a meat thermometer registers 160°. Cool the veal to room temperature. Pour the cooking juices into a jar, refrigerate, and remove the fat after it has congealed on the surface. Reserve for the gravy.

To make the gravy, sauté the mushrooms in the butter until softened. Add the tarragon and parsley and blend in the cornstarch. Add the reserved cooking juices and bring to a simmer, stirring constantly. The sauce will be slightly thickened.

When the veal has cooled, remove the strings and press the spinach mixture firmly over the top and sides.

Roll out the dough into a sheet 15 inches square, or large enough to cover the veal. Invert the veal over the pastry so that the spinach is on the bottom. Pull up the sides of the pastry to encase the veal, overlapping at the seam, and press the seam to seal. Overlap and seal the ends, cutting off any excess dough. Carefully invert onto a baking pan so that the seam side is underneath. Decorate with leaves cut from scraps of dough and brush the top and sides of the pastry with egg yolk glaze. Cut a few air vents in the top of the crust. (The recipe may be prepared ahead to this point. If you are going to complete the cooking the next day, cover with plastic wrap and refrigerate. Remove from the refrigerator at least 2 hours before baking to make sure that the veal returns to room temperature, or it will not heat through.)

To complete cooking, preheat the oven to 425°. Bake the veal for 30 to 40 minutes or until the crust is well browned. Reheat the gravy and pour into a sauceboat. Serve the veal on a platter surrounded by parsley.

YIELD: 12 SERVINGS

WATERCRESS, MUSHROOM, AND ENDIVE SALAD

FOR THE VINAIGRETTE

⅔ cup olive oil
2 tablespoons plus 2 teaspoons white wine vinegar
1 garlic clove, peeled and cut in half

FOR THE SALAD

4 large Belgian endive
1 pound firm white mushrooms, cleaned, trimmed, and sliced
2 large bunches watercress
Salt
Fresh-ground pepper

Combine the ingredients for the vinaigrette at least 1 hour before serving to allow time for the garlic to marinate.

Cut the endive in half lengthwise and then slice across into ¾-inch pieces. Combine the endive, mushrooms, and watercress in a salad bowl. Just before serving, discard the garlic clove and toss the vinaigrette with the salad. Add salt and pepper to taste.

YIELD: 12 SERVINGS

MOCHA MOUSSE WITH CHOCOLATE-ALMOND BRITTLE

This is not a rich dark mousse, but a blend of coffee and chocolate that is light in flavor and texture. It is shot through with pieces of homemade chocolate brittle.

FOR THE BRITTLE

½ cup blanched, slivered almonds
4 ounces Baker's German's Sweet Chocolate
2 teaspoons unsalted butter

FOR THE MOUSSE

6 eggs, separated
¾ cup plus 1 tablespoon
   sugar
1 cup light cream or half and
   half
1 tablespoon plus 1 teaspoon
   instant coffee
2 ounces Baker's semi-sweet
   baking chocolate, cut into
   small pieces

1 envelope plus ¾ teaspoon
   unflavored gelatin
½ cup cold water
1 teaspoon vanilla
3 tablespoons amaretto
   liqueur
2 cups heavy cream

To make the brittle, preheat the oven to 350°. Spread the nuts on a baking sheet and toast for 5 to 6 minutes, or just until very lightly colored. Spread in one layer over an area roughly 8 inches in diameter on a sheet of wax paper. Break the chocolate into small pieces and put it in the top of a double boiler with the butter. Stir constantly over hot water until the chocolate is melted. Remove from the heat, continue stirring until it is smooth and shiny, and then pour it over the almonds to cover them completely. If necessary, spread it a bit with a knife so that you have one solid, thin sheet of chocolate. Let stand, or refrigerate, until hardened. Then break it into ½-inch pieces.

To make the mousse, beat the egg yolks with ¼ cup of the sugar until light. Add the light cream, instant coffee, and the chocolate. Place the mixing bowl over a pan of simmering water and cook, stirring continuously, until the chocolate is melted and the mixture is quite thick. Remove from the heat.

Sprinkle the gelatin over the cold water to soften; dissolve over low heat, stirring constantly. Stir the dissolved gelatin into the mocha custard. Add the vanilla and amaretto and cool to room temperature.

Beat the egg whites until they hold soft peaks. Continue beating until stiff but not dry while gradually adding ½ cup sugar. Whip the cream with the remaining tablespoon of sugar until it holds soft peaks. Fold the mocha custard into the whipped cream and then fold in the beaten egg whites. Gently mix in the chocolate brittle pieces, turn into a glass serving bowl, and chill until set.

YIELD: 10 TO 12 SERVINGS

A Midwinter Buffet

FONDUE CROUSTADES

MUSHROOM CROUSTADES

CARBONNADES DE BOEUF

RICE[†]

BAKED PARSNIPS OR
PURÉED PARSNIPS (page 97)

GREEN SALAD[†]

LEMON-RASPBERRY MOUSSE

CARBONNADES de Boeuf, a splendid beef stew flavored with onions, mustard, and beer, is an ideal entrée for a winter buffet. A hearty and aromatic dish, it is designed to warm the spirits and satisfy appetites stimulated by wind-chill factors. Nothing on this menu requires a knife, an advantage if it is the sort of buffet that does not involve a dinner table. Parsnips go particularly well with carbonnades and are at the peak of their season in mid to late winter. They are equally good baked with a slight glaze or puréed with cream. Since this is a buffet, it does not include a first course but rather a few hors d'oeuvres to serve with drinks. After the robust entrée, a light and tart Lemon-Raspberry Mousse is a fitting dessert.

Advance Preparation   The Carbonnades de Boeuf may be made two days in advance. The hors d'oeuvres, parsnips, and Lemon-Raspberry Mousse may all be prepared a day before serving.

FONDUE CROUSTADES

For this hot hors d'oeuvre, little cups of toasted bread are filled with a grated cheese mixture containing flavorings traditionally used in a fondue.

24 slices soft white bread*

FOR THE CHEESE MIXTURE

*6 ounces Emmenthaler or
   Gruyère cheese, grated
1½ teaspoons flour
1 very small garlic clove,
   peeled and pressed*

*A pinch of nutmeg
Fresh-ground white pepper
6 tablespoons dry white
   wine
1 tablespoon kirsch*

2–3 shallots, peeled and sliced paper-thin

Preheat the oven to 375°.

Flatten each slice of bread with a rolling pin. Cut into circles with a 3-inch cookie cutter and carefully press them into ungreased miniature muffin tins (1¼-inch diameter at base). Bake for 12 minutes or until lightly browned, and cool on a wire rack.

Combine the grated cheese, flour, garlic, nutmeg, and pepper in a mixing bowl. Put the wine and kirsch into a saucepan and simmer until reduced to 3 tablespoons. Cool and stir into the cheese mixture. (The recipe may be prepared ahead to this point. Cover and refrigerate the cheese and put the croustades in an airtight tin.)

* Firm bread cannot be molded into the muffin tins without breaking.

Place a slice of shallot in the bottom of each croustade. Fill with the cheese mixture and bake at 375° for 5 to 7 minutes, or until the cheese is melted. Serve immediately.

YIELD: 24 HORS D'OEUVRES

MUSHROOM CROUSTADES

Rounds of French bread toasted with a mushroom-cheese mixture.

2 tablespoons unsalted butter
12 ounces mushrooms, cleaned, trimmed, and minced
2 tablespoons minced shallot
1 garlic clove, peeled and minced
Salt
Fresh-ground pepper
½ cup grated Jarlsberg cheese
¼ cup fresh-grated Parmesan cheese
2 tablespoons sour cream
French bread

Melt the butter in a large skillet, add the mushrooms, shallot, and garlic, and cook over moderately high heat until all the moisture has evaporated. Stir as the mixture dries out to prevent scorching. Remove from the heat, season with a little salt and pepper, and cool. Stir in the Jarlsberg, Parmesan, and sour cream. Cut rounds of French bread about ¼ inch thick. If the slices are more than 2 inches in diameter, cut each in half. Spread each slice with the mushroom mixture and place on a cookie sheet. Cover tightly with plastic wrap until serving.

To serve, place the croustades under the broiler and cook for a minute or two, until toasted. Be careful not to burn them.

YIELD: APPROXIMATELY 24 HORS D'OEUVRES

CARBONNADES DE BOEUF

This is a traditional Belgian beef stew, flavored with beer, onions, and bacon. It is an interesting change of pace from the usual boeuf bourgignon and a good, hearty meal for a blustery night. Like most stews, it is better if made a day or two ahead of time and reheated before serving.

½ pound sliced bacon, cut into dice
2 pounds yellow onions, peeled and sliced
1½ tablespoons minced garlic
6 pounds lean, boneless beef chuck, cut into strips approximately 2½ inches long, 1 inch wide, and ⅜ inch thick
Salt
Fresh-ground pepper
Approximately ¼ cup olive oil

¼ cup minced fresh parsley
½ teaspoon dried thyme
2 bay leaves
3 tablespoons Dijon mustard
2 tablespoons light brown sugar, packed
1 tablespoon tomato paste
3 cups beer
2½ cups beef stock or broth
2 tablespoons cornstarch
1 tablespoon cold water
1 tablespoon red wine vinegar

Fry the bacon in a very large skillet until crisp. Remove with a slotted spoon and reserve. In 2 tablespoons of the bacon fat, sauté the onions and garlic until very soft, but do not brown. Transfer them to a large, heavy oven-proof casserole.

Lightly season the beef with salt and pepper. Heat 1 tablespoon of the olive oil in the skillet and add as much beef as will fit in one layer without crowding. Brown on both sides over high heat, and as the beef is cooked, transfer it to the casserole with the onions. Cook the remaining beef in the same way, adding more oil to the pan as necessary.

Preheat the oven to 325°. Add the reserved bacon, the parsley, thyme, and bay leaves to the casserole. Stir the mustard, sugar, and tomato paste into the beer and broth, and pour the mixture into the casserole. Cover tightly, put it in the oven, and cook for approximately 2 hours, or until the meat is very tender but not falling apart. Strain off the cooking juices, cool, and degrease. Stir the cornstarch into the cold water and 1 tablespoon vinegar. Add to the degreased cooking juices and pour the mixture into a saucepan. Bring to a simmer, stirring. The gravy will thicken slightly. Taste and add another tablespoon vinegar if necessary. Return the gravy to the casserole. (The recipe may be prepared in advance to this point.)

To serve, preheat the oven to 375°. Put the covered casserole in the oven and reheat for 20 minutes.

YIELD: 12 SERVINGS

BAKED PARSNIPS

Peter Rabbit had a nearly fatal weakness for carrots and radishes, but there is no record of his risking life or limb for a parsnip. I suspect he was content to let Mr. McGregor have them. I once asked the grocer how many parsnips I would need to serve twelve people. "Not many," was the reply. "Most people don't like them." I, however, find them a delicious vegetable that is often overlooked. They reach their peak in flavor and sweetness in the late winter months.

3 pounds parsnips
⅓ cup Madeira
¼ cup light brown sugar, packed
2 tablespoons unsalted butter, cut into small bits

Peel the parsnips and cut off the stem ends. Quarter or halve the larger ones so that they are of uniform thickness. Put in a saucepan, cover with water, and bring to a boil. Boil for about 3 minutes, or just until they are tender enough to be pierced with a metal skewer. Do not overcook, they should remain firm. Put them in a buttered baking dish in one layer, cut side up. Sprinkle with the Madeira and sugar and dot with butter. (They may be prepared ahead to this point.)

Preheat the oven to 375°. Bake the parsnips for 30 minutes, or until tender and slightly browned around the edges.

YIELD: 12 SERVINGS

PUREED PARSNIPS. Prepare 1½ times the recipe on page 97.

LEMON-RASPBERRY MOUSSE

A tart lemon mousse with streaks of raspberry purée swirled through.

One 10-ounce package frozen
  raspberries in syrup,
  defrosted
2 teaspoons confectioners'
  sugar
5 eggs, separated
1 cup plus 1 tablespoon sugar

⅔ cup lemon juice
1 envelope unflavored
  gelatin
¼ cup cold water
Grated zest of 1 lemon
1¼ cups heavy cream

Drain the raspberries well and reserve the syrup for another use. Press the berries through a fine sieve to extract the seeds. You should have about ⅓ cup of thick purée. Stir in the confectioners' sugar and reserve.

Lightly beat the egg yolks in the top of a double boiler or a small, heavy saucepan. Add ¼ cup sugar and the lemon juice and cook, stirring constantly over simmering water or low heat, until thick. Do not let the mixture boil.

Soften the gelatin in the cold water and dissolve over low heat, stirring. Add the dissolved gelatin and the lemon zest to the lemon custard and cool the mixture to room temperature.

Beat the egg whites until they hold firm peaks. Continue beating as you gradually add ¾ cup sugar. Whip the cream in a large mixing bowl with the remaining tablespoon of sugar until stiff. Fold in the cooled custard mixture and the beaten egg whites.

Turn half of the mousse into a glass serving bowl. Drizzle with half of the raspberry purée. Add the rest of the lemon mousse and drizzle the remaining raspberry purée over the top. Holding a knife vertically, swirl the raspberry purée through the mousse with a couple of figure-eight turns. Do not overmix; the raspberry should remain in streaks. Cover the bowl with plastic wrap and chill until firm.

YIELD: 8 CUPS OR 10 TO 12 SERVINGS

A Moroccan Lamb Dinner

BEEF AND ORANGE CONSOMMÉ

(page 101)

MOROCCAN LAMB WITH COUSCOUS

GREEN SALAD WITH AVOCADO†

PEARS WITH ALMOND CUSTARD SAUCE

I spent some time in Morocco many years ago but never knew what I was eating. Unconcerned with food in those days, I was more interested in shopping, sightseeing, and bargaining in the market-places. I do remember once eating something unusual sold by a street vendor and then regretting it. So while I wish I could claim to have coaxed this recipe from some swarthy chef in a dark Moroccan café, the truth is, I first encountered it in Rochester, New York, in the kitchen of our friends, Susan and Richard O'Brien. It is a splendid, subtly flavored lamb stew, as good in America as it must have been in Marrakesh.

Advance Preparation The Beef and Orange Consommé and the Moroccan Lamb may be prepared a day or two ahead, but add the orange juice to the consommé and prepare the couscous just before serving. The Pears with Almond Custard Sauce may be cooked one day ahead and refrigerated separately.

MOROCCAN LAMB WITH COUSCOUS

This is a wonderful recipe of lamb stewed with tomatoes, onions, and raisins, and served with couscous, a coarse semolina.

½ cup medium dry sherry
¾ cup yellow raisins
Olive oil
2½ pounds cubed lamb, cut from the leg
1 pound yellow onions, chopped coarse (2¾ cups)
4 large garlic cloves, minced
One 28-ounce can Italian tomatoes, well-drained and chopped*
1 cup chicken stock

1 teaspoon ground turmeric
¼ teaspoon ground coriander
A large pinch of dried red pepper flakes
A 2-inch strip of orange peel
1–2 teaspoons cornstarch or arrowroot
1 cup sliced almonds
1 cup pitted black olives
Salt

FOR THE COUSCOUS

1½ cups precooked couscous
1½ cups chicken broth

Put the sherry and raisins in a small saucepan, bring to a boil, remove from the heat, and reserve.

Heat a little olive oil in a large Dutch oven and brown the lamb on all sides. Do this in several batches, so as not to crowd the pan, adding more oil if necessary. Transfer the lamb to a platter as it is browned. Pour off all but a little of the oil, lower the heat, and sauté the onions and garlic until soft, but do not brown. Return the lamb to the casserole, and add the raisins and sherry, the tomatoes, chicken stock, spices, and orange peel. Cover tightly, bring to a simmer, and cook gently for 1½ hours, or just until the lamb is tender.

---

* In season, 1¼ pounds peeled and chopped fresh tomatoes can be substituted.

Discard the orange peel. Dissolve the cornstarch or arrowroot in a little water and gradually stir it into the simmering stew, adding just enough to thicken the broth slightly. Add the almonds and olives, and correct the seasoning, if necessary. Serve with the couscous on the side.

To make the couscous, measure it into a casserole or vegetable dish with a tight-fitting lid. Bring the chicken broth to a boil and stir it into the couscous. Cover and let stand for about 5 minutes. (No longer, or it will dry out.) Stir with a fork to separate the grains before serving.

YIELD: 6 SERVINGS

PEARS WITH ALMOND CUSTARD SAUCE

Poached pears in a sauce flavored with amaretto.

FOR THE PEARS

2 cups dry white wine
1/2 cup water
1 cup sugar
1 teaspoon vanilla extract

1 cinnamon stick or 1/4
   teaspoon ground
   cinnamon
6 pears

FOR THE SAUCE

6 egg yolks, lightly beaten
1/4 cup heavy cream
3/4 cup milk
1/4 cup sugar

1 teaspoon vanilla extract
1 tablespoon plus 1
   teaspoon amaretto
   liqueur

Combine the wine, water, sugar, vanilla, and cinnamon in a heavy enameled saucepan and bring to a simmer. Peel each pear, cut in half lengthwise, and remove the core and stem. As it is peeled, drop into the wine mixture. Adjust the heat so that the liquid barely simmers and cook the pears until they are tender but not too soft. Remove the pan from the heat and let the pears cool in the syrup; then place in the refrigerator to chill.

To make the sauce, in a small, heavy enameled saucepan, whisk together the egg yolks, cream, milk, and sugar over low heat until the mixture is thick. Remove from the heat, turn into a bowl, and stir in the vanilla and amaretto. Cool on a wire rack and then cover and chill until serving.

To serve, place 2 pear halves on each dessert plate and spoon some of the sauce over them.

YIELD: 6 SERVINGS

SPRING

An Impressionist Luncheon

SORREL AND MINT SOUP (page 176)

WALNUT AND KIWI CHICKEN SALAD

MELBA TOAST[†]

STRAWBERRY-CASSIS ICE

As warm weather approaches, we are apt to be more concerned with the visual appeal of food, as if the summer kitchen were required to compete with the extravagant gestures of the garden. Lightness, too, becomes an important factor in dining, hearty soups and stews giving way to salads, fish, and an abundance of fresh fruit and vegetables. This luncheon is designed for that time in spring when there is a certain balmy languor in the air and a promise of warmer days to follow. The entrée combines chicken and walnuts with cool green kiwi fruit, cucumbers, scallions, avocados, and watercress, all dressed in a lime vinaigrette. Dessert is a fresh and bright Strawberry-Cassis Ice.

Advance Preparation   Make the Strawberry-Cassis Ice a few days before serving, the soup one day ahead. Prepare the Chicken Salad on the morning of the luncheon and toss with the vinaigrette just before serving.

WALNUT AND KIWI CHICKEN SALAD

A light and cooling chicken salad tossed in a lime vinaigrette.

FOR THE SALAD

3 large chicken breasts, split
*   in half*
3 cups chicken broth
1 large cucumber
6 kiwi
1 large avocado

⅓ cup chopped scallions with
*   tender green ends*
¾ cup broken walnuts,
*   toasted**
1 bunch watercress

FOR THE VINAIGRETTE

½ cup walnut or olive oil
2 tablespoons lime juice
2 tablespoons white wine vinegar

Put the chicken breasts and the broth in a large skillet. Partially cover and bring to a simmer. Cook gently for 20 minutes, or just until the chicken is cooked through. Do not overcook or it will be dry. Drain, and when cool enough to handle, strip off the skin and bones. Cut the meat into strips, about 2½ inches long and ½ inch wide, following the grain. Peel and seed the cucumber and slice lengthwise into strips about 2½ inches long and ¼ inch thick. Peel the kiwi and slice crosswise. Cut the avocado in half, peel it, discard the pit, and slice lengthwise. Wrap the avocado slices tightly in plastic wrap to prevent discoloring.

To serve, combine the chicken, cucumber, kiwi, avocado, scallions, walnuts, and watercress in a bowl. Mix the ingredients for the vinaigrette and toss with the salad just before serving.

YIELD: 6 TO 8 SERVINGS

* Spread in a baking pan and toast for 5 to 7 minutes in a 350° oven.

STRAWBERRY-CASSIS ICE

---

4 pints strawberries
⅔ cup sugar
6 tablespoons cassis syrup

Rinse and dry the strawberries. Hull them and cut each in half. Put the berries and sugar in a large kettle and slowly bring to a simmer. Cook gently, stirring frequently, for 5 or 6 minutes, or until the berries are soft. Purée in a food processor, reserving the juice. Turn into a bowl or freezer container and stir in the reserved strawberry juice and the cassis syrup. Freeze until firm. Break into chunks and purée, in four batches, in a food processor until smooth but not liquefied. As each batch is puréed, return it to the freezer before it has a chance to melt. Freeze until firm.

YIELD: 5½ CUPS OR 6 TO 8 SERVINGS

A Pasta Supper

ASPARAGUS VINAIGRETTE

LINGUINE CORNARO OR
LINGUINE WITH SMOKED SALMON

GREEN SALAD[†]

RHUBARB AND STRAWBERRY TART

I am always amazed by the variety of ways in which pasta is served in Italy. Each restaurant has its own inventive specialty, such as a sauce of tiny shellfish hidden among pappardelle (ribbon macaroni), or a combination of fresh vegetables for pasta primavera. For the pasta dinner that follows, the menu begins with a light appetizer of Asparagus Vinaigrette. Then you may choose to make either of two recipes for the pasta course: Linguine Cornaro with fresh artichokes, chèvre, ham, and cream, or Linguine with Smoked Salmon, also in a cream sauce, and flavored with dill and lemon zest. Either of these dishes constitutes a filling entrée and should not, as in Italy, be the prelude to greater things such as roast meat. Follow the pasta with a simple green salad and then a Rhubarb and Strawberry Tart to celebrate spring.

Advance Preparation The Asparagus Vinaigrette and the Rhubarb and Strawberry Tart may be prepared a day before serving.

Prepare the ingredients for either pasta dish on the day of the party so that the last-minute work of cooking the pasta will be minimal.

ASPARAGUS VINAIGRETTE

2 *pounds asparagus*
Salt
¼ *cup olive oil*
1 *tablespoon plus 2 teaspoons*
  white wine vinegar

1 *tablespoon lemon juice*
1 *garlic clove, peeled and*
  halved

Trim the ends and scales off the asparagus, wash well, and lay flat in a large skillet. Add about 1 inch of water and salt and bring to a simmer. Cook gently, partially covered, for 5 to 7 minutes, or just until tender but still firm. Drain well and transfer to a shallow bowl or Pyrex dish. Combine the remaining ingredients and pour over the asparagus. Marinate for several hours, turning the stalks a few times in the vinaigrette. Remove the garlic clove before serving. Serve chilled or at room temperature.

YIELD: 4 TO 6 SERVINGS

LINGUINE CORNARO

For this splendid pasta dish, the linguine is lightly coated with cream, tossed with a large quantity of fresh parsley and lemon zest, and combined with fresh artichoke hearts, chèvre, and ham. It is a substantial and satisfying dish.

4 medium-size globe artichokes
Salt
Vegetable oil
8 ounces white linguine
½ cup light cream
3 tablespoons unsalted butter, cut into small pieces

⅛ teaspoon grated garlic
3 ounces mild chèvre without rind, coarsely crumbled
4 ounces sliced baked ham, cut into 1½-inch strips
1 cup minced fresh parsley
Grated zest of 1½ lemons
Fresh-ground pepper

Cut off and discard the top third of the artichoke leaves and the stems. Wash well under cold running water and stand them upright in a large enameled or stainless steel saucepan. Cover with water and simmer, covered tightly, for 45 minutes, or until the bases are tender. Drain well. When cool enough to handle, strip off all the outer leaves and discard or reserve for another use. Cut the artichoke hearts in half, scrape out the chokes, and cut each half lengthwise into 2 or 3 pieces. Cover and reserve.

Bring a very large pot of water to a rolling boil. Add salt and a little vegetable oil and the linguine and cook al dente, until tender but not soft. Drain well in a colander, turn into a bowl, and toss with the cream, butter, and garlic. Add the reserved artichoke hearts, the chèvre, ham, parsley, lemon zest, and ground pepper to taste and toss well. Serve immediately.

YIELD: 4 SERVINGS

LINGUINE WITH SMOKED SALMON

If you like smoked salmon, this is a delicious way to serve it. It is a filling dish, however, so serve small portions.

Salt
Vegetable oil
8 ounces linguine
¼ cup sour cream
*½ cup light cream or half-
   and-half*
½ cup minced fresh parsley
*1½ teaspoons minced fresh
   dill weed or ½ teaspoon
   dried*

Grated zest of 1 large lemon
*⅓ pound smoked Nova
   Scotia salmon, shredded
   (not salty)*
Fresh-ground pepper

Bring a large pot of water to a boil. Add salt, a little vegetable oil, and the linguine. Cook until tender but firm, and drain in a colander. Add the remaining ingredients and toss to combine. (Salt will not be necessary.) Serve immediately.

YIELD: 4 SERVINGS

RHUBARB AND STRAWBERRY TART

The rhubarb is baked in its tart shell and then covered with whole fresh strawberries glazed to a deep red with raspberry jelly. It is an appropriate and appealing dessert with which to inaugurate the spring season.

*One partially baked 9-inch
   tart shell (page 14)*
1½ pounds rhubarb
3 tablespoons tapioca
1¼ cups sugar

*1½ tablespoons unsalted
   butter, melted*
1 teaspoon grated lemon rind
2 pints strawberries
¼ cup red raspberry jelly

Prepare and bake the tart shell according to the directions on page 14 and cool on a wire rack before filling.

Preheat the oven to 375°. Wash the rhubarb and chop into ½- to ¾-inch pieces, discarding any leaves. You should have 4 generous cups. Combine the tapioca and sugar in a large mixing bowl. Add the rhubarb, melted butter, and lemon rind, and stir to combine thoroughly. Let stand at room temperature for 20 minutes or longer. Turn the mixture into the cooled pie shell and bake, loosely covered with aluminum foil, for 30 minutes. Remove the foil and bake 30 minutes longer, basting the surface of the filling with the juices that accumulate in the crust. Remove from the oven and cool on a wire rack.

Wash and hull the strawberries. Drain, hulled side down, on several layers of paper towels for 1½ to 2 hours. When the tart has cooled, arrange the strawberries on top in concentric circles, completely covering the surface. Melt the raspberry jelly in a small metal cup or saucepan and simmer for 1 or 2 minutes. Using a pastry brush, cover each strawberry and the top edge of the tart shell with the raspberry glaze.

YIELD: 6 TO 8 SERVINGS

A Lenten Supper

ISTANBUL ARTICHOKES OR

GNOCCHI VERDI (page 277)

SEAFOOD RISOTTO

ARUGOLA AND MUSHROOM SALAD[†]

PEARS AND CHEESE[†]

HERE is a meal that you might serve in Lent. It is not an austere menu, but it does show some restraint and excludes meat. The custom of saying grace before a meal has, unhappily, all but disappeared in modern times, and it is usually a nice surprise to find it still observed. Should you be so inclined on this occasion, seize the opportunity before anyone has a chance to lift his spoon. A New York friend of mine was once entertained at a dinner party on a visit to New Orleans. The host made a great ceremony of serving the lobster bisque and enjoined his guests to start right in, lest the soup get cold. My friend, eager to oblige, dutifully picked up her spoon and dug in. She then noticed, with mounting unease, that she was the only one to do so. After the last person had been served, the host said grace. Puzzled and humiliated, my friend turned to her dinner partner, protesting, "But he said to start." He leaned over to her and whispered, "They say it, but they don't mean it."

It is hard to know who was more embarrassed, my own friend or

Mr. Jones who, as reported in *The Lyttelton Hart-Davis Letters*, tucked into the salted almonds before grace. This did not go unnoticed by the presiding dean, who offered thanks "For all that we are about to receive and for all that Mr. Jones has already received."

Advance Preparation   Cook the Artichokes the morning of the party or the day before if you are serving them chilled. If hot, prepare them ahead and cook them just before serving. The Gnocchi may be made a day ahead and heated before serving. Prepare the ingredients for the Risotto early on the day of the party. The rice itself must be cooked at the last minute.

ISTANBUL ARTICHOKES

My husband's recipe, and very good.

6 large artichokes	*2 medium yellow onions,*
1 tablespoon sugar	*peeled and sliced*
½ cup lemon juice	*½ a large Valencia or navel*
⅔ cup olive oil or (half olive	*orange*
and half vegetable oil)	*A large pinch of crushed*
1 cup water	*red pepper*
¾ teaspoon salt	

Wash the artichokes well. Cut off the stems and the top third of the leaves of each, and then snip off the thorny tips of the remaining leaves with a pair of shears. Set the artichokes upright in an enameled or stainless steel pot. Add the remaining ingredients, scattering the onion and orange slices on top of the artichokes. Cover tightly and simmer for 1 hour (no less, or the sauce won't be thick enough, nor the flavor right).

Serve hot or chilled, in individual bowls, spooning some of the sauce, onions, and orange slices over each serving.

YIELD: 6 SERVINGS

SEAFOOD RISOTTO

A creamy Italian rice mixture containing mussels, scallops, and shrimp.

3 pounds mussels, scrubbed
2 garlic cloves, peeled and
  minced
4 tablespoons minced shallot
1 bay leaf
½ cup water
½ pound large, raw,
  unshelled shrimp
4 tablespoons unsalted butter
1 pound bay scallops
3½ tablespoons lemon juice
1 small fennel bulb, trimmed
  and chopped fine (1 cup)

1¼ cups Arborio Italian
  rice*
Approximately 1½ cups
  reserved shellfish stock
1½ cups chicken broth
1½–2 cups water
⅓ cup pine nuts, lightly
  toasted†
⅓ cup minced fresh parsley
Fresh-ground pepper

Put the mussels in a large, heavy, lidded kettle with half the garlic, half the shallots, the bay leaf, and ½ cup water. Cover tightly, bring to a simmer, and cook for 5 to 7 minutes, or until the shells have opened wide and the mussel meat is firm and opaque. Discard any mussels that fail to open. Set aside 8 to 12 smaller mussels for garnish and remove the rest from their shells. Strain and reserve the broth.

Shell and devein the shrimp. Melt 2 tablespoons of the butter in a large skillet, add the shrimp and scallops, sprinkle with 2 tablespoons of the lemon juice, and sauté for 2 or 3 minutes, or just until the shrimp turn pink and the scallops are cooked through. Remove from the pan, add to the shelled mussels, and reserve. Add the pan juices to the reserved mussel broth. (The dish may be prepared ahead to this point.)

* If Italian rice is not available, substitute American short- or medium-grain rice, but not long-grain.
† Spread in a pan and bake at 350° for 5 or 6 minutes.

Melt the remaining butter in the pan, add the fennel and the rest of the garlic and shallots, and cook over low heat until the fennel is tender, but do not brown. Add the rice and cook, stirring, until it becomes transparent and then milky in color. Meanwhile, combine the reserved shellfish broth, the chicken broth, and 1½ cups water in a saucepan and heat to simmering. Keep it hot on a back burner while you cook the rice.

When the rice is opaque, add about ⅓ cup of the hot broth mixture. Simmer gently, uncovered, stirring occasionally. Continue to add the broth and water, ⅓ to ½ cup at a time, as the liquid in the pan is absorbed. Keep the heat low so that it barely simmers. Cook until the rice is tender and creamy but not gummy. This will take 30 to 40 minutes. Add hot water if additional liquid is required to complete cooking the rice. When the rice is cooked, add the mussels, shrimp, and scallops, and cook, stirring, for about a minute or until the shellfish is reheated. Stir in the pine nuts, parsley, and remaining lemon juice. Season with pepper and serve immediately. Garnish each serving with a couple of unshelled mussels.

YIELD: 4 TO 6 SERVINGS

A Special Dinner in Shad Season

SORREL AND MINT SOUP

SHAD WITH ROE AND
ASPARAGUS MOUSSE FILLING

MINT AND CHIVE MOUSSELINE SAUCE

STEAMED FIDDLEHEADS OR
STEAMED PEAS[†]

GREEN SALAD WITH WATERCRESS[†]

RHUBARB SHERBET WITH
STRAWBERRIES

T H E following menu is a celebration of spring, featuring delicacies that appear early in the season, promising the bounty of the months to come. Sorrel and mint, two gifts from the spring garden, are combined in a lovely tart soup to begin the meal. The entrée is shad, a prized North Atlantic fish available in March and April. Here it is prepared with a stuffing of asparagus mousse and shad roe, and served with Mint and Chive Mousseline Sauce. Fiddleheads, the uncurled fronds of certain ferns, are a wonderful spring vegetable with an indescribable earthy, nutty flavor. Learn to recognize them and garner them wild along the banks of streams, or from a special greengrocer. If they are not available, steamed peas would be an appropriate alternative. On a menu such as this, dessert would have to include strawberries; here they garnish a homemade Rhubarb Sherbet, a tart and colorful conclusion to the meal.

Advance Preparation   The soup may be made a day ahead, as well as the asparagus filling for the shad. Cook the roe, stuff the shad, and prepare the Mint and Chive Mousseline a few hours before serving. The fiddleheads can be prepared for cooking well in advance and then simply steamed before serving. The Rhubarb Sherbet can be made a few days before the party.

SORREL AND MINT SOUP

Sorrel and mint are among the first herbs to appear in spring, growing side by side in my neighbor's garden. This seemed to suggest a natural affinity, which I thought might be used to culinary advantage. My experiments produced a delicately flavored chilled soup. Because the sorrel is puréed without being cooked, it retains its fresh green color.

2 tablespoons unsalted butter
3 tablespoons flour
3½ cups chicken stock or
   broth
3 egg yolks, lightly beaten
¾ pound sorrel leaves
   without stems (6 cups
   packed)

½ cup sour cream
1 cup plus 2 tablespoons
   heavy cream
¼ cup plus 1 tablespoon
   minced fresh mint
   leaves

FOR THE GARNISH

Sprigs of mint

Melt the butter in a saucepan and blend in the flour. Add the chicken broth gradually, whisking to blend. Bring to a simmer and cook for 1 or 2 minutes. Stir a little of the hot broth into the beaten egg yolks. Return the yolks to the pan and cook over medium-low heat for about 15 minutes, stirring constantly, until thickened. Do not allow to boil. Remove from the heat and cool to room temperature.

After the broth has cooled, purée the sorrel, in batches, in a food processor, adding a little of the broth mixture. Turn into a bowl and add the remaining broth. Whisk in the sour cream; then add the heavy cream and mint. Taste and add a little salt if necessary. Chill, tightly covered, until serving. Garnish each serving with a sprig of fresh mint.

YIELD: 6 CUPS OR 6 TO 8 SERVINGS

SHAD WITH ROE AND ASPARAGUS MOUSSE FILLING

Shad, a prized North Atlantic fish, is exceptional in flavor and texture and, in my opinion, equalled only by salmon. But it is the more valued because of its brief season, available from March until May when the fish enter the rivers along the coast to breed. It is a highly perishable fish and must be eaten soon after it is caught. For this recipe, baked shad fillets encase sautéed roe and an asparagus mousse filling that is subtly flavored with mint. The dish is served with a light Mint and Chive Mousseline Sauce.

½ *tablespoon unsalted butter*
1 *pair shad roe*
Olive oil
2 *large shad fillets (1 pound each)*
2 *tablespoons minced fresh chives*

1 *tablespoon minced fresh mint leaves*
1 *tablespoon lemon juice*
Salt
Mint and Chive Mousseline Sauce (recipe follows)

FOR THE ASPARAGUS FILLING

1½ pounds fresh asparagus
Salt
1½ tablespoons unsalted
   butter
2 tablespoons flour
½ cup sour cream

1 egg yolk, lightly beaten
2 teaspoons lemon juice
½ cup fine, fresh bread
   crumbs*
2 tablespoons minced, fresh
   mint leaves

FOR THE GARNISH

Watercress
Lemon wedges

To make the asparagus filling, wash the asparagus and trim off the tough ends and scales. Lay flat in a large skillet, add about 1 inch of water and a little salt, partially cover, and bring to a simmer. Cook gently, just until tender (5 to 7 minutes for medium-size asparagus). Drain well and cut ¾-inch off the tips. Cut each tip in half lengthwise and reserve. Chop the stems course and purée them in a food processor. Turn into a mixing bowl and drain off any excess liquid that accumulates at the bottom of the bowl. Melt the butter in a saucepan and blend in the flour. Add the sour cream and cook, stirring, until the mixture simmers and thickens. Add the egg yolk off the heat, return to the stove, and cook over low heat, stirring, for about 5 minutes. Do not allow to simmer. Remove from the heat, add 2 teaspoons lemon juice, the bread crumbs, 2 tablespoons minced mint, and salt to taste. Stir in the puréed asparagus and reserved asparagus tips and refrigerate until cool and thickened.

Melt ½ tablespoon butter in a saucepan, add the roe, cover, and cook over medium heat for 4 minutes on each side. Remove from the heat and reserve. The roe will be partially cooked, not cooked through.

Oil the bottom of a baking dish. Cut six 12-inch lengths of kitchen string and lay them across the bottom of the dish at 2-inch intervals.

---

* About 2 slices firm white bread, crusts trimmed, pulverized in a food processor.

Lay one shad fillet, skin side down, over the string. Cover with half the asparagus mousse. Separate the two sections of roe and lay them end to end along the length of the shad, on top of the mousse. Spread the rest of the mousse over the roe. Place the other shad fillet, skin side up, on top of the filling, pulling out the flaps of each fillet to make sides. Tie with the string. Sprinkle the chives, 1 tablespoon mint leaves, 1 tablespoon lemon juice, and a little salt over the fish. Cover the pan tightly with aluminum foil and bake for 40 minutes. Transfer to a heated platter and remove the strings. Garnish with watercress and lemon wedges. Serve the Mint and Chive Mousseline Sauce on the side.

YIELD: 6 SERVINGS

MINT AND CHIVE MOUSSELINE SAUCE

An herb-flavored hollandaise with whipped cream folded in. My method of making the hollandaise is unorthodox, but it works. The sauce can be made a few hours before serving.

4 egg yolks	*2 teaspoons minced fresh*
¼ pound (1 stick) unsalted	*mint*
butter	*Salt*
2 tablespoons lemon juice	*Fresh-ground white pepper*
1 teaspoon minced fresh	*¼ cup heavy cream*
chives	

All the ingredients, except the herbs, should be well-chilled. Make the sauce 1 or 2 hours before serving. Lightly beat the egg yolks in a small, heavy saucepan or skillet. (Enameled iron is best; do not use aluminum.) Add the stick of butter in 1 piece, the lemon juice, chives, and mint. Cook over very low heat, stirring constantly by spearing the stick of butter with a fork and swirling it around the bottom of the pan. Keep the heat low or the eggs will scramble.

When the butter has melted, stir constantly with a wire whisk until the sauce is thick. Remove from the heat and whisk for a few seconds to stop the cooking. Season to taste, cover, and keep in a warm, but not hot, place. Whip the cream until it holds soft peaks. Cover and keep at room temperature. Just before serving, fold together the hollandaise and whipped cream and turn into a sauceboat.

YIELD: ABOUT 1 CUP

STEAMED FIDDLEHEADS

Fiddleheads—or the furled fronds of certain edible ferns—grow wild along the banks of streams and rivers and in the woods in the northeastern part of the United States. Their season is brief—a few weeks in early spring. If you cannot harvest them yourself, look for them in fancy greengrocers. They are among the prized delicacies of this season.

4 cups (12 ounces) fiddleheads
Salt
2 tablespoons unsalted butter

Wash the ferns well in a few changes of water, rubbing off any brown husks that cling to the stems. Put them in a steamer basket over boiling water, cover the pot tightly, and cook for 15 to 20 minutes, or until tender. Turn into a serving dish and toss with salt and the butter.

YIELD: 6 SERVINGS

RHUBARB SHERBET WITH STRAWBERRIES

An unusual sherbet combining rhubarb and cassis. It does not require an ice cream freezer.

*3 pounds rhubarb, washed
    and chopped
1 ¾ cups sugar
Grated zest of 1 lemon
6 tablespoons crème de
    cassis liquer or 8
    tablespoons cassis syrup*

*½ cup reserved rhubarb
    juice
1 cup heavy cream*

FOR THE GARNISH

*2 pints fresh strawberries
Sugar
Crème de cassis or cassis syrup*

Preheat the oven to 325°. Put the rhubarb, 1½ cups sugar, and the lemon zest in a heavy casserole, cover, and bake until soft (30 to 40 minutes). Drain, reserving the juice, and purée the rhubarb in a food processor. Stir in the cassis.

Boil down ½ cup of the reserved rhubarb juice to ¼ cup and stir it into the rhubarb purée. Freeze until firm.

Whip the cream with the remaining ¼ cup sugar. Break the frozen rhubarb into chunks and purée it, in small batches, in a food processor until smooth. The mixture should have the consistency of frozen juice concentrate. Turn into a mixing bowl and fold in the whipped cream. Cover with plastic wrap and refreeze immediately.

Rinse, hull, and slice the strawberries. Just before serving, mix them with a little sugar and cassis. Spoon some of the berries over each serving of sherbet.

YIELD: 6 CUPS SHERBET OR 8 SERVINGS

A Dinner for Six, Remembering Asolo

SAUTÉED MUSHROOMS

GAME HENS WITH
CHICKEN LIVER SAUCE

BRAISED LEEKS OR
POTATOES WITH HAZELNUT STUFFING

GREEN SALAD WITH ARUGOLA[†]

TIRAMI SU

ASOLO is a small Italian town in the Veneto, mounted in a jewel-like setting among the foothills of the Dolomites. There is a magnificent view in every direction—dark cypress trees set against green hills, deep, lush valleys, a Renaissance monastery perched on the summit of a neighboring hill, and everywhere flowers in the foreground and a backdrop of cool blue mountain peaks. Comfortably situated in the midst of this natural splendor is a man-made splendor, the Villa Cipriani, with its own enchanting gardens and enticing kitchen. At one end of the dining room, one can look across the valley to the ancient, still-inhabited monastery. My husband used to say it stood there as a silent reproach to the high living enjoyed by the hotel patrons; I, on the other hand, maintained that the good monks probably looked down on us with condescenion, confident that they enjoyed the rarest vintages. One evening the menu offered small hens with chicken liver sauce, and they were delicious. I savored that dish, mentally filing the flavors for future use. The entrée for this meal is my own version of that recipe. It is accompanied by Braised Leeks or Potatoes with Hazelnut Stuffing. The dessert is Tirami Su, a Venetian specialty, here reinterpreted.

Advance Preparation   The dessert may be made a day before serving. The leeks may be prepared a day ahead and baked just before serving. Sauté the chicken livers for the sauce early in the day; it will then take little time to finish it after the hens have cooked. The mushrooms for the appetizer must be sautéed just before serving. The potatoes can be prepared early on the day of the party and reheated before serving.

SAUTÉED MUSHROOMS

These are flavored with shallots, celery, and Madeira, and served over large garlic croutons.

FOR THE CROUTONS

2 tablespoons unsalted butter
1 garlic clove, peeled and halved
6 slices French bread

FOR THE MUSHROOMS

1 tablespoon olive oil   *⅓ cup Madeira*
2 tablespoons unsalted butter   *Salt*
1 tablespoon minced shallot   *Fresh-ground pepper*
2 large celery stalks, sliced   *¼ cup minced fresh*
thin crosswise   *parsley*
1 pound mushrooms, cleaned
and trimmed; large ones
halved

To make the croutons, melt the butter in a frying pan with the garlic. Add the bread and sauté over moderate heat until lightly browned on both sides. Remove from the pan and keep warm.

To cook the mushrooms, remove the garlic clove from the crouton pan. Add the olive oil and 2 more tablespoons butter. Add the shallot and celery and sauté over low heat for a minute. Add the mushrooms and sauté over very high heat, stirring, until browned. Sprinkle with the Madeira and cook until the moisture evaporates. Remove from the heat and stir in the parsley. Place a crouton on each plate and top with the mushrooms.

YIELD: 6 SERVINGS

GAME HENS WITH CHICKEN LIVER SAUCE

The sauce is made of crisp sautéed bits of chicken liver combined with pan juices and Marsala. It is important to use very fresh livers and a good quality Marsala.

3 game hens, each about 1½ pounds, split in half
1½ tablespoons unsalted butter, softened
Salt
Fresh-ground pepper

FOR THE SAUCE

1 tablespoon unsalted butter
1 garlic clove, peeled and
   minced
2 tablespoons minced shallot
1 pound chicken livers
4 tablespoons olive oil

Pan juices
Approximately ¾ cup
   chicken stock or broth
2 teaspoons cornstarch
3 tablespoons Marsala

FOR THE GARNISH

Watercress

Rinse the hens and dry well. Place them in a roasting pan, cut sides down, and rub the skin with the softened butter. Season with salt and pepper.

To make the sauce, melt 1 tablespoon butter in a very large, heavy skillet. Gently sauté the garlic and shallot until soft, but do not brown. Remove from the pan and reserve. Cut the chicken livers into very small bits with a sharp carving knife.* Heat the oil in the skillet and sauté the chopped livers briefly over moderately high heat, stirring frequently, until they begin to get crisp and browned. Remove from the heat and reserve with the garlic and shallot.

To cook the hens, preheat the oven to 350°. Roast the hens for about 55 minutes, basting occasionally with the pan juices, until the skins have browned. Keep them warm while you finish making the sauce. Pour the pan juices into a Pyrex measuring cup and skim off the fat. Add enough chicken stock to make 1¼ cups. Put the livers, garlic, and shallot in a small stainless steel or enameled saucepan and add the pan juices and stock. Dissolve the cornstarch in the Marsala and add to the sauce. Bring to a simmer, stirring until slightly thickened. To serve, place each half hen on a dinner plate and spoon some of the sauce over it. Garnish the plate with watercress.

YIELD: 6 SERVINGS

---

* It will be easier to mince the livers if you place them in the freezer until they are slightly firm, but not frozen.

BRAISED LEEKS

---

9 *medium leeks*   ⅓ *cup fresh-grated*
1 *tablespoon unsalted butter*   *Parmesan cheese*
1 *tablespoon vegetable oil*   1½ *tablespoons sesame*
1 *cup chicken broth*   *seeds*

Cut off and discard the roots and green ends from the leeks. Wash well under cold running water, spreading the cut ends to rinse out the sand and dirt. Dry well.

Heat the butter and oil in a large skillet. Add the leeks and brown lightly on all sides. Pour in the broth, cover tightly, and simmer for 25 to 35 minutes, or until the leeks are very tender. Drain. (The dish may be prepared ahead to this point.)

Carefully cut each leek in half lengthwise and put them in a single layer, cut side up, in a baking dish. Sprinkle with the Parmesan and sesame seeds.

To serve, preheat the oven to 350°, and bake for 15 to 20 minutes.
YIELD: 6 SERVINGS

POTATOES WITH HAZELNUT STUFFING

---

3 *large, thick-skinned*   6 *tablespoons heavy cream*
   potatoes   ¾ *cup ground hazelnuts**
7½ *tablespoons unsalted*   *Salt*
   butter   *Fresh-ground pepper*

Preheat the oven to 375°.

Scrub the potatoes, prick all over with a fork, and bake for 1 hour, or until they are soft in the center. Remove from the oven, cool slightly, and cut in half lengthwise. Carefully scoop out the flesh

---

* Raw cashew nuts may be substituted for hazelnuts in this recipe.

without tearing the skins. Mash the potatoes with the butter. Mix in the cream, hazelnuts, and salt and pepper to taste. Refill the shells.

To serve, preheat the oven to 350°, and heat the potatoes for 15 minutes. Turn on the broiler and brown for 1 or 2 minutes.

YIELD: 6 SERVINGS

TIRAMI SU

This dessert is a Venetian specialty made with mascarpone, a fresh cheese not widely available in the United States. It is close in texture and flavor to a very thick cream, and I have found a combination of lightly whipped cream and ricotta to be a satisfactory substitute. The dessert is flavored with chocolate, coffee, and coffee liqueur, and laced with pieces of sponge cake—related in texture to a *zuppa inglese*. It should be served in small glass or china dessert bowls. Tirami Su means "Lift me up," and it is guaranteed to do so.

FOR THE SPONGE CAKE

2 eggs, lightly beaten
¼ cup sugar
½ teaspoon vanilla extract
¼ cup plus 2 tablespoons flour

FOR THE CHEESE MIXTURE

1 pound (2 cups) creamy
*   ricotta**
2⅔ cups heavy cream
½ cup sugar
2 teaspoons vanilla extract
1 tablespoon plus 1 teaspoon
*   ground espresso coffee*

4 ounces Baker's German's
*   Sweet Chocolate, grated*
4 tablespoons Tia Maria
*   liqueur*

* Be sure to use a very fresh ricotta; the flavor should have no suggestion of sourness.

To make the sponge cake, preheat the oven to 350°. Butter and lightly flour a round of wax paper to fit the bottom of a 7- or 8-inch cake pan.

Combine the eggs and sugar in a large mixing bowl and set over a pan of simmering water. Stir continuously until the eggs are quite warm, but do not let them cook. Remove from the heat, stir in the vanilla, and beat the mixture with an electric mixer until it is as thick as crème Chantilly, very light in color, and tripled in volume. This will take 5 to 7 minutes. Sift the flour over the beaten eggs and fold together gently but thoroughly. Turn into the prepared pan, spread evenly with a spatula, and bake in the center of the preheated oven for 18 to 20 minutes, or until a toothpick tests clean. Remove from the pan, peel off the wax paper, and cool on a wire rack, top side up.

To make the cheese mixture, purée the ricotta in a food processor or blender until it is completely smooth. In a very large mixing bowl, whip the cream lightly with the sugar and vanilla, just until thickened but not stiff. It should not be firm enough to hold a shape when the beater is lifted. Stir in the ricotta and then add the ground coffee and grated chocolate.

To assemble the dessert, sprinkle the sponge cake with 2 tablespoons of the Tia Maria and tear it into small pieces (about 1 inch). Fold the cake and the remaining Tia Maria into the cheese mixture. Turn into a glass bowl and chill before serving. If desired, grate a little chocolate over the top of the dessert to garnish.

YIELD: 8 TO 10 SERVINGS

A Scaloppine Party for Eight

BEET AND CLARET SOUP (page 57)

VEAL SCALOPPINE FOSCARI

PARSLEY AND LEMON RICE

ASPARAGUS VINAIGRETTE (page 167)
OR GREEN SALAD†

LEMON AND ALMOND CAKE

WHILE there are many appealing ways to serve veal scaloppine, it is usually a last-minute preparation and therefore not a convenient party dish. In the recipe that follows, however, both the veal and its sauce can be cooked ahead of time and successfully reheated just before serving. It is important to buy tender white veal, and the scallops should be sliced thin and pounded even thinner with a wooden mallet. Lemon and Parsley Rice goes very well with this dish, as does either Asparagus Vinaigrette or a green salad. The dessert is an airy cake composed of two almond sponge layers filled with lemon mousse.

Advance Preparation   The Beet and Claret Soup, the Asparagus Vinaigrette, and the Lemon and Almond Cake may be made a day before serving. The Veal Scaloppine Foscari may be prepared several hours before serving.

VEAL SCALOPPINE FOSCARI

Sautéed whole mushrooms and veal scallops are served in a light cream sauce, discreetly flavored with anchovies, tarragon, and dry vermouth. While it may seem unorthodox to do so, the veal and sauce can be prepared ahead of time and then combined and reheated just before serving.

2 pounds veal scallops, pounded very thin
Flour
6 tablespoons unsalted butter (approximately)
Olive oil
5 anchovy fillets (4 if large), boned
2 garlic cloves, minced
3 tablespoons minced shallot

1½ tablespoons minced fresh tarragon or 1 scant teaspoon dried
1 pound small whole mushrooms, cleaned and trimmed*
½ cup dry vermouth
1½ cups light cream or half-and-half
Fresh-ground white pepper

Dredge the veal lightly in flour. Heat 1 tablespoon butter and 1 tablespoon oil in a large skillet. When it is quite hot, add as many veal scallops as will fit without crowding the pan. Cook about a minute on each side over high heat to brown slightly. Transfer to a platter and brown the remaining veal in the same way, adding more butter and oil as necessary. Remove from the pan and reserve.

Clean out the pan if the flour has burned on the bottom. Melt 2 tablespoons butter in the skillet, add the anchovies, and stir until dissolved. Add the garlic, shallot, tarragon, and mushrooms. Cook over moderate heat, stirring occasionally, until the mushrooms are tender. Remove from the pan with a slotted spoon and transfer to a

---

* If the mushrooms are large, cut them in halves or quarters.

bowl. Add the vermouth to the juices in the pan and add any juices that accumulate in the bowl of mushrooms. Turn up the heat and simmer, stirring, until the liquid is reduced by half. Add the cream and simmer, stirring constantly, until the sauce is reduced by about ⅓ and is slightly thickened. It should have the consistency of heavy cream. Be careful not to reduce the sauce too much (taste it as it simmers) or it will be too salty and too rich. It should be a light sauce. (The recipe may be prepared ahead to this point.)

To serve, reheat the sauce in the skillet. Add the veal and mushrooms and simmer for 1 or 2 minutes, or just until heated through. Season with pepper, but do not add salt. Serve immediately.

YIELD: 8 SERVINGS

PARSLEY AND LEMON RICE

1 ⅔ *cups uncooked rice*
Salt
3 tablespoons unsalted butter, cut into small pieces
1 cup minced fresh parsley
Grated zest of 1 large lemon

Bring a very large pot of water to a rolling boil. Add salt and the rice and boil for 15 to 20 minutes, or until the rice is tender but still firm. Drain in a colander and rinse under hot tap water. Toss with the butter, parsley, and lemon zest and serve.

YIELD: 8 SERVINGS

ASPARAGUS VINAIGRETTE. Prepare double the recipe on page 167.

LEMON AND ALMOND CAKE

This cake is composed of two very thin, light sponge cake layers made with ground almonds and separated by a fluffy lemon mousse filling. It is a good, light dessert with which to conclude a meal.

FOR THE CAKE LAYERS

3 eggs
6 tablespoons sugar
¼ teaspoon almond extract
½ teaspoon vanilla extract
3 tablespoons flour

4 ounces blanched almonds,
*   ground*
2–3 tablespoons amaretto
*   liqueur*

FOR THE LEMON MOUSSE

4 eggs, separated
½ cup lemon juice
¾ cup plus 2 tablespoons
*   sugar*
2 teaspoons unflavored
*   gelatin*

¼ cup cold water
Grated zest of 1 lemon
1 cup heavy cream

FOR THE TOPPING

Confectioners' sugar

Preheat the oven to 350°. Line two 9-inch round cake pans with buttered and floured wax paper. Combine the eggs and sugar in a mixing bowl. Set over a pan of barely simmering water and heat, stirring constantly, until the eggs feel quite warm, but do not let them cook. Remove from the heat and beat with an electric mixer for 5 to 8 minutes, until very light, thick, and tripled in volume. Beat in the almond and vanilla extracts. Sift the flour over the top, sprinkle with the ground almonds, and fold all together gently but thoroughly. Turn into the prepared cake pans and bake for 15 to 20 minutes, or until the cake springs back when pressed lightly and a toothpick tests clean. Loosen the edges with a knife and invert onto a cake rack. Carefully peel off the wax paper and cool. When the cake is cool, sprinkle the surface of each layer with 1½ tablespoons amaretto.

To make the lemon mousse filling, line a 9-inch round cake pan with buttered wax paper. Combine the egg yolks, lemon juice, and ½ cup sugar in a small, heavy saucepan. Cook over low heat, stirring constantly, until thick. Soften the gelatin in the cold water and dissolve over low heat, stirring constantly. Add the gelatin and grated lemon zest to the custard and cool to room temperature. Beat the egg whites until they hold soft peaks. Continue beating as you gradually add ¼ cup sugar. Whip the cream with the remaining 2 tablespoons sugar until it holds soft peaks. Fold the egg whites and cream into the cooled custard. Turn into the prepared cake pan and refrigerate until set.

To assemble the cake, place one cake layer on a serving plate. Loosen the edges of the lemon mousse with a knife and invert onto the cake layer. Peel off the wax paper and shave a little off the edges of the mousse if it is larger than the cake. Place the other cake layer on top. Refrigerate until shortly before serving time. Dust the top of the cake with confectioners' sugar just before serving.

YIELD: 8 SERVINGS

A Special Italian Dinner
for Four

MUSHROOM ANTIPASTO

CHICKEN AND ARTICHOKES IN
LEMON-ANCHOVY SAUCE

PARSLEY AND LEMON RICE (page 191)
OR PAGLIA E FIENO WITH CHÈVRE

ARUGOLA AND BOSTON
LETTUCE SALAD[†]

CHOCOLATE-AMARETTI CAKE

EACH of the dishes on this menu was inspired by Italian cuisine. It is my version of a meal you might have in northern Italy. The basis for the antipasto is funghi trifolati, mushrooms sautéed in a classic Italian style. For this dish, they are combined, in a lemon vinaigrette, with salami, Jarlsberg, olives, minced onion, and parsley. This antipasto can be served in lettuce cups as a first course, or with thin rounds of French bread as an hors d'oeuvre to have with drinks. The entrée is a sauté of chicken scaloppine and artichoke hearts—fresh and pure flavors accented by a simple lemon-butter-anchovy sauce. With the chicken, serve either rice mixed with lemon rind and a large handful of minced fresh parsley, or a dish of green and white fettuccine in a sauce of light cream and crumbled chèvre. To clear the palate, a salad of Boston lettuce and arugola or watercress, and then a creamy, dark, one-layer chocolate cake for dessert.

Advance Preparation   The Mushroom Antipasto and the Chocolate-Amaretti Cake may be made the day before serving. Prepare the artichokes for the entrée early on the day of the party; the final sautéeing for this dish must be done at the last minute. Have all the ingredients ready for the rice or pasta side dish; then boil and assemble before serving.

MUSHROOM ANTIPASTO

2 tablespoons unsalted butter
2 anchovy fillets
12 ounces mushrooms, cleaned, trimmed, and sliced
1 garlic clove, peeled and pressed
2 tablespoons dry white wine
1 tablespoon lemon juice
Fresh-ground black pepper
3 tablespoons capers

3–4 ounces Jarlsberg cheese, cut into small julienne strips
4 ounces hard salami, cut into small julienne strips
1/4 cup pitted black olives, preferably Calamata, halved
1/4 cup minced red onion
3 tablespoons minced fresh parsley

FOR THE VINAIGRETTE

3 tablespoons olive oil
2 teaspoons wine vinegar
2 teaspoons lemon juice

Melt the butter in a large, heavy skillet. Add the anchovy fillets and mash them with the back of a spoon to dissolve. Add the mushrooms and garlic and cook gently for a few minutes. Sprinkle with the wine and lemon juice, turn up the heat, and cook until the liquid evaporates, stirring to prevent scorching. Remove from the heat and season generously with pepper.

Turn the mushrooms into a bowl and let stand until cool. Add the capers, cheese, salami, olives, onion, and parsley.

Combine the ingredients for the vinaigrette and toss with the mushroom mixture just before serving.

YIELD: 1½ TO 2 CUPS OR 4 SERVINGS

CHICKEN AND ARTICHOKES IN LEMON-ANCHOVY SAUCE

This is a lovely, light dish for spring. Chicken breasts, boned and cut thin like scaloppine, are sautéed quickly with fresh artichoke hearts and served with a lemon-butter sauce flavored with anchovies, capers, and herbs.

2 large artichokes
2 large chicken breasts,
  skinned, boned, and cut
  in half
Fine, dry bread crumbs
6 tablespoons unsalted
  butter

1 large or 2 small anchovy
  fillets, boned
1 tablespoon lemon juice
1 tablespoon capers
¼ teaspoon dried rosemary
1 generous tablespoon
  minced fresh parsley

FOR THE GARNISH

Parsley sprigs

Trim the stems and top third of the leaves off the artichokes. Put them in a saucepan, cover with water, add salt, and cover tightly. Bring to a boil and boil gently for 20 to 30 minutes, or until the bottoms can be pierced easily with a metal skewer. Drain well. When cool enough to handle, strip off all the outer tough leaves, leaving only those that are completely edible. Cut each artichoke in half lengthwise and scrape out the chokes. Cut each half into 2 or 3 wedges.

Cut each half chicken breast horizontally into 2 thin scallops. Press the bread crumbs into the chicken pieces, coating well on both sides. Melt 2½ tablespoons of the butter in a very large skillet over moderate heat. Add the anchovy and stir to dissolve. When the butter is foaming, put the chicken and artichoke wedges in the skillet and sauté for 3 minutes on each side, or just until the chicken is cooked through. Do not overcook or it will be dry. Transfer to a serving platter and keep warm. Stir the lemon juice, capers, rosemary, and parsley into the pan juices. Remove from the heat, add the remaining 3½ tablespoons butter and stir until melted. Spoon the sauce over the chicken and artichokes and garnish the platter with fresh parsley.
YIELD: 4 SERVINGS

PARSLEY AND LEMON RICE. Prepare half the quantity on page 191.

PAGLIA E FIENO WITH CHÈVRE

We frequently had paglia e fieno in Venice. It is a mixture of green and white pasta, usually served with cream and butter.

Salt
Vegetable oil
3 ounces green fettuccine
3 ounces white fettuccine
1½ tablespoons unsalted
  butter, cut into small
  pieces

¼ cup light cream
2 ounces mild, rindless
  chèvre cheese, such as
  Montrachet, crumbled
  coarse
Fresh-ground pepper

Bring a large pot of water to a rolling boil. Add salt and a little vegetable oil and the pasta. Boil until tender but slightly firm. Drain well in a colander and turn into a serving bowl. Toss with the butter, cream, chèvre, and pepper. Add a little extra cream if the pasta does not seem moist enough.

YIELD: 4 SERVINGS AS A SIDE DISH

CHOCOLATE-AMARETTI CAKE

This is a very creamy one-layer cake made without flour. It has a rich chocolate flavor with a hint of almond. If desired, serve whipped cream flavored with a little sugar and amaretto liqueur.

*8 ounces semisweet
  chocolate (not chocolate
  chips)
¼ pound unsalted butter
5 eggs, separated
½ cup plus 1 tablespoon
  sugar*

*2 tablespoons amaretto
  liqueur
⅓ cup ground amaretti
  (hard Italian macaroons)
1 tablespoon unsweetened
  cocoa, sifted*

FOR THE GARNISH

Confectioners' sugar

Butter a round 9-inch cake pan. Cut a piece of wax paper to fit the bottom of the pan, and butter and flour the paper. Preheat the oven to 350°.

Break the chocolate into small pieces and melt it with the butter in the top of a double boiler over hot, not simmering, water, stirring constantly.

Beat the egg yolks until thick and light, gradually adding ¼ cup of the sugar. Stir in the melted chocolate mixture and the amaretto liqueur.

Beat the egg whites until they hold soft peaks. Continue beating until stiff as you gradually add the remaining sugar. Fold ¼ of the

beaten whites into the chocolate mixture. Sprinkle the ground amaretti and cocoa over the top, then add the rest of the whites, folding
everything together carefully but thoroughly. Turn into the prepared
pan, spreading the batter evenly with a spatula. Bake for 25 to 30
minutes. When done, the cake will be dry near the edges and moist
in the center. Do not overcook or the cake will lose its creamy quality.
Transfer to a wire rack and loosen the edges with a knife. Cool in
the pan for 20 minutes. Invert onto the rack, peel off the wax paper,
and complete cooling. Turn onto a cake platter, bottom side up, as the
top will crack slightly in cooling. Dust with confectioners' sugar just
before serving.

YIELD: 8 SERVINGS

A Lamb Dinner for Ten

JERUSALEM ARTICHOKE SOUP

LEG OF LAMB WITH MUSHROOM,
SPINACH, AND PROSCIUTTO STUFFING

SLICED BEETS WITH GARLIC-CRUMB
TOPPING OR
POTATO-CHEESE GALETTE (page 103)

FENNEL, ENDIVE, AND
WATERCRESS SALAD

MAPLE-WALNUT ROLL

THIS menu, for a special dinner party in spring, features a boned and marinated leg of lamb. It is prepared with a savory stuffing of sautéed mushrooms, scallions, a few spinach leaves, and chopped prosciutto that creates a colorful marbleized pattern in the center of each slice. Two sauces accompany the lamb: a pan gravy flavored with rosemary; and Salsa Verde, a thick parsley sauce served at room temperature. The meal begins with an unusual hot soup of Jerusalem artichokes. With the lamb, serve crisp Potato-Cheese Galette or sliced beets flavored with garlic and dill. The salad is an elegant mixture of fennel, endive, and watercress, and, in recognition of maple-sugaring season, dessert is a walnut roll filled with a creamy maple mousse.

Advance Preparation The Jerusalem Artichoke Soup and the Maple-Walnut Roll may be made a day ahead. Stuff the lamb and prepare either vegetable early on the day of the party so that everything will be ready for the oven. After the lamb has roasted, increase the oven temperature and put in the potatoes or beets to cook while the meat is resting and being carved.

JERUSALEM ARTICHOKE SOUP

A delicately flavored and unusual creamed soup.

3 pounds Jerusalem artichokes
3 tablespoons lemon juice
2 cups cold water
2 tablespoons unsalted butter
1 large yellow onion, peeled and chopped
2 garlic cloves, peeled and minced

2 large potatoes, peeled and sliced thin
2 cups chicken stock or broth
1¾ cups heavy cream
Salt
Fresh-ground pepper
A pinch of tarragon

Peel and slice the artichokes and drop them into a bowl with the lemon juice and water. Melt the butter in a large enameled or stainless steel saucepan and sauté the onions and garlic until softened, but do not brown. Drain the artichokes and add them to the pan; sauté briefly. Add the sliced potatoes and the chicken stock, cover the pan tightly and simmer until the vegetables are tender. Drain, reserving the broth, and purée the vegetables in a food processor, adding the broth in a thin stream. Stir in the cream, seasoning, and tarragon, and reheat before serving.

YIELD: APPROXIMATELY 8 CUPS OR 10 SERVINGS

LEG OF LAMB WITH MUSHROOM, SPINACH AND PROSCIUTTO STUFFING

1 boned leg of lamb, about 4¾ pounds after boning (7½ pounds before), with skin and some of the fat removed

FOR THE MARINADE

3 garlic cloves, pressed
¼ cup lemon juice
¼ cup dry vermouth
¼ cup olive oil
⅓ cup chopped fresh mint leaves

1½ teaspoons minced fresh rosemary or ½ teaspoon dried

FOR THE STUFFING

½ pound mushrooms, cleaned and sliced
1 tablespoon unsalted butter
¼ cup chopped scallions
1½ cups parsley sprigs

1½ cups coarse-chopped raw spinach leaves
¼ pound thin-sliced prosciutto, cut into ¾-inch squares

FOR THE PAN GRAVY

Pan juices
1 tablespoon flour
1 teaspoon minced fresh rosemary or ⅓ teaspoon dried
1¼ cups beef broth

1 recipe Salsa Verde, page 52.
Watercress or parsley

Put the lamb in a large, shallow bowl with the ingredients for the marinade. Cover loosely and marinate in the refrigerator for 12 to 24 hours, turning the lamb over occasionally.

To make the stuffing, sauté the mushrooms in the butter until soft. Turn into a bowl and combine with the scallions, parsley, spinach, and prosciutto.

Preheat the oven to 500°. Remove the lamb from the marinade. Strain and reserve the marinade for basting. Stuff the lamb and tie securely with kitchen string at 1½-inch intervals. Transfer to a roasting pan and roast for 15 minutes. Lower the oven temperature to 350° and cook for 1½ to 1¾ hours longer, or until a meat thermometer registers 150°. While the lamb is roasting, baste occasionally with the marinade.

When the lamb is done, transfer it to a heated platter and let it rest while you make the gravy. Degrease the pan juices. Blend in the flour, stirring rapidly with a wire whisk. Add the rosemary and broth and heat to simmering on top of the stove. (It is easiest to do this in the roasting pan where the liquid will be shallow.)

Slice the lamb, adding any juices to the gravy. Garnish the platter with watercress or parsley. Pass the Salsa Verde and the gravy separately.

YIELD: 10 SERVINGS

SLICED BEETS WITH GARLIC-CRUMB TOPPING

3 pounds trimmed beets (8 medium-large)	2 tablespoons lemon juice
4 slices white bread	2 tablespoons fresh dill weed or 1 teaspoon dried
1 large garlic clove, peeled and pressed	4 tablespoons unsalted butter, melted

Scrub the beets and cook in boiling water until tender. Plunge into cold water, peel, and slice ¼ inch thick. Butter a large shallow baking dish and arrange the beets in a slightly overlapping layer in the dish.

Trim the crusts from the bread and dry in a 350° oven, turning once. Cool, crumble coarse, and combine with the garlic, lemon juice, and dill. Scatter the mixture over the beets and drizzle the melted butter on top. (The dish may be prepared in advance to this point.)

To serve, preheat the oven to 350°. Cook the beets, uncovered, for 20 minutes, or until they are heated through and the topping is crisp.

YIELD: 10 TO 12 SERVINGS

POTATO-CHEESE GALETTE. Prepare double the recipe on page 103, using 2 round 9-inch pans.

FENNEL, ENDIVE, AND WATERCRESS SALAD

1 medium-large fennel bulb
4 Belgian endive
3 bunches watercress

FOR THE VINAIGRETTE

⅓ cup olive oil
1 tablespoon white wine vinegar
1 teaspoon lemon juice

Trim off and discard the green stalks from the fennel. Cut it in half lengthwise and then slice each half crosswise into thin slivers. Cut the endive in half lengthwise and then slice across at 1-inch intervals. Combine the fennel, endive, and watercress in a salad bowl. Combine the ingredients for the vinaigrette and toss with the salad just before serving.

YIELD: 10 SERVINGS

MAPLE-WALNUT ROLL

A walnut cake roll with a maple mousse filling.

FOR THE CAKE

6 eggs, separated
⅔ cup sugar
1 teaspoon vanilla extract
1½ cups walnuts, ground
A pinch of cream of tartar

FOR THE MAPLE FILLING

2 eggs, separated
7 tablespoons pure maple
  syrup
1½ teaspoons unflavored
  gelatin

3 tablespoons cold water
⅔ cup heavy cream
1 tablespoon brandy
A pinch of cream of tartar

FOR GARNISH

Confectioners' sugar

To make the cake, preheat the oven to 350°. Line a 10-by-15-inch jelly roll pan with wax paper, and butter and flour the paper and the sides of the pan. With an electric mixer, beat the egg yolks until light and thick, gradually adding ⅓ cup of the sugar. Stir in the vanilla and ground walnuts. Wash the beaters and then beat the egg whites until frothy. Add the cream of tartar and beat until they hold firm peaks. Continue beating while gradually adding the remaining ⅓ cup sugar. Fold the nut mixture into the beaten whites and turn into the prepared pan, leveling the batter with a spatula. Bake for 15 minutes, or until the cake is lightly browned and a toothpick tests clean. Dampen a clean cotton or linen dish towel with cold water and wring it out. Place the cake, in the pan, on a wire rack and cover with the towel. When cool, transfer to the refrigerator to chill.

To prepare the filling, lightly beat the egg yolks in a small, heavy saucepan and add the maple syrup. Cook over low heat, stirring with a wire whisk, until thickened. Remove from the heat and let cool. Soften the gelatin in the cold water and dissolve over low heat, stirring constantly. Cool just to room temperature. Whip the cream with the brandy until it holds soft peaks. Continue beating while adding the dissolved gelatin in a thin stream. Beat the egg whites until frothy; add the cream of tartar and beat until stiff. Whisk the maple custard into the whipped cream and then fold in the egg whites. Chill until firm.

Place 2 long, overlapping sheets of wax paper on the counter and dust with confectioners' sugar. Take the cake out of the refrigerator and loosen the edges with a knife. Unmold onto the wax paper, and peel the paper off the bottom of the cake. Spread with the maple cream. Roll up the cake from the long side by lifting the wax paper and turning the cake onto itself. It will crack a bit at the sides. Lift the roll onto a serving platter and cover loosely with wax paper. (If tightly covered, the cake will become soggy when refrigerated.) Refrigerate until serving. Just before serving, sift confectioners' sugar over the top of the cake.

YIELD: 10 TO 12 SERVINGS

A Celebratory Dinner

AVOCADO AND SHRIMP COCKTAIL

CHICKEN HADRIAN

PURÉED SPINACH (page 133)

GREEN SALAD WITH ARUGOLA[†]

PEAR, CHOCOLATE, AND
HAZELNUT TORTE

THIS is the sort of dinner you would serve to celebrate a special event—a birthday, a going-away party, a welcome-back party. The entrée is a convenient dish for entertaining as it is prepared ahead of time, with only the final baking done before serving. Suprêmes of chicken, covered with a mushroom-feta-ham mixture, are steamed in foil and moistened with their own juices and a little Marsala. The appetizer is a variation on an old favorite—a festive combination of shrimp and avocado in a mildly curried Russian dressing. The dessert is, in itself, a cause for celebration, and, indeed, it was originally created for my husband's birthday, perhaps the ultimate distinction. As you consider making this cake (a composition of hazelnut layers, pear cream filling, and chocolate icing), it may be appropriate to reflect upon the wisdom of Jean Anthelme Brillat-Savarin, nine-teenth century philosopher and gourmand: ". . . beauty consists above all in roundness of form and gracefully curving lines. The most elegant outfit and cleverest dressmaker cannot hide certain absences, nor conceal certain angles; and it is a common saying that with every pin she removes, a thin woman, however beautiful she may seem, loses something of her charm." And, in case you are still unconvinced, he observes further, with undisguised contempt, that thin women "are easily bored at table and live only for cards and scandal."* Go ahead and make the cake.

Advance Preparation   The Puréed Spinach and the Pear, Chocolate, and Hazelnut Torte may be made the day before the party. Prepare the Avocado and Shrimp Cocktail and the Chicken Hadrian on the day of serving. The entrée can be made ahead up to the final 15-minute baking. Reheat the spinach for about 20 minutes at 350°.

AVOCADO AND SHRIMP COCKTAIL

A delicious combination, easily prepared.

> *2 medium-large avocados*
> *Lemon juice*
> *32 medium cooked, shelled, and deveined shrimp*

FOR THE DRESSING

> *½ cup mayonnaise*
> *¾ cup sour cream*
> *¼ cup ketchup*
> *2 tablespoons minced fresh mint leaves*
> *A large pinch of curry powder*

---

* Jean Anthelme Brillat-Savarin, *The Philosopher in the Kitchen,* trans. by Anne Drayton. Penguin Books, 1970.

FOR THE GARNISH

Mint sprigs

Peel the avocados, cut in half lengthwise, discard the pits, and slice crosswise ¼ inch thick. Dip each slice into lemon juice to prevent discoloring. Place in a bowl with the shrimp. Combine the ingredients for the dressing and mix with the shrimp and avocado. Cover and chill. Serve in individual glass bowls or cocktail cups or goblets. Garnish each serving with a sprig of mint.

YIELD: 8 SERVINGS

CHICKEN HADRIAN

This is a Roman-style chicken with a Greek influence. Boned and skinned chicken breasts are sautéed briefly in butter and then steamed in their own juices under a blanket of sautéed mushrooms, ham, and feta cheese. Use a mild and creamy feta and rinse it if it is too salty.

½ pound firm white mushrooms, cleaned and trimmed
2½ tablespoons minced shallots
5 tablespoons unsalted butter
3 ounces thin-sliced baked ham, cut into ½-inch squares

3 tablespoons minced fresh parsley
5 tablespoons Marsala
Fresh-ground pepper
6 ounces feta cheese, cut into ½-inch dice
4 large, whole chicken breasts, skinned, boned, and cut in half

FOR THE GARNISH

Watercress or parsley

Cut any large mushrooms into halves or quarters and then slice about ⅛ inch thick. Sauté them, with the shallots, in 1 tablespoon butter over medium heat for a few minutes. When they begin to render their juices, add the ham, parsley, 2 tablespoons Marsala, and some pepper, and turn up the heat. Cook, stirring, until the moisture evaporates. Turn the mushroom mixture into a bowl. When cool, mix with the feta cheese.

Melt 2 tablespoons butter in the skillet and sauté 4 of the chicken breast halves for 2 minutes on each side over medium heat to brown slightly. They should remain underdone or pink inside. Remove, melt the remaining 2 tablespoons butter in the skillet, and sauté the remaining chicken in the same way.

Preheat the oven to 350°.

Place a very long sheet of aluminum foil in a shallow baking pan. Put the chicken breasts close together on top of the foil, and drizzle with the pan juices and 3 tablespoons Marsala. Spoon equal portions of the mushroom-feta mixture on top of each breast half, pressing it down firmly to fit it all on. Pull up the ends of the sheet of foil to encase the chicken, folding over and crimping the edges to seal at the top and sides so that you have an airtight package. (The recipe may be prepared ahead to this point. If you do not proceed with the final baking right away, put the chicken in the refrigerator and remove about 20 minutes before baking to return to room temperature.)

Bake for no longer than 15 minutes. The chicken will be dry if it is overcooked. To serve, place on a heated platter or individual plates, spoon the pan juices over the chicken, and garnish with watercress or parsley.

YIELD: 8 SERVINGS

PEAR, CHOCOLATE, AND HAZELNUT TORTE

A two-layer cake made with ground hazelnuts, a pear-cream filling, and chocolate icing.

FOR THE CAKE LAYERS

*½ pound hazelnuts
 (a generous 1 ½ cups)
4 eggs, lightly beaten
½ cup plus 1 tablespoon
 sugar*

*1 teaspoon vanilla extract
Grated zest of 1 lemon
4 tablespoons unsalted
 butter, melted*

FOR THE PEAR FILLING

*2 tablespoons lemon juice
1 ½ pounds Bosc or Anjou
 pears (4 large), peeled,
 cored, and chopped fine
¼ cup plus 2 teaspoons
 sugar*

*1 teaspoon vanilla extract
½ teaspoon unflavored
 gelatin
2 tablespoons cold water
2 teaspoons brandy
½ cup heavy cream*

FOR THE ICING

*4 ounces Baker's German's Sweet Chocolate
2 ½ tablespoons unsalted butter
1 tablespoon curaçao*

To make the cake, preheat the oven to 350°. Spread the hazelnuts in a baking pan and cook for 6 minutes. Do not turn off the oven. Put them in a coarse linen towel and rub vigorously to remove as much of the skins as possible. Grind the nuts in 2 batches in a food processor, using an off-on motion, so that they are partly pulverized and partly chopped fine. Reserve.

Butter and lightly flour 2 pieces of wax paper cut to fit the bottom of 2 round 9-inch cake pans.

Mix the eggs and sugar in a large mixing bowl and set over a pan of boiling water. Stir until the eggs are quite warm, but do not let them cook. Remove from the heat, add the vanilla, and beat with an electric mixer for 5 to 8 minutes, until the eggs are very pale in color, tripled in volume, and have the consistency of lightly whipped cream. First fold in the nuts and lemon zest, and then the melted butter, combining thoroughly but taking care not to deflate the eggs. Turn into the prepared cake pans and bake for 20 to 25 minutes, or until a toothpick tests clean. Loosen the edges of the cakes with a knife and invert onto a cake rack. Peel off the wax paper and cool to room temperature.

To make the filling, put the lemon juice in a heavy saucepan. Add the pears and ¼ cup of the sugar and bring to a simmer. Cook 15 to 20 minutes, stirring as the sauce thickens, until most of the liquid has evaporated and the mixture is almost as thick as applesauce. Add the vanilla and remove from the heat.

Soften the gelatin in the cold water and dissolve over low heat, stirring constantly. Stir into the pear sauce and cool to room temperature.

Whip the cream with the brandy and the remaining 2 teaspoons sugar until it holds soft peaks. Fold into the cooled pear mixture.

After the cake layers have cooled, spread the filling evenly over one layer and refrigerate until set. Remove from the refrigerator and cover with the other cake layer.

To make the chocolate icing, break the chocolate into very small pieces and put it in the top of a double boiler with the butter and curaçao. Stir constantly over hot, not simmering, water until the chocolate has melted. Be careful not to overheat it. Pour the melted chocolate over the top of the cake and spread evenly with a knife, allowing it to drip a little over the edges. Refrigerate the cake if you are not serving it soon and remove from the refrigerator about ½ hour before serving.

YIELD: 8 SERVINGS

An Old-Fashioned Sunday Dinner

MUSHROOM TIMBALES (page 115)

ROAST BEEF WITH
ORANGE-MADEIRA SAUCE

POTATO-ONION CASSEROLE

GREEN SALAD†

BRIE†

CHOCOLATE-LEMON LAYER CAKE

A standing rib roast of beef, crisply browned on the outside, rare within, served with potatoes and at least one green vegetable was a special Sunday dinner when I was a child. I still consider it a festive meal, even though it is the sort of food that has fallen out of vogue in our current search for novelty. Just before embarking on his trip around the world, Phileas Fogg dined on roast beef, his customary midday meal taken at the Reform Club. I would guess that he had his fill of exotic cuisines in the course of the next eighty days, and was rather pleased, on the eighty-first, to return to the Reform Club for dinner. The following roast beef dinner begins with individual

Mushroom Timbales. The beef is served with a gravy of pan juices, flavored with orange and Madeira. The dessert is a layer cake created for a friend's birthday: almond sponge layers filled with lemon mousse and topped with a chocolate glaze.

Advance Preparation   The Chocolate-Lemon Layer Cake may be made a day before serving. The Mushroom Timbales may be prepared several hours, or even a day, before cooking, but they should be at room temperature before they are put in the oven. The Potato-Onion Casserole may be prepared several hours ahead of baking time.

MUSHROOM TIMBALES. Follow the instructions for appetizer servings made in individual ramekins or custard cups on page 116 and cook for 20 minutes at 350°.

ROAST BEEF WITH ORANGE-MADEIRA SAUCE

A classic rib roast with a sauce made from the pan juices and flavored with orange juice, Madeira, and chutney. Try to get the first ribs, which are less fatty.

> *One 7½–8 pound standing rib roast of beef*
> *Salt*
> *Fresh-ground pepper*
> *Allspice*

FOR THE SAUCE

> *1 tablespoon unsalted butter*
> *1 tablespoon flour*
> *¾–1 cup beef stock or*
>   *broth*
> *1 tablespoon Madeira*

> *1½ tablespoons juice from*
>   *a jar of Major Grey's*
>   *chutney, preferably Sun*
>   *Brand*
> *¼ cup fresh orange juice*

FOR THE GARNISH

Watercress

Preheat the oven to 350°.

Season the beef with salt, pepper, and a little ground allspice. Put the beef in a roasting pan and cook for 18 to 20 minutes per pound, or until a meat thermometer registers 140°, for rare beef.

While the beef is cooking, melt the butter in a small saucepan. Blend in the flour and cook briefly over low heat. Gradually whisk in ¾ cup of the beef stock, and the Madeira and chutney juice. Reserve. When the roast is done, degrease the pan juices and add to the gravy, along with any juice that accumulates when carving the beef. You should have at least ½ cup pan juices. Taste the gravy and adjust flavorings, supplementing with additional beef stock if necessary. Reheat the gravy, stir in the orange juice, and serve. Garnish the roast beef platter with watercress.

YIELD: 8 SERVINGS

POTATO-ONION CASSEROLE

A hearty side dish flavored with grated cheese.

*1 pound yellow onions,
peeled and sliced thin
(3 cups)
1 tablespoon olive oil
2½ pounds red potatoes
3½ tablespoons unsalted
butter*

*5 ounces Jarlsberg cheese,
grated (1¼ cups)
2 ounces Parmesan cheese,
grated (½ cup)*

Sauté the onions in the olive oil until soft and transparent, but do not brown.

Peel the potatoes and slice ⅛ inch thick. As they are sliced, drop them into a bowl of cold water to prevent discoloring. Butter a heavy casserole that is about 8 inches in diameter and 4 inches deep (2-quart capacity). Cover the bottom of the dish with 2 layers of potato slices and dot with about 2 teaspoons of the butter. Scatter ¼ of the onions on top and sprinkle with some of the Jarlsberg and Parmesan. Continue layering in this manner, but use up all the onions before the last layer of potatoes. The top layer should consist of potatoes, butter, and cheese. Cover the casserole tightly with a lid or aluminum foil. (Up to this point, the dish may be prepared several hours in advance of serving.)

To serve, preheat the oven to 350°. Bake the casserole for about 1½ hours, or until the potatoes are tender. When cooked, uncover the casserole and brown for a minute or two—under the broiler if it will fit.

YIELD: 8 TO 10 SERVINGS

CHOCOLATE-LEMON LAYER CAKE

Two white génoise cake layers made with ground almonds are filled with a deep, fluffy layer of tart lemon mousse. The top of the cake is glazed with dark chocolate icing.

FOR THE CAKE LAYERS

6 eggs
⅔ cup sugar
1 teaspoon grated lemon zest
⅓ cup flour

8 ounces blanched, slivered
  almonds, ground
6 tablespoons unsalted
  butter, melted and cooled

FOR THE LEMON MOUSSE FILLING

4 eggs, separated
¾ cup plus 1 tablespoon
  sugar
½ cup lemon juice

2 teaspoons unflavored gelatin
¼ cup cold water
Grated zest of 1 lemon
1 cup heavy cream

FOR THE CHOCOLATE ICING

4 ounces Baker's German's Sweet Chocolate
2½ tablespoons unsalted butter

To make the cake layers, preheat the oven to 350°. Line the bottoms of two 9-inch round cake tins with buttered and floured wax paper. Combine the eggs and sugar in a large mixing bowl. Set over a pan of simmering water and stir until the mixture is quite warm, being careful not to let the eggs cook. Remove from the heat, add the lemon zest, and beat with an electric mixer for 5 to 8 minutes, or until the eggs are very pale in color, tripled in volume, and have the consistency of lightly whipped cream. Fold in the ground almonds and flour; then add the melted butter, combining thoroughly with a rubber spatula but taking care not to deflate the eggs. Turn into the prepared pans and bake for 18 to 20 minutes, or until a toothpick tests clean and the cake springs back when pressed lightly. Cool in the pans on a wire rack; then unmold and peel off the wax paper.

To make the lemon mousse filling, line a 9-inch round cake pan with buttered wax paper. Combine the egg yolks, ½ cup sugar, and the lemon juice in a small, heavy saucepan. Cook over low heat, stirring constantly, until thick. Remove from the heat. Soften the gelatin in the cold water and dissolve over low heat, stirring constantly. Add the gelatin and grated lemon zest to the custard and cool to room temperature. Beat the egg whites until they hold soft peaks. Continue beating as you gradually add ¼ cup sugar. Whip the cream with the remaining tablespoon of sugar until it holds soft peaks. Fold the egg whites and cream into the cooled custard. Turn into the prepared cake pan and refrigerate until set.

To assemble the cake, place one cake layer on a serving plate. Loosen the edges of the lemon mousse with a knife and invert onto the cake layer. Peel off the wax paper. Place the other cake layer on top.

To make the icing, cut the chocolate into very small pieces and put it in the top of a double boiler with the butter. Stir continuously over hot water until it has melted. Remove from the heat and continue stirring until the chocolate is smooth and shiny. Pour it over the top of the cake all at once and spread evenly with a knife, allowing some to drip over the sides. Refrigerate the cake until shortly before serving.

YIELD: 1 LARGE LAYER CAKE OR 8 TO 10 SERVINGS

A Duck Dinner

CHILLED BEET SOUP

LIME-AND-HONEY-GLAZED DUCK
WITH MANGO

RICE[†]

GREEN BEANS VINAIGRETTE OR
GREEN SALAD[†]

STRAWBERRY-LEMON TART

R OAST duck is an easy dish to cook, and when served imaginatively, it can be the basis for a party menu. In this recipe it is glazed with lime and honey and garnished with sautéed mango. The menu includes Chilled Beet Soup, which goes particularly well with duck, and a Strawberry-Lemon Tart for dessert.

Advance Preparation   The Chilled Beet Soup, the beans, and the Strawberry-Lemon Tart may be prepared a day before serving.

CHILLED BEET SOUP

Grated fresh gingerroot gives this soup an extraordinary flavor. It blends beautifully with the beets, contributing a refreshing, slightly piquant taste.

1½ pounds trimmed fresh beets

2 cups beef stock or strong broth

1 large tomato, peeled, cored, and seeded

⅓ cup minced red onion

1 large garlic clove, peeled and cut in half

1 tablespoon plus ½ teaspoon grated fresh gingerroot

¾ cup sour cream

1 tablespoon lime juice

Peel the beets and slice ¼ inch thick. Simmer, covered, with the beef stock, tomato, onion, garlic, and gingerroot for 30 to 40 minutes, or until the beets are tender. Remove from the heat and strain, reserving the broth. Purée in a food processor. Stir in the reserved broth, the sour cream, and lime juice. Chill before serving.

YIELD: APPROXIMATELY 4½ CUPS OR 4 TO 6 SERVINGS

LIME-AND-HONEY-GLAZED DUCK WITH MANGO

One 4½–5 pound duck, quartered
1 large lime
2½ tablespoons light honey
Salt

FOR THE GARNISH

1 mango
1 tablespoon unsalted butter
2 tablespoons brown sugar, packed
1 tablespoon brandy

Rinse and dry the duck pieces and remove all visible fat. Grate the lime zest; combine the zest with the honey and reserve. Squeeze the lime juice and pour it into a shallow dish just large enough to hold the duck. Marinate the duck pieces cut side down in the lime juice at room temperature for about an hour.

Preheat the oven to 375°. Place the duck on a rack in a roasting pan. Sprinkle with salt and prick the skin all over. Roast for about 1 hour and 40 minutes, pricking the duck skin occasionally to release the fat and draining the fat from the pan as necessary. The duck is done when the flesh feels tender and the thigh juices run clear. Remove from the oven and spread the lime and honey mixture over the skin. Roast for 5 minutes longer to glaze, but do not let the honey burn.

Prepare the garnish about 15 minutes before the duck is finished cooking. Peel and slice the mango. Melt the butter and sugar in a large skillet over low heat. Add the mango slices and sauté them on both sides over moderately high heat, sprinkling with the brandy. Stir and cook just until tender and slightly glazed. They should not get too soft.

Arrange the duck pieces and mango on a heated platter and serve.
YIELD: 4 SERVINGS

GREEN BEANS VINAIGRETTE

Be sure to buy tender, young, and very fresh green beans, as older ones are often tough and woody. Fresh beans will snap in half easily.

FOR THE VINAIGRETTE

¼ cup olive oil
2 tablespoons white wine vinegar
1 garlic clove, peeled and cut in half

FOR THE BEANS

¾ pound green beans
2½ tablespoons minced red onion
1½ tablespoons minced fresh tarragon
Salt

Combine the ingredients for the vinaigrette at least 1 hour before preparing the beans.

Rinse the beans and snap off the stem ends. Place in a steamer basket and cook, tightly covered, over boiling water just until they are tender. They should remain slightly crisp. Drain and toss in the vinaigrette while they are still warm. Discard the garlic clove and add the minced onion, tarragon, and salt to taste.

YIELD: 4 SERVINGS

STRAWBERRY-LEMON TART

This tart has a lemon custard filling and is covered with glazed fresh strawberries.

FOR THE PASTRY

1 ½ cups flour
3 tablespoons sugar
Grated zest of 1 large lemon
5 tablespoons cold unsalted
  butter, cut up

3 tablespoons chilled
  vegetable shortening
2–3 tablespoons water

FOR THE LEMON FILLING

1 tablespoon unsalted butter
1 tablespoon flour
⅓ cup lemon juice
½ cup plus 1 tablespoon
  light cream or half-and-
  half

⅓ cup sugar
Grated zest of 1 large
  lemon
4 egg yolks

FOR THE BERRIES AND GLAZE

1 quart strawberries
2 tablespoons apple jelly
3–4 tablespoons red raspberry jelly

To make the pastry, combine the flour, sugar, and lemon zest in a large mixing bowl. Lightly rub in the butter and vegetable shortening with the tips of your fingers. Add enough water to form the mixture into a dough. Knead 1 or 2 turns, wrap in wax paper, and chill until firm enough to roll out.

Preheat the oven to 375°. Roll out the dough between lightly floured sheets of wax paper into a circle to fit a 9-inch tart pan. Line the pan with the dough, doubling it at the sides. Cover the pastry with aluminum foil and fill with dried beans or rice. Bake for 20 minutes. Remove the foil and beans, prick the bottom of the pie shell, and bake 10 minutes longer or until lightly browned. Cool on a wire rack.

To make the lemon filling, melt the butter in a small, heavy saucepan. Add the flour, stir to blend, and gradually whisk in the lemon juice and cream, stirring until smooth. Add the sugar and lemon zest and cook, stirring continuously over medium heat for 5 to 7 minutes, until the mixture is quite thick. Lightly beat the egg yolks, add a little of the hot lemon mixture, and then add the yolks to the saucepan, stirring vigorously. Cook over medium heat for 5 minutes longer, stirring constantly, or until the custard is very thick and smooth. Do not boil. Remove from the heat and cool to room temperature.

Wash and hull the strawberries and drain thoroughly on several layers of paper towels, hulled side down. Let stand for 1 hour or longer.

Melt the apple jelly in a small saucepan or stainless steel measuring cup. Brush the inside and top edges of the pastry shell with the melted jelly and allow to set. When the custard is cool, spoon it into the tart shell. Arrange the berries side by side over the custard, hull side down. Melt the raspberry jelly, let simmer for a few minutes, and then brush it over each berry.

YIELD: 6 TO 8 SERVINGS

A Far Eastern
Shrimp Dinner

CEYLON COCONUT SHRIMP

LIME RICE

ASPARAGUS WITH LEMON BUTTER[†]

CUCUMBER AND WATERCRESS SALAD[†]

FROZEN STRAWBERRY MOUSSE OR
STRAWBERRIES AND ORANGE
SECTIONS IN CURAÇAO[†]

THIS is a light menu to serve at a dinner party anticipating warm weather; it should be a welcome change from the usual winter diet of heavy roasts and stews. The shrimp are served over lime-flavored rice in a very mild sauce based on milk, coconut, lime, and a delicate blend of Eastern spices. It is another treasure from my husband's bachelor days, when he collected exotic and unfamiliar dishes with which to dazzle his friends. Asparagus accompanies the entrée, with either fruit or Frozen Strawberry Mousse for dessert.

Advance Preparation The Frozen Strawberry Mousse may be made several days before serving. Prepare all the ingredients for the shrimp dish early on the day of the party. The entire dish can then be finished in 5 minutes just before serving. Boil the rice just before cooking the shrimp and keep warm.

CEYLON COCONUT SHRIMP

This exotic dish can be made very quickly and simply and is a welcome change from the usual dinner party fare.

3 pounds raw, unshelled medium-large shrimp	*1½ teaspoons minced garlic*
1½ cups sliced onion	*¾ teaspoon grated fresh gingerroot*
1 tablespoon unsalted butter	*2 tablespoons minced shallot*
3¼ cups milk	
¼ teaspoon ground turmeric	*1 cinnamon stick*
⅛ teaspoon ground coriander	*1 cup grated sweetened coconut*
A pinch of chili powder	*3 tablespoons lime juice*

FOR THE GARNISH

1 cup sliced almonds, lightly toasted*

Shell and devein the shrimp and reserve. Sauté the onion in the butter until soft, but do not brown.

In a large, heavy stainless steel or enameled saucepan, combine the milk with the sautéed onions, the turmeric, coriander, chili powder, garlic, gingerroot, shallot, cinnamon stick, and coconut. Do not add the lime juice. Heat, stirring constantly to prevent the milk from scorching, and do not let the mixture simmer. Add the shrimp and continue cooking below the simmering point for 3 or 4 minutes, or just until the shrimp are pink and firm. Remove from the heat and

---

* To toast the almonds, preheat the oven to 350°. Spread the almonds on a baking sheet and toast for 5 to 6 minutes, until very lightly colored but not browned.

stir for a few minutes to cool slightly. Whisk in the lime juice. Serve over hot rice and garnish each serving with sliced almonds.

YIELD: 8 SERVINGS

LIME RICE

Salt
2 cups uncooked long-grain rice
3 tablespoons unsalted butter, cut into small pieces
Grated zest of 2 limes

Bring a very large pot of water to a rolling boil. Add about a tablespoon of salt and the rice, and stir. Boil for 15 to 17 minutes, or until the rice is tender but still firm. Drain in a colander and rinse under hot tap water. Turn into a serving bowl and stir in the butter and lime zest.

YIELD: 8 SERVINGS

FROZEN STRAWBERRY MOUSSE

This mixture is less creamy than the usual—somewhere between a mousse and a sorbet in texture. It has a pronounced strawberry flavor, enhanced by the addition of cassis syrup. It is garnished with sliced fresh berries.

3 pints strawberries
1 envelope plus ½ teaspoon unflavored gelatin
¼ cup cold water
¼ cup cassis syrup

1 cup sugar
½ cup water
4 egg whites
⅛ teaspoon cream of tartar
¾ cup heavy cream

FOR THE GARNISH

1–2 pints fresh strawberries
Sugar
Cassis syrup

Rinse, hull, and dry the strawberries and purée in a food processor. Turn into a heavy saucepan or kettle and slowly bring to a simmer. Boil gently for 8 to 10 minutes, stirring frequently. Remove from the heat and skim off the foam. Soften the gelatin in the cold water and dissolve over low heat, stirring constantly. Stir into the puréed berries. Add the cassis syrup, allow to cool, and then set in the refrigerator while proceeding with the recipe. (Check it from time to time to make sure it doesn't set.)

Combine the sugar and ½ cup water in a small, heavy saucepan. Bring to a boil and cook until a candy thermometer registers 230° to 234° (or a little of the syrup can be formed into a soft ball when dropped in a glass of ice water). While the syrup is cooking, beat the egg whites until frothy. Add the cream of tartar and continue beating until they hold firm peaks. Add the hot syrup in a thin stream while beating continuously with an electric mixer. After the syrup has been absorbed, beat the egg whites for 5 minutes longer until cool and very stiff. Whip the cream until it holds soft peaks.

If the strawberry purée has not yet thickened, place the bowl over a larger bowl filled with ice cubes and stir until the mixture is thick and syrupy, but do not let it set. Fold the whipped cream into the beaten egg whites and then fold in the strawberry purée. Turn into a serving bowl, cover with plastic wrap, and freeze until firm.

To prepare the garnish, rinse, hull, and dry the strawberries. Slice or cut in half. A couple of hours before serving, sweeten them with a little sugar and cassis.

To serve, remove the mousse from the freezer about ½ hour before serving to soften slightly. Garnish each serving of mousse with some of the sliced berries.

YIELD: 8 TO 10 SERVINGS

A Dinner for Joseph Brodsky

JELLIED BEET SOUP

CHICKEN CATHAY

PARSLEY AND LEMON RICE (page 191)

GREEN SALAD[†]

RHUBARB SHERBET WITH
STRAWBERRIES (page 181)

WE entertain many visiting poets in Rochester and Washington, and the parties are always lively—full of laughter, noisy conversation, and literary anecdotes. While it is a challenge to provide food and drink equal to these occasions, I feel confident that everyone would have a good time even if there were a disaster in the kitchen. The following menu was served to our friend Joseph Brodsky, when he came to Rochester to read at the University. I was told that he liked Chinese food and so prepared this American version of Oriental cuisine. The entrée is a mixture of chicken, nuts, celery, and scallions in a teriyaki marinade. Serve it with Parsley and Lemon Rice. The dessert is thoroughly Western, but very good: a cassis-flavored rhubarb sherbet garnished with fresh strawberries.

Advance Preparation   The Rhubarb Sherbet may be made several days before the party. The Jellied Beet Soup and the Chicken Cathay may be made one day ahead, but do not add the nuts to the chicken dish until just before serving.

JELLIED BEET SOUP

6 cups peeled and sliced beets
    (8 medium or 2 ¼ pounds
    trimmed)
6 cups strong, clear beef
    stock or broth
1 large garlic clove, peeled
    and cut in half

2 envelopes plus 2
    teaspoons unflavored
    gelatin
6 tablespoons cold water
3–4 tablespoons strained,
    fresh lime juice

FOR THE GARNISH

Sour cream
Minced fresh chives
Lime wedges

Put the beets in a large saucepan with the beef stock and garlic. Cover tightly, bring to a simmer, and cook for 15 minutes. Strain the soup and discard the solids. You should have 5¾ cups. Soften the gelatin in the cold water and dissolve over low heat, stirring constantly. Stir into the beet soup. Add 3 to 4 tablespoons lime juice, according to taste. Refrigerate until set.

Serve in small glass bowls. Place a spoonful of sour cream on top of each serving and sprinkle the chives over the sour cream. Place a lime wedge beside each bowl.

YIELD: 8 SERVINGS

CHICKEN CATHAY

An oriental-style dish combining strips of marinated chicken breast with walnuts, cashews, celery, and scallions. In preparing this recipe, do not add salt, as the chicken is well seasoned with soy sauce.

4 small chicken breasts, split, skinned, and boned
1½ cups raw cashews
1½ cups walnuts
Vegetable oil
6 cups celery, cut diagonally ½ inch wide and 1½ inches long

1½ cups scallions, cut diagonally into 1-inch lengths
Approximately ¼ cup flour
2 eggs, lightly beaten
1½ cups water
2 tablespoons cornstarch

FOR THE MARINADE

¾ cup medium dry sherry
½ cup Kikkoman Milder, salt reduced soy sauce*
⅞ cup water
1 tablespoon brown sugar

1 teaspoon grated fresh gingerroot
2 garlic cloves, peeled and pressed

Cut the chicken into strips about ½ inch wide and 2½ inches long. Combine the ingredients for the marinade in a large bowl. Add the chicken, cover with plastic wrap, and refrigerate for 6 to 8 hours.

Preheat the oven to 350°. Spread the cashews and walnuts on a large baking sheet and toss with 1 tablespoon vegetable oil. Bake for 5 to 8 minutes, until very lightly toasted but not browned. Drain on paper towels to absorb the excess oil, and reserve.

Heat a little oil in a large skillet, add the celery, and stir-fry over moderately high heat until slightly softened but still crisp. Remove from the pan and reserve. Add the scallions and cook very briefly to soften a bit. Reserve with the celery.

---

* It is important to use this soy sauce, as the salt content is reduced by half.

After the chicken has marinated, drain it well, reserving the marinade. Dredge in the flour and then toss in a bowl with the beaten eggs. Heat a little oil in the skillet and sauté the chicken in several batches over medium-high heat, tossing to brown on all sides. This should take only a couple of minutes; be careful not to overcook it. As it is cooked, transfer to a platter. Stir the reserved marinade into the pan. Dissolve the cornstarch in a little of the water and stir into the pan with the remaining water. Gradually bring to a simmer, stirring with a whisk. (The recipe may be prepared in advance to this point.) To serve, reheat the sauce and then add the chicken, celery, and scallions. Cook very briefly, just until hot. Add the cashews and walnuts and serve immediately.

YIELD: 8 SERVINGS

A Quick and Easy
Ham Dinner

AVOCADO AND SHRIMP
COCKTAIL (page 208)

HAM FLAVORED WITH PORT, APPLE,
AND APRICOT

PURÉED BEETS

ARUGOLA, MUSHROOM, AND
FETA SALAD

FRESH STRAWBERRIES WITH
CURAÇAO†

WHEN you are pressed for time, a baked ham can be an appetizing and practical solution to a dinner party. The recipe that follows is not for a country ham which is highly flavored and needs little embellishment, but rather for boned, precooked ham. Since the recipe calls for a cut portion, you will be able to select one that is lean. If the ham is too salty, it may be soaked or blanched before baking. Puréed Beets accompany the entrée, with fresh strawberries for dessert.

Advance Preparation   The Puréed Beets may be made one day ahead. Marinate the ham the day before cooking it. Prepare the Avocado and Shrimp Cocktail on the day of the party.

HAM FLAVORED WITH PORT, APPLE, AND APRICOT

For this recipe, the ham is marinated in port and cider or apple juice and glazed with apricot preserves. The marinade is used for the sauce. Be sure to buy a ham that is lean and not heavily salted. I use a portion of boned ham cut lengthwise so that the bottom is flat; it is easier to carve and the pieces are smaller. If you use a large-cylindrical-shaped ham, allow more cooking time as it is twice as thick.

One 3–3½ pound precooked, boneless ham portion, cut lengthwise	Apricot preserves
	1 teaspoon Dijon mustard
	1 tablespoon brandy
¾ cup apple juice or cider	2½ teaspoons cornstarch
½ cup ruby port	

Marinate the ham in the apple juice and port overnight, turning once or twice. (Use a glass, ceramic, or enamel pan.)

Preheat the oven to 350°. Put the ham in a baking pan, pour in the marinade, and cover the pan tightly with aluminum foil. Bake for about 40 minutes, or until the ham is tender and a meat thermometer registers 140°. Drain the marinade into a saucepan. Spread the surface of the ham with apricot preserves and bake, uncovered, for 10 minutes longer.

Whisk the mustard and brandy into the pan juices. Dissolve the cornstarch in a tablespoon of cold water and stir into the sauce. Cook, stirring, until the mixture simmers and thickens. Pour into a heated sauceboat.

YIELD: 6 SERVINGS

PURÉED BEETS

The beets are flavored with garlic, ginger, and sour cream. It is a colorful accompaniment to a roast, and easy to prepare.

3 pounds trimmed fresh beets
1 ½ teaspoons grated fresh
  gingerroot
1 large garlic clove, peeled
  and pressed

1 ½ tablespoons lemon juice
Salt
⅔ cup sour cream

Wash the beets and boil in water to cover until tender. Drain and peel. Cool to room temperature and purée in a food processor. Turn into a 6-to-8-cup casserole and stir in the ginger, garlic, lemon juice, and salt to taste. (The dish may be prepared in advance to this point.)

To serve, preheat the oven to 350°. Stir the sour cream into the beet purée. Cover the casserole and heat for 20 minutes.

YIELD: 8 SERVINGS

ARUGOLA, MUSHROOM, AND FETA SALAD

FOR THE VINAIGRETTE

½ cup olive oil
2 tablespoons white wine vinegar
1 large garlic clove, peeled and cut in half

2 large bunches arugola
½ pound firm, white mushrooms, cleaned, trimmed, and
  sliced
¼ pound mild feta cheese, crumbled
Fresh-ground pepper

Combine the ingredients for the vinaigrette at least 1 hour before serving to allow time for the garlic to marinate.

Wash and dry the arugola and discard any roots or tough ends. Combine in a salad bowl with the mushrooms, feta, and pepper. Toss with the vinaigrette just before serving.

YIELD: 6 SERVINGS

SUMMER

A Tropical Lunch

MANGO CHICKEN SALAD

TOASTED SYRIAN BREAD WITH
SESAME SEEDS (page 312)

RASPBERRY-ALMOND ICE

THIS is my impression of the sort of entrée one might be served
under the palm trees on a South Sea island, although I cannot speak
with any authority on that exotic cuisine. My intention was to prepare a chicken salad that did not, for a change, have a creamy or
mayonnaise dressing. Tropical ingredients, such as mango, avocado,
and ginger, punctuated by fresh mint, seemed both novel and fitting
accompaniments to chicken; the dressing is a cooling lime and ginger
vinaigrette. Dessert is a delicious combination of raspberry ice and
almond paste, made without an ice cream machine.

Advance Preparation The Raspberry-Almond Ice may be made
several days before serving. Make the Chicken Salad on the day of
the party.

MANGO CHICKEN SALAD

FOR THE DRESSING

7 tablespoons olive oil
3 tablespoons lime juice
2 tablespoons white wine vinegar
I tablespoon syrup from a jar of preserved ginger stem
I garlic clove, peeled and cut in half

FOR THE SALAD

3 whole chicken breasts, cut
in half
3 cups chicken broth
I ½ cups peeled, sliced
mango
I large avocado, peeled and
sliced

¼ cup thin-sliced preserved
ginger stem
¼ cup minced fresh mint
leaves

FOR THE GARNISH

Spinach or lettuce leaves

Combine the ingredients for the dressing and reserve.

Poach the chicken, partially covered, in simmering broth in a large skillet for 20 minutes, or just until cooked through. Be careful not to overcook or it will be dry. Drain, and when cool enough to handle, strip the skin and bones from the chicken and cut it into julienne strips, about 2½ inches long and ½ inch wide, following the grain of the meat.

In a mixing bowl, combine the chicken with the mango, avocado, ginger, and mint. Just before serving, remove the garlic clove from the dressing and gently toss the dressing and salad. Serve on a bed of spinach or lettuce leaves.

YIELD: 6 SERVINGS

RASPBERRY-ALMOND ICE

---

4 pints raspberries
1 cup sugar
½ cup almond paste (not "marzipan")

Wash the berries and drain well. Put them in a large, heavy kettle with the sugar. Slowly bring to a simmer, stirring occasionally. Cook for 1 or 2 minutes. Remove from the heat and strain through a fine sieve to remove the seeds, pressing through as much pulp as possible.

Put the almond paste in a food processor and, with the motor running, add the raspberry purée in a thin stream. Freeze until firm. Break into chunks and purée, in batches, in a food processor until smooth but not liquefied. Refreeze immediately.

YIELD: APPROXIMATELY 1 QUART OR 6 SERVINGS

A Cooling, Summery Lunch
for House Guests

CHILLED TOMATO AND
PEACH SOUP (page 288)

COLD CURRIED SHRIMP

TOASTED SYRIAN BREAD (page 312)

HONEYDEW ICE

I think of this menu as a convenient one to serve house guests because, although it is quite special, it does not require a lot of preparation. Each item on the menu is light and noncreamy—cooling food
for humid summer days. The dressing for the shrimp is essentially a
lime vinaigrette, with a subtle suggestion of curry flavoring. The
chilled tomato soup, flavored with fresh peaches, complements the
curried entrée. The Honeydew Ice is a very smooth and refreshing
concoction, its flavor heightened by the addition of melon liqueur.

Advance Preparation The Honeydew Ice may be made several
days in advance, and the Chilled Tomato and Peach Soup the day
before serving. Prepare the Cold Curried Shrimp on the day it is
served.

CHILLED TOMATO AND PEACH SOUP. Prepare half the recipe on page 288.

COLD CURRIED SHRIMP

Shrimp, avocado, cucumber, and herbs are combined in a mildly curried vinaigrette dressing. It is a light and refreshing hot-weather dish.

FOR THE DRESSING

6 tablespoons olive oil
3 tablespoons lime juice
1 tablespoon juice from a jar of Major Grey's chutney, preferably Sun Brand

⅓ teaspoon curry powder
A pinch of ground coriander
1 garlic clove, peeled and cut in half

FOR THE SALAD

1½ pounds raw, unshelled large shrimp
Salt
3 tablespoons lime juice
1 medium-small cucumber

¼ cup minced fresh chives
¾ cup chopped fresh mint leaves
1 large or 2 small avocados

Combine the ingredients for the dressing 1 hour or more before needed to allow time for the garlic to marinate.

Shell and devein the shrimp. Bring a large pot of water to a boil. Add salt and the shrimp and cook 2 minutes or just until the shrimp are pink and firm. Drain and toss immediately with the lime juice. Cool to room temperature.

Peel the cucumber, quarter lengthwise, and discard the seeds. Slice into julienne strips, about ¼ inch wide and thick and 2½ to 3 inches long. Drain off any lime juice not absorbed by the shrimp. Combine the shrimp, cucumber, chives, and mint leaves in a salad bowl, and cover and refrigerate until serving.

To serve, peel and halve the avocado. Discard the pit and slice crosswise about ¼ inch thick. Add to the salad. Discard the garlic clove and toss the dressing with the salad.

YIELD: 4 SERVINGS

HONEYDEW ICE

An interesting, delicately flavored ice. Its pale jade color is enhanced by a garnish of kiwi fruit or frosted green grapes.

1 medium-size, ripe honeydew melon (3½ pounds or more)
3 tablespoons light honey
3–4 tablespoons Midori melon liqueur

FOR THE GARNISH

Peeled and sliced kiwi fruit or frosted green grapes*

Cut the melon in half, discard the seeds, and purée enough of the fruit to make 4 cups. Stir in the honey and 3 tablespoons of the melon liqueur. Place in the freezer until firm. Break the ice into chunks and purée it, in several batches, in a food processor until smooth but not liquefied. Return each batch to the freezer as it is processed to keep it from melting. After it is puréed, taste and stir in a little more melon liqueur if desired. Then freeze until firm.

Serve the ice in glass dessert bowls, garnished with 2 or 3 kiwi slices or a small bunch of frosted grapes.

YIELD: APPROXIMATELY 1 QUART OR 6 SERVINGS

* To frost grapes, dip small clusters in lightly beaten egg white and then dredge in granulated sugar. Dry on a wire rack.

A Casual Seaside Supper

PROSCIUTTO AND HONEYDEW MELON[†]

MUSSEL AND RICE SALAD

SLICED TOMATOES WITH
FRESH BASIL[†]

BLUEBERRY SORBET

T H E entrée for this meal is a cooling salad composed of steamed mussels and rice, flavored with herbs, capers, lemon zest, and pine nuts, and marinated in a lemon vinaigrette. Beginning with an appetizer of prosciutto and melon and ending with Blueberry Sorbet, it is an uncomplicated meal, equally suitable for lunch or supper. It is the sort of casual shellfish dinner I can easily imagine eating at the beach, and it would be particularly appealing in hot and humid weather.

Advance Preparation   The Blueberry Sorbet may be made several days before serving. The Mussel and Rice Salad is best made the same day it is served. If pressed, you can make it a day ahead, but do not add the lemon zest until an hour or two before serving.

MUSSEL AND RICE SALAD

FOR THE VINAIGRETTE

6 tablespoons olive oil
3 tablespoons lemon juice
1 garlic clove, peeled and cut in half

FOR THE SALAD

4 pounds mussels
2 garlic cloves, peeled and minced
2 tablespoons minced shallot
1 ½ tablespoons minced fresh tarragon or ¾ teaspoon dried
⅓ cup dry white wine
Salt
1 cup uncooked long-grain rice

½ cup minced fresh parsley
⅓ cup chopped fresh mint leaves
¼ cup capers, well drained
¼ cup chopped scallions
¼ cup pine nuts
1 ¼ teaspoons grated lemon zest
Fresh-ground pepper
1 bunch watercress

Combine the ingredients for the vinaigrette at least 1 hour before serving.

Scrub and beard the mussels. Put the garlic, shallot, tarragon, and wine into a large, heavy pot. Add the mussels, cover tightly, and bring to a boil. Cook for 5 to 7 minutes, or until the mussels have opened wide, and the meat is firm and opaque. Discard any mussels that fail to open. Remove the rest from their shells and reserve. Strain the broth and reserve ½ cup.

Bring a large pot of water to a boil and add salt and the rice. Boil for 15 to 17 minutes, or until the rice is tender but still firm. Drain in a colander and rinse under hot tap water. Turn into a bowl, stir the reserved ½ cup mussel broth into the hot rice, and let stand until the broth is absorbed.

When the rice is cool, combine it with the mussels, parsley, mint, capers, scallions, pine nuts, lemon zest, and pepper.

Just before serving, remove the garlic clove from the vinaigrette and toss the dressing and salad together. Mix in the watercress. Serve the salad chilled or at room temperature.

YIELD: 4 SERVINGS

BLUEBERRY SORBET

A soft-textured sorbet with an intense blueberry flavor.

> *2 pints blueberries*
> *2 tablespoons lime juice*
> *¾ cup sugar*
> *I egg white*

Wash and dry the blueberries and place in a large, heavy pot with the lime juice and ½ cup of the sugar. Slowly bring to a boil and boil gently for 20 minutes, stirring often to prevent scorching. (A candy thermometer should register 220°.) Remove from the heat and purée in a food processor. Cool to room temperature.

Beat the egg white until it holds firm peaks. Continue beating as you gradually add the remaining ¼ cup sugar. Fold into the puréed blueberries. Place in the freezing compartment of your refrigerator and freeze until firm.

YIELD: APPROXIMATELY 3 CUPS OR 4 SERVINGS

A Venetian-Style Supper
for Four or Six

INSALATA CAPRESE

PAGLIA E FIENO BARBARO

ENDIVE AND WATERCRESS SALAD†

PEACHES WITH ZABAGLIONE

PAGLIA e fieno, a combination of green and white fettuccine, is a popular dish in Italy. In the recipe that follows it is combined with sautéed mushrooms, as well as bits of prosciutto, chèvre cheese, parsley, and cream. It is a filling dish and therefore the rest of the menu is light. Beginning with a tomato and mozzarella salad and ending with fresh peaches with zabaglione, it is the sort of meal one might be served in a restaurant in Venice.

Advance Preparation The Zabaglione may be made a day before serving, but do not slice the peaches until you are ready to serve them. The Insalata Caprese may be assembled a few hours before serving. The pasta itself must be cooked at the last minute, but all the other ingredients can be prepared and assembled several hours in advance.

INSALATA CAPRESE

FOR EACH SERVING

3 large slices of a peeled, ripe tomato
3 slices mozzarella cheese, preferably fresh mozzarella

Chopped, fresh basil leaves
Olive oil
Salt
Fresh-ground pepper

On each appetizer plate, alternate the slices of tomato and mozzarella. Sprinkle generously with chopped basil and drizzle with a little olive oil. Add salt and pepper just before serving.

PAGLIA E FIENO BARBARO

½ pound mushrooms, cleaned, trimmed, and sliced
3 tablespoons unsalted butter
Salt
Fresh-ground pepper
6 ounces green fettuccine
6 ounces white fettuccine
4 ounces thin-sliced prosciutto, fat trimmed, and cut into ½-inch squares

4 ounces mild, rindless chèvre, such as Montrachet, crumbled
¼ cup minced fresh parsley
Grated zest of 1 large lemon
¾ cup light cream

Sauté the mushrooms in 1 tablespoon of the butter in a large skillet over high heat for a few minutes to brown slightly. Season with salt and pepper and set aside.

Bring a large pot of water to a boil. Add salt and a little vegetable oil and the pasta. Cook until tender but still firm. Drain in a colander. Turn into a heated serving dish and toss with 2 tablespoons butter and the remaining ingredients, adding as much of the cream as needed to moisten the pasta. Serve immediately.

YIELD: 4 TO 6 SERVINGS

PEACHES WITH ZABAGLIONE

The following zabaglione has less sugar and less Marsala than traditional recipes. The result is a denser, less sweet custard that does not separate when chilled.

> *12 egg yolks*
> *½ cup sugar*
> *4–5 tablespoons Marsala*
> *2 cups sliced peaches*

In a large, heat-proof mixing bowl, beat the egg yolks with an electric mixer until light. Gradually beat in the sugar and Marsala. Set over a pan of simmering water and cook until thick, stirring constantly with a wire whisk. The sauce may be served warm or cooled to room temperature and refrigerated until serving.

Serve in wine goblets or small glass dessert bowls. Place some of the peaches in the bottom of each and top with the custard.

YIELD: 4 TO 6 SERVINGS

A Provençal Supper for Six

TOMATO AND MUSSEL SOUP

GARLIC BREAD[†]

GREEN SALAD WITH ARUGOLA[†]

MANGO-GINGER ICE OR FRESH FRUIT[†]

THE Tomato and Mussel Soup on this menu began as a quick improvisation when we entertained friends unexpectedly. I was grateful for the inspiration as it was one of those rewarding moments in the kitchen when everything turned out right. The soup is robust, although unthickened—an elaboration on the traditional moules à la marinière that includes sautéed tomatoes, basil, and Greek olives. It has the virtue of being both light and satisfying, and requires little more than garlic bread and a salad to complete the meal. To follow this spicy, aromatic soup, dessert is a cooling mango ice given character by bits of preserved ginger.

Advance Preparation   The Mango-Ginger Ice may be made several days before serving. Much of the preparation for the soup, such as scrubbing the mussels, cooking the tomatoes, chopping the basil, and grating the Parmesan, can be done early in the day, but the soup itself cannot be made ahead of time.

TOMATO AND MUSSEL SOUP

Ideal for a summer lunch or supper entrée, this soup has a Provençal character. The mussels are steamed in wine and herbs and served in their shells surrounded by a broth pungently flavored with tomatoes, garlic, basil, and Greek olives. A bowl of grated Parmesan should be served on the side, as well as a couple of large empty bowls in which to discard the mussel shells.

1 ¾ pounds fresh tomatoes
1 tablespoon olive oil
3 extra-large garlic cloves,
    peeled and minced

¼ cup minced shallot
½ teaspoon dried basil
A large pinch of dried hot
    red pepper flakes

FOR THE MUSSELS

7 pounds mussels
2 cups dry white wine
4 garlic cloves, peeled and minced
⅓ cup minced shallot
1 teaspoon dried basil

½ cup minced fresh basil
6 ounces Calamata olives, halved and pitted
1 cup fresh-grated Parmesan cheese

Dip each tomato in boiling water to facilitate peeling. Core, peel, and chop coarse. Put the olive oil in a large skillet, add the garlic and shallot, and sauté very gently for 1 minute. Be careful not to brown. Add the tomatoes, ½ teaspoon dried basil, and red pepper flakes, and sauté over moderately high heat until the tomatoes are very soft and just begin to break down. Remove from the heat and reserve.

To prepare the mussels, rinse them well, scrubbing if they are sandy, and remove the beards. Put the wine, garlic, shallot, and dried basil in a very large pot. Add the mussels, cover tightly, and cook 5 to 8 minutes, or until the shells open wide and the mussel meat is opaque. With a slotted spoon, transfer the mussels to a large bowl and keep in a warm place. Reheat the tomato mixture. Strain the mussel broth through a fine sieve into the tomatoes, simmer briefly, and add the fresh basil and olives. Ladle the soup into large soup plates and pile in the mussels, in their shells. Pass the Parmesan separately.

YIELD: 6 SERVINGS

MANGO-GINGER ICE

4 medium-size, ripe Florida mangoes
¾ cup sugar
⅔ cup water
¼ cup syrup from a jar of preserved ginger stem
¼ cup fine-diced preserved ginger stem

FOR THE GARNISH

Fresh mint

Peel the mangoes and cut the flesh off the large center pits. Purée in a food processor. You should have about 3½ cups.

Combine the sugar and water in a small saucepan. Bring to a boil and boil to the soft ball stage or 234° on a candy thermometer. Add the sugar syrup and the ginger syrup to the mango purée and place in the freezing compartment of the refrigerator until firm.

Break the ice into chunks and purée, in batches, in a food processor until smooth but not liquefied. Stir in the diced ginger and re-freeze immediately.

Garnish each serving with a sprig of fresh mint.

YIELD: APPROXIMATELY 1 QUART OR 6 SERVINGS

An Informal Patio Supper

MUSSELS RÉMOULADE

INSALATA DI PASTA VERDE

FRESH FRUIT AND CHEESE[†] OR

LEMON AND ALMOND CAKE (page 192)

THE basis for this menu is a cooling salad of green pasta mixed with tomatoes, black olives, herbs, and feta cheese. It is a simple and colorful entrée for a hot evening and can be made in minutes. Mussels Rémoulade are suggested for an appetizer, but should you want something simpler, a chilled cucumber soup or gazpacho would be appropriate. Serve fruit and cheese for dessert, or Lemon and Almond Cake, a light sponge cake with a lemon mousse filling.

Advance Preparation   The Lemon and Almond Cake may be made a day ahead. The Mussels Rémoulade and pasta salad can be prepared early on the day they are served.

MUSSELS RÉMOULADE

The mussels are steamed as for moules à la marinière and then chilled and served in their shiny blue-black shells, topped with a rémoulade sauce.

3 pounds mussels, bearded and scrubbed
½ cup dry white wine
2 garlic cloves, peeled and minced
2 tablespoons minced shallot
1 bay leaf

FOR THE RÉMOULADE SAUCE

1 egg yolk
2 teaspoons Düsseldorf or
  Dijon mustard
2 teaspoons lemon juice
½ cup light olive oil (or half
  vegetable oil and half
  olive oil)

½ cup sour cream
1 ½ tablespoons minced
  fresh parsley
1 tablespoon minced fresh
  chives or tender green
  scallion ends
1 ½ teaspoons dry vermouth

FOR THE GARNISH

Mussel half-shells
Minced parsley
Lettuce

Put the mussels in a very large, heavy pot with the wine, garlic, shallot, and bay leaf. Cover tightly and simmer for 5 to 7 minutes, or until the mussel shells are wide open and the meat is opaque and firm. Discard any mussels that fail to open. Remove the mussel meats from their shells and refrigerate. Clean and reserve a half-shell for each mussel meat.

To make the sauce, beat the egg yolk with the mustard and lemon juice, using an electric mixer or a wire whisk. Slowly add the olive oil, drop by drop. As the mixture thickens, add the oil in a very thin stream, beating continuously. Fold in the sour cream, parsley, chives, and vermouth. Chill until serving.

To serve, arrange about 8 half-shells on top of a lettuce leaf for each serving. Place the mussels in the shells, spoon a little sauce over each mussel, and sprinkle minced parsley over the sauce.

YIELD: 6 SERVINGS

INSALATA DI PASTA VERDE

A light and easy pasta salad for evenings when it's too hot to cook and almost too hot to eat.

FOR THE VINAIGRETTE

> ¾ cup olive oil
> 4½ tablespoons lemon juice
> 1 garlic clove, peeled and cut in half

FOR THE SALAD

> Vegetable oil
> Salt
> 12 ounces green fettuccine
> 6 large ripe tomatoes, peeled and chopped coarse
> 1½ cups small pitted black olives
> ¾ pound feta cheese, rinsed if salty and cut into ½-inch chunks
>
> 1½ cups chopped fresh mint or basil leaves
> ¼ cup minced fresh chives
> Salt
> Fresh-ground pepper
> 1 large bunch arugola or watercress (optional)

Combine the ingredients for the vinaigrette at least 1 hour before serving.

Bring a large pot of water to a boil. Add a little vegetable oil, salt, and the pasta. Cook until tender but not soft. Drain well. Remove the garlic clove and toss the vinaigrette with the pasta. Cool to room temperature and add the tomatoes, olives, feta cheese, mint or basil, chives, and seasoning to taste. Refrigerate. Just before serving, add the arugola or watercress, if desired.

YIELD: 6 SERVINGS

A Casual Country Dinner

SPARERIBS WITH BARBECUE SAUCE

KENTUCKY CORN PUDDING

SLICED TOMATOES WITH
FRESH BASIL[†]

U.T.'S PEACH TORTE

THIS is a good menu for entertaining informally—no-fuss, down-home cooking that simply tastes good. The entrée is spareribs cooked in a spicy, dark barbecue sauce. I know a number of people addicted to ribs, and I am in complete sympathy with their habit. Buy the small ribs, however, rather than the "country style" which, although meatier, are less tender and likely to be dry. The rest of the menu is rich in summer's bounty, depending on fresh produce that is best gathered from your own garden or a farmer's market: tomato and basil salad; Kentucky Corn Pudding; and a delicious peach torte, a gift from a Southern friend.

Advance Preparation The Barbecue Sauce for the ribs may be made a day ahead. The ribs are precooked before baking in the sauce, and this initial cooking can be done early in the day. The Kentucky Corn Pudding and the Peach Torte may be prepared several hours in advance of the actual baking.

SPARERIBS WITH BARBECUE SAUCE

These ribs are glazed with a dark, rich barbecue sauce, of the Chinese restaurant variety.

5 ¼–5 ½ pounds baby spareribs

FOR THE SAUCE

1 teaspoon cornstarch
½ cup plus 1 tablespoon
  ketchup
2 tablespoons soy sauce
1 tablespoon lime juice

3 medium garlic cloves,
  peeled and pressed
2 tablespoons hoisin sauce*
2 ½ tablespoons light
  honey

Preheat the oven to 325°. Wrap the ribs in a large sheet of heavy-duty aluminum foil, folding the edges tightly to seal. Place in a large, shallow baking pan and bake for 50 to 60 minutes.

To make the sauce, mix the cornstarch with the ketchup. Stir in all the remaining ingredients except the honey and reserve.

Remove the ribs from the oven and increase the temperature to 350°. Discard the aluminum foil and cut the ribs apart. Put them back in the roasting pan and coat them with the sauce. Bake for 15 to 25 minutes, depending on the thickness of the ribs. Carefully baste with the pan juices, drizzle the honey over the ribs, and bake for 5 minutes longer, watching so that the honey doesn't burn.
YIELD: 6 SERVINGS

* Hoisin sauce is available at oriental markets and gourmet departments of some supermarkets.

KENTUCKY CORN PUDDING

This is a glorified version of a corn pudding, with the height and airy texture of a soufflé. The recipe comes from Kentucky via our friend Bryan Leithauser.

6–8 *ears of corn (or enough*   *1 teaspoon salt*
   to make 4 cups kernels)   *1 ¾ cups heavy cream*
¼ pound unsalted butter   *1 ¾ cups milk*
¼ cup flour   *7 eggs, lightly beaten*
⅓ cup sugar

Strip the husks and silk from the corn and cut off enough kernels to make 4 cups. Melt the butter in a deep, 2-quart, flame-proof casserole. Stir in the corn. Combine the flour, sugar, and salt, and add to the corn mixture. Stir in the cream, milk, and eggs.

   Preheat the oven to 350°. Bake the pudding for 50 to 55 minutes, or until it is browned on top and a knife tests clean.

YIELD: 8 SERVINGS

U.T.'S PEACH TORTE

An improvisation, by our friend U. T. Summers, on an old Southern recipe. It consists chiefly of peaches and nuts lightly bound in a crusty batter. It is best served warm and topped with whipped cream.

FOR THE TORTE

2 eggs
1 cup plus 2 tablespoons
   sugar
¼ cup flour
2½ teaspoons baking powder
⅛ teaspoon salt

2 cups peeled and sliced
   peaches
½ cup chopped walnuts
1 teaspoon grated lemon
   zest
1 teaspoon vanilla extract

FOR THE TOPPING

1 cup heavy cream
2 teaspoons sugar
1½–2 tablespoons amaretto liqueur

Preheat the oven to 325°. Generously butter an 8-by-12-inch pan.

Beat the eggs with an electric mixer until light. Continue beating while gradually adding the sugar. Stir in the remaining ingredients for the torte. Turn into the prepared pan and bake for 30 to 35 minutes, or until the the top is brown and crusty.

To make the topping, whip the cream with the sugar and amaretto until it holds soft peaks.

Serve the cake while it is warm. Cut into large squares and top each serving with a large spoonful of whipped cream.

YIELD: 6 TO 8 SERVINGS

An Innovative Dinner for Six

TOMATO AND CHÈVRE SALAD

SAUTÉED SHRIMP AND SCALLOPS
WITH CAPPELLETTI

TOASTED FRENCH BREAD[†]

GREEN SALAD[†]

STRAWBERRY-CASSIS ICE (page 165)

IN Italy, cappelletti—little squares of pasta folded over a filling of meat, cheese, or spinach—are served like ravioli in a sauce, or in a clear chicken broth. But in this recipe, I decided to treat them as a component of a "sauté": equal parts of shrimp and scallops are sautéed and mixed with cooked cappelletti. A little cream with bits of sautéed tomatoes and a handful of fresh basil is then stirred into the mixture. It is a splendid dish and, with the proper organization, one that can be prepared without too much trouble. The cappelletti can be made in advance and stored in the freezer. The shellfish takes only a few minutes to cook, and if everything is prepared and ready, the last-minute work is chiefly a matter of assembly. It is not a recipe to prepare for more than six, however, because the shrimp and scallops cannot be cooked properly in larger quantities. Serve the entrée with nothing more than thin rounds of buttered and toasted French bread, and follow with a green salad. For the appetizer, a fresh and simple combination of sliced tomatoes and chèvre; and a cooling and colorful Strawberry-Cassis Ice for dessert.

Advance Preparation   The cappelletti may be made several days ahead and frozen until needed. The Strawberry-Cassis Ice may also be made several days before serving. The shrimp and scallops must be sautéed at the last minute.

TOMATO AND CHÈVRE SALAD

An attractive and delicious appetizer modeled on the Italian Insalata Caprese that combines mozzarella and tomatoes. Both salads are the essence of simplicity and provide light and colorful summer fare.

FOR EACH SERVING

> *1 medium-size ripe tomato*
> *1½–2 ounces French chèvre**
> *Salt*
> *1 teaspoon minced fresh chives*
> *Olive oil*

Immerse the tomato in boiling water for several seconds so that it can be peeled easily. Peel, core, and cut it crosswise into ¼-inch-thick slices. Cut an equal number of thin slices of the chèvre. Arrange alternate slices of tomato and chèvre overlapping in a crescent pattern on a serving plate. Sprinkle lightly with salt and scatter the chives on top. Drizzle a little olive oil over each serving.

---

* Use a mild, rindless chèvre, such as Montrachet. The amount of cheese needed will depend on the diameter of the log, as more slices can be cut from a long, narrow log. A 300-gram (11 ounce) log of Montrachet will serve 6 to 8 people.

SAUTÉED SHRIMP AND SCALLOPS WITH CAPPELLETTI

The shrimp and scallops are combined with spinach-filled cappelletti, bits of tomato and chopped basil, and lightly sauced with cream. It is a very appealing and novel combination. The cappelletti can be made several days ahead and frozen.

FOR THE CAPPELLETTI FILLING

Two 10-ounce packages fresh spinach
1 egg yolk
1 cup ricotta cheese
⅓ cup grated Parmesan cheese
Salt
Fresh-ground pepper

FOR THE PASTA DOUGH

1 cup all-purpose, unbleached flour
⅛ teaspoon salt
1 egg
2 teaspoons olive oil
Approximately 1½ tablespoons water

FOR THE SEAFOOD MIXTURE

2 medium tomatoes, peeled, seeded, and chopped
2½ tablespoons unsalted butter
3 tablespoons minced shallot
1 pound bay scallops
1 pound medium-large raw shrimp, shelled and deveined
¼ cup dry white wine
⅔ cup heavy cream
1 tablespoon unsalted soft butter mixed with 1 tablespoon flour
Approximately 54 cappelletti
⅔ cup chopped fresh basil

To make the filling for the cappelletti, wash the spinach, discarding the stems and any wilted leaves. Cook in a large, covered pot in the water clinging to the leaves. Drain well in a colander. When it is cool enough to handle, press out the moisture, a handful at a time. With a large kitchen knife, chop the spinach fairly fine. In a mixing bowl, combine it with the egg yolk, ricotta, Parmesan, a little salt, and pepper. Cover with plastic wrap and refrigerate until needed.

To make the pasta, combine the flour and salt in a large, broad-bottomed mixing bowl. Make a well in the center and add the egg, oil, and 1 tablespoon water. Mix with a fork, slowly incorporating the flour into the center. Add enough additional water to make a firm dough. Knead briefly. Cut the dough in half and wrap half in wax paper.

Place 2 long sheets of wax paper on the counter and dust lightly with flour. Roll half the dough at a time through a pasta machine, beginning on the first setting. Fold in half and repeat, rolling it through on setting 1 or 2, until the dough is smooth and no longer looks mottled. Tighten the rollers to the next setting and run the dough through once or twice without folding it in half. Proceed in this way to the higher settings. As the strip of dough becomes too long and unwieldy, cut it into sections about 18 inches long. Place all the strips except the one you are working with on the floured wax paper and cover with another sheet of wax paper and a damp towel to keep them from drying out. When all the dough has been rolled thin (through the highest setting), cut one strip at a time into 2-inch squares, keeping the rest covered. Place a half-teaspoonful of the spinach filling in the center of each square. Fold the square in half to form a triangle, pressing the edges together firmly to seal. (If the edges seem dry, moisten with a little water.) Fold down the middle point of the triangle and press the 2 ends together to seal. You should have a little pouch with a handle. (The Italians call them "little hats.") As each cappelletto is made, place it, uncovered, on the floured wax paper. If you are not cooking the cappelletti right away, dry for 1 hour and then place on a baking sheet in 1 layer and freeze. When they are frozen, transfer them to an airtight container and return to the freezer. You should have about 54 cappelletti. A little less won't matter, as 7 to 9 per serving is adequate.

When you are ready to proceed with the recipe, bring a very large pot of water to a boil. While the water is heating, sauté the chopped tomatoes in ½ tablespoon butter in a very large skillet.

Cook over high heat, stirring, until the moisture evaporates. Remove the tomatoes from the pan and reserve. Wipe out the skillet, and sauté the shallots in 1 tablespoon butter until soft. Reserve in the pan.

When the water boils, add salt and a little vegetable oil and the cappelletti. Stir gently a few times to dislodge any that stick to the bottom of the pot. Cook them at a simmer. Frozen cappelletti will take about 7 minutes total cooking time, 4 minutes after they have floated to the top. When they are cooked, use a slotted spoon to transfer them to a colander. (Pouring them out may break them.) Keep in a warm place while you proceed with the recipe.

Add the scallops to the skillet containing the shallots. Cook over very high heat for a couple of minutes, just until they turn opaque. Remove from the pan and keep warm. Drain off any liquid from the pan. Add the remaining tablespoon butter to the pan and sauté the shrimp over moderately high heat, sprinkling with the wine, for 2 minutes, or just until they turn pink. Remove from the pan and add to the scallops. Add the cream and sautéed tomatoes to the skillet and blend in the butter-flour mixture, stirring. Bring to a boil and cook for a minute or two until the sauce is slightly thickened. Remove the pan from the heat. Stir in the seafood, cappelletti, and basil, and serve immediately.

YIELD: 6 SERVINGS

Dinner with an Indonesian Flavor

BOMBAY ICE

JAVA BEEF STEW

ORANGE AND COCONUT RICE (page 41)

BEETS VINAIGRETTE

BLUEBERRIES AND GREEN GRAPES
IN LEMON YOGURT

WHILE beef stews, being hearty, heat-sustaining fare, properly belong to the winter kitchen, I have experimented with one that strikes me as a summer stew. It is inspired by Indonesian cuisine, combining meat, fruit and nuts, and seems an appropriate meal for hot weather. It is served with a mixture of rice, grated coconut, and orange rind. The appetizer is an unusual chutney-flavored ice.

Advance Preparation The Bombay Ice may be made several days in advance. The Java Beef Stew may be made a day or two ahead, but do not add the fruit and nuts until shortly before serving. The Beets Vinaigrette may be prepared a day ahead. Prepare the dessert on the day it is to be served.

BOMBAY ICE

This unusual ice combines fresh mangoes, ginger, and chutney. It can be served as an appetizer preceding a lamb, beef, or duck dinner, or as an accompaniment to an entrée curry.

2 medium-size, ripe Florida
    mangoes (1½ pounds)
6 tablespoons sugar
⅓ cup water
2 tablespoons syrup from a
    jar of preserved ginger
    stem

2 tablespoons juice from a
    jar of Major Grey's
    chutney, preferably Sun
    Brand
2 tablespoons fine-diced
    preserved ginger stem

FOR THE GARNISH

Fresh mint

Peel the mangoes and cut the flesh off the large center pits. Purée in a food processor. You should have about 1¾ cups.

Combine the sugar and water in a small saucepan. Bring to a boil and boil to the soft ball stage, or 234° on a candy thermometer. Add the sugar syrup, ginger syrup, and chutney juice to the mango purée and place in the freezer until firm.

Break the ice into chunks and purée it in a food processor until smooth but not liquefied. Stir in the diced ginger stem and refreeze immediately.

Garnish each serving with a sprig of fresh mint.

YIELD: APPROXIMATELY 1 PINT OR 4 SMALL SERVINGS

JAVA BEEF STEW

Orange, mango, mint, cashews, and currants contribute a slightly exotic flavor to this summer version of a beef stew.

¾ cup coarse-chopped, raw cashew nuts
1½ pounds lean, boneless beef chuck, cut into 1¼-inch cubes
Salt
Fresh-ground pepper
3 tablespoons vegetable oil
3 medium-size yellow onions, peeled and chopped
1 medium-size sweet red pepper, cored, seeded, and cut into julienne strips
2 garlic cloves, peeled and minced

1½ tablespoons flour
¾ teaspoon curry powder
1½ cups beef stock or broth
1½ cups tomato juice
¼ cup dried currants
⅓ cup minced fresh mint leaves
A small strip of orange zest
1 large or 2 small oranges, peeled, cut into sections, and seeded
1 mango, peeled, seeded, and chopped coarse

Preheat the oven to 350°. Spread the cashew nuts in a pan and toast in the oven for 5 to 7 minutes, or until very light colored. Reserve.

Season the beef with salt and pepper and brown in a large skillet in the oil. As the beef is browned, remove it from the pan and reserve. Add a little more oil to the pan if necessary and sauté the onions, pepper, and garlic until slightly softened, but do not brown. Blend in the flour and curry powder. Add the beef stock and tomato juice and bring to a simmer, stirring until slightly thickened. Return the beef to the pan and add the currants, mint leaves, and orange zest. Cover the pan tightly and simmer for 1½ hours, or until the meat is tender. Add the orange and mango and cook, covered, for an additional 5 minutes, or until the mango is tender but still firm. Discard the orange zest. Stir in the cashew nuts just before serving. Serve with Orange and Coconut Rice.

YIELD: 4 SERVINGS

ORANGE AND COCONUT RICE. Prepare half the recipe on page 41.

BEETS VINAIGRETTE

4 medium beets (1–1½ pounds trimmed)
2 tablespoons minced red onion
1 teaspoon minced fresh dill weed

FOR THE VINAIGRETTE

3 tablespoons olive oil
1 tablespoon red wine vinegar
1 garlic clove, peeled and cut in half

Combine the ingredients for the vinaigrette at least 1 hour before cooking the beets.

Trim and wash the beets. Cook in boiling, salted water until tender. Drain, immerse in cool water for a few seconds, and peel. Slice about ⅛ inch thick and toss with the vinaigrette while still warm. Discard the garlic clove, add the onion and dill, cool to room temperature, and chill until serving.

YIELD: 4 SERVINGS

BLUEBERRIES AND GREEN GRAPES IN LEMON YOGURT

A simple and light summer dessert. You may substitute crème fraîche for the yogurt if you don't care about calories.

> *8 ounces plain yogurt*
> *Grated zest of 1 large lemon*
> *1 tablespoon light honey*
> *1½ cups blueberries, washed and dried*
> *1½ cups seedless green grapes, washed and dried*

Combine all the ingredients, chill, and serve.

YIELD: 4 SERVINGS

A Simple and Elegant
Italian Dinner for Four

PROSCIUTTO AND HONEYDEW MELON†

CHICKEN MALCONTENTA

PARSLEY AND LEMON RICE (page 191)

ARUGOLA AND BIBB LETTUCE SALAD†

STRAWBERRIES IN CASSIS CREAM OR

PEACHES WITH ZABAGLIONE (page 250)

THROUGHOUT the history of modern gastronomy, dishes have been named to honor famous people, very often opera singers— Chicken Tetrazzini and Peach Melba, for example. And I would hope that the great Italian chefs have for some time been arranging the culinary immortality of Luciano Pavarotti. My own inventiveness has found a different source of inspiration. You will come across the names of some of the great villas of the Veneto throughout this book. The entrée that follows is, with all respect, named for a Palladian masterpiece, the Villa Foscari, popularly known as La Malcontenta.

The menu is one to prepare for just a few special friends because, while the entrée is quick and easy to make, it must be done at the last minute. The other items on this menu are composed of simple, fresh ingredients and require almost no preparation.

Advance Preparation   Make the Strawberries in Cassis Cream on the same day as the party. If you are serving Sliced Peaches with Zabaglione, the zabaglione may be made a day ahead, but slice the peaches just before serving.

CHICKEN MALCONTENTA

Bite-size pieces of boneless chicken are briefly sautéed with cherry tomatoes, pine nuts, and a quantity of fresh basil and parsley. While it is not a "prepare-ahead" dish, it can be made quickly and easily when entertaining a small number of guests. It is a colorful and delicious combination, intended to please everyone but the chicken.

2 whole chicken breasts,	*¼ cup pine nuts*
split, skinned, and boned	*¾ cup chopped fresh basil*
Fine, dry bread crumbs	*½ cup minced fresh parsley*
1 large garlic clove, peeled	*1 tablespoon lemon juice*
and halved	*Salt*
8 tablespoons unsalted butter	*Fresh-ground pepper*
1 pint small cherry tomatoes,	
stemmed and washed	

Rinse the chicken and dry well with paper towels. Cut it into bite-size pieces, about 1½ inches square, and sprinkle with the bread crumbs, pressing them firmly into the chicken on all sides. Put the garlic in a large skillet, add 3 tablespoons butter, and melt it slowly over low heat. Discard the garlic, add the chicken pieces, and cook over high heat, turning to brown both sides, for 3 or 4 minutes, or just until cooked through. Transfer to a heated platter and keep warm. Lower the heat under the skillet and add ½ tablespoon butter if it seems dry. Add the cherry tomatoes and pine nuts and cook for about 5 minutes, stirring occasionally, until the tomatoes are tender, but do not let their skins break. Add the tomatoes and nuts to the chicken. Wipe out the skillet with a paper towel. Cut the remaining butter into small pieces and add it to the pan with the basil, parsley, and lemon juice. Remove the pan from the heat and stir until the butter is melted and the sauce homogenized. Spoon it over the chicken and tomatoes and stir to combine. Sprinkle with salt and pepper, and serve immediately.

YIELD: 4 SERVINGS

PARSLEY AND LEMON RICE. Prepare half the recipe on page 191.

STRAWBERRIES IN CASSIS CREAM

Strawberries folded into a mixture of whipped cream, strawberry purée, and cassis.

> *3 pints strawberries*
> *4 tablespoons sugar*
> *1 cup heavy cream*
> *¼ cup cassis syrup*

Wash and hull the berries and dry on paper towels. Purée 1 pint in a food processor or blender. You should have about 1 cup purée. Turn the purée into a heavy saucepan, add 2 tablespoons sugar, and bring to a simmer. Simmer for 10 minutes, stirring frequently and skimming off the foam. You should have about ⅔ cup. Cool to room temperature and then place in the refrigerator until cold and thick.

Whip the cream with 1 tablespoon sugar and the cassis and refrigerate. Cut the remaining strawberries into halves or quarters and refrigerate.

To serve, toss the berries with the remaining tablespoon sugar. Combine the strawberry purée with the whipped cream and fold in the sliced berries. Serve in small glass dessert bowls.

YIELD: 6 SERVINGS

A Special Fish Dinner

INSALATA DI MARE OR

GNOCCHI VERDI

LAKE TROUT WITH SORREL SAUCE

FUSILLI D'ESTATE (page 286)

PEACH-MERINGUE CAKE

WHEN the weather turns warm, I start checking the fish market for lake trout. It is a fine-textured, moist, and delicately flavored fish, often called "salmon trout" because of its pink flesh. In this recipe, its flavor and color are set off to advantage by the green sorrel sauce. The accompanying side dish is composed of cold spiral pasta mixed with plenty of fresh tomatoes, mint, spinach, avocado, and black olives. This simple but colorful entrée is surrounded by a Venetian-inspired menu. The appetizer, often found on antipasto tables in Italy, is a mixture of shell fish and artichokes in a lemon vinaigrette. Or, if you perfer, serve gnocchi made from spinach and ricotta cheese. For dessert, a peach and meringue cake, an idea borrowed from Ristorante Campiello in Venice.

Advance Preparation Either appetizer may be made a day in advance; if you are making the Insalata di Mare, do not add the lemon zest until shortly before serving. The sorrel sauce may be made a day ahead. Prepare the pasta salad the day of the party, but do not add the tomatoes until an hour or two before serving. Make the Peach-Meringue Cake on the day of the party.

INSALATA DI MARE

Shrimp, clams, mussels, and artichoke hearts are combined in a lemon vinaigrette and seasoned with capers, herbs, and celery.

FOR THE VINAIGRETTE

> *1 cup olive oil*
> *6 tablespoons lemon juice*
> *2 tablespoons white wine vinegar*
> *1 small garlic clove, peeled and pressed or grated*

FOR THE SALAD

> *1 pound medium-size raw, unshelled shrimp*
> *4 dozen soft shell (littleneck) clams (5 pounds)*
> *5 pounds mussels*
> *½ cup dry white wine*
> *½ pound cooked artichoke hearts, fresh or frozen*
> *¼ cup minced fresh parsley*

> *3 tablespoons minced chives*
> *3 tablespoons well-drained capers*
> *¼ cup thin-sliced celery heart*
> *1 tablespoon fresh dill weed or ½ teaspoon dried*
> *Grated zest of 1 small lemon*

FOR THE GARNISH

> *Lemon wedges*

In a large, shallow mixing bowl, combine the ingredients for the vinaigrette and reserve.

Shell and devein the shrimp. Bring a large pot of water to a boil, add the shrimp and cook for 2 minutes, or just until they turn pink. Drain in a colander and toss in the vinaigrette while they are still warm.

Wash the clams well and put them in a large steamer basket. (Cook them in two batches, if necessary.) Pour about an inch of water into a large pot, put in the basket of clams, cover tightly, and steam for 5 to 10 minutes, or just until they open. Remove the clams from their shells and add to the bowl of shrimp.

Scrub and beard the mussels and put them in a large pot with the wine and ½ cup water. Cover tightly and cook 5 to 8 minutes, or until the shells open wide and the mussels are opaque. Remove them from their shells and combine with the clams and shrimp.

Cut the cooked artichoke hearts into ½-inch-wide wedges. Add them to the bowl of shellfish, along with the parsley, chives, capers, celery heart, dill, and lemon zest. Toss, cover with plastic wrap, and refrigerate until serving.

Serve in small glass bowls or on a lettuce leaf and garnish each serving with a lemon wedge.

YIELD: 10 APPETIZER SERVINGS

GNOCCHI VERDI

These green dumplings made with spinach and cheese can be served as an appetizer or a vegetable side dish. They can be made ahead of time and reheated before serving.

Three 10-ounce packages fresh spinach
6 tablespoons all-purpose flour
1 ½ pounds skim milk ricotta, well drained
¾ cup grated Jarlsberg cheese

6 tablespoons fresh-grated Parmesan cheese
3 eggs, lightly beaten
¾ teaspoon ground coriander
Fresh-ground pepper

FOR THE TOPPING

> *2–3 tablespoons unsalted butter, melted*
> *1 tablespoon fresh-grated Parmesan cheese*
> *3 tablespoons grated Jarlsberg cheese*

Wash the spinach, discarding the stems and any wilted leaves. Put it in a large enamel or stainless steel pot with the water clinging to the leaves. Slowly bring to a boil and simmer for several minutes, until the spinach is thoroughly cooked. Drain well in a colander, pressing out as much moisture as possible by squeezing it through your hands a little at a time. Chop the spinach fine and put it in a mixing bowl. Blend in the flour, ricotta, Jarlsberg, Parmesan, eggs, coriander, and pepper. Chill for about an hour, or until firm.

Sprinkle 2 large sheets of wax paper with flour and pour a small mound of flour into one corner for flouring your hands. Dip the palms of your hands in the flour and, with a spoon, scoop up a heaping tablespoonful of the spinach mixture. Roll very gently between your palms to form a ball 1½ to 1¾ inches in diameter. Flatten slightly, and set on the floured wax paper. Make the rest of the gnocchi in the same way, reflouring your hands before forming each one.

Butter a large, shallow Pyrex baking dish (or one that you can serve from) and set it next to the stove. Bring a very large pot of water to a boil and add 1 tablespoon salt. Lift one of the gnocchi off the wax paper with a knife and carefully lower into the boiling water. Poach until it rises to the surface (about a minute). Remove it with a slotted spoon, drain for a moment, and then set it in the buttered baking dish. Repeat with the remaining gnocchi, poaching 4 at a time after you have successfully made the first one. Set them in the baking dish in overlapping rows. (If you are preparing these ahead of time, cover the dish with plastic wrap and refrigerate.)

To serve, preheat the oven to 375°. Sprinkle the melted butter, Parmesan, and Jarlsberg over the gnocchi. Bake uncovered for 15 minutes, or just until heated through. Be careful not to overcook or the gnocchi will dry out and darken.

YIELD: 50 TO 55 GNOCCHI OR 8 SERVINGS

LAKE TROUT WITH SORREL SAUCE

Lake trout, a pink-fleshed and delicately flavored fish, is served on a pool of bright green sorrel sauce. Because the sorrel is not really cooked but puréed in a food processor and added to the sauce, it retains its fresh color.

FOR THE SAUCE

3 tablespoons unsalted butter
3 tablespoons flour
1 cup plus 2 tablespoons fish stock or bottled clam juice

2 tablespoons dry white wine
3 tablespoons heavy cream
1 ½ cups fresh young sorrel leaves, packed

FOR THE FISH

Olive oil
2 tablespoons minced shallot
4 pounds lake trout fillets

¼ cup dry white wine
Salt
Fresh-ground pepper

FOR THE GARNISH

Minced parsley

To make the sorrel sauce, melt the butter in a heavy, 1-quart saucepan. Stir in the flour and gradually blend in the fish stock and wine. Bring to a boil, stirring constantly. Add the cream and allow to cool. Wash and dry the sorrel leaves, discarding the stems and any thick ribs. Mince fine in a food processor. With the motor running, slowly add a little of the cooled sauce in a fine stream to make a purée. Blend in the remainder of the sauce and return to the saucepan. Reserve.

To cook the fish, preheat the oven to 375°. Lightly coat the bottom of a large baking dish with olive oil and sprinkle with half the shallots. Put in the fish, skin side down, and rub a little oil into the flesh of each fillet. Sprinkle with the wine, the remaining shallots, and seasoning to taste. Cover the pan tightly with aluminum foil and bake for 20 minutes, or just until the fish flakes and is cooked through.

Gently heat the sauce, stirring. Do not allow it to simmer or it will lose its fresh color. Spoon the sauce onto a heated serving platter. Lay the trout on top and sprinkle with minced parsley.

YIELD: 8 SERVINGS

PEACH-MERINGUE CAKE

This is my own version of a remarkable dessert I had at Campiello's, a splendid restaurant in Venice. The cake was composed of layers of meringue and sponge cake and filled with apricots and custard. In Italy, the apricots worked beautifully, but after experimenting with our local fruit, I found peaches more dependable in flavor and texture.

FOR THE CAKE BATTER

> *3 eggs*
> *⅓ cup sugar*
> *1 teaspoon vanilla extract*
> *½ cup plus 1 tablespoon flour*
> *4 tablespoons unsalted butter, melted*

FOR THE MERINGUE

> *4 egg whites*
> *⅛ teaspoon cream of tartar*
> *1 cup sugar*
> *1 teaspoon vanilla extract*

FOR THE FILLING

4 egg yolks	*2–3 tablespoons Marsala*
¼ cup flour	*1 teaspoon vanilla*
3 tablespoons sugar	*3 medium peaches*
1 ¼ cups milk, scalded	

Cut rounds of wax paper to fit the bottom of two 9-inch cake tins and butter and flour the paper.

To make the cake batter, in a large mixing bowl, lightly beat the eggs and sugar. Place the bowl over a pan of simmering water and stir until the eggs are quite warm. Remove the bowl from the heat and beat with an electric mixer for 7 or 8 minutes, or until the mixture has the consistency of lightly whipped cream and has tripled in volume. Beat in the vanilla. Sift the flour on top and gently fold it in with a rubber spatula. Drizzle the melted butter over the batter and fold it in gently but thoroughly. Turn the batter into the prepared cake pans and reserve.

Preheat the oven to 325°.

To make the meringue, beat the egg whites until frothy. Add the cream of tartar and continue beating until stiff but not dry. Gradually beat in the sugar, then add the vanilla. Continue beating for a few minutes until the meringue is very dry. Place the meringue on top of both pans of cake batter in large spoonfuls. Spread gently with a knife to distribute evenly over the top of each cake. Bake the cakes for 40 minutes, or until a toothpick inserted in the center of the meringues tests clean. (When baked, the meringue will rise in uneven mounds and crack slightly.) Cool the cakes in the pan on a wire rack.

To make the filling, in a small, heavy saucepan, beat together the egg yolks, flour, and sugar. Gradually add the scalded milk, whisking until smooth. Add 2 or 3 tablespoons Marsala, according to taste, and cook over medium-low heat, stirring constantly, until the custard is very thick. Stir in the vanilla, cool to room temperature, and then chill thoroughly.

(It is best to wait until a few hours before serving to assemble the cake, as the texture of the meringue is better if it has not been refrigerated. Leftovers, however, should be kept under refrigeration.)

To assemble the cake, run a knife around the edges of the cake pans. Reserve the better looking meringue layer for the top. Invert the other layer, meringue side down, onto a cake plate and peel off the wax paper. Spread the cold custard over the cake. Peel and slice the peaches and arrange them over the custard. Turn the other cake layer out of the pan gently, taking care not to break the meringue, and peel off the wax paper. Place it on top of the filling, meringue side uppermost.

YIELD: 8 SERVINGS

A Garden Buffet

MINT CANAPÉS

MELON CUBES WRAPPED IN PROSCIUTTO[†]

COUNTRY PÂTÉ

FUSILLI D'ESTATE

GORGONZOLA AND ST. ANDRE CHEESE[†]

FRENCH BREAD[†]

PEACHES, PLUMS, AND GRAPES[†]

APRICOT FLORENTINES (page 86) OR
CHOCOLATE-AMARETTI CAKE (page 198)

HERE is an easy buffet for summer entertaining. Since there are no hot dishes and no last-minute preparation, the entire meal can be laid out on the buffet table while you circulate and enjoy the party. The meal is a simple country spread, appropriate for a "cocktail buffet" or "picnic supper" invitation. The pâté is a coarse-textured variety, made without liver and substantial but not rich. This version of a pasta salad is particularly refreshing, employing quantities of fresh tomatoes and chopped mint leaves, and accented with grated lemon zest. It is, moreover, an elastic menu: quantities can be doubled or tripled to accommodate a large crowd.

Advance Preparation   The Country Pâté is best when made two or three days before serving. Both the Apricot Florentines and the Chocolate-Amaretti Cake can be made a day ahead, but the cookies should not be made if the weather is very humid. The pasta salad should be made the day of the party, with the tomatoes added an hour or two before serving. Make the Mint Canapés the same day they are served.

MINT CANAPÉS

If you have an uncontrollable mint patch in your back yard, this recipe should deplete the supply. It makes an unusual and brisk-flavored summer hors d'oeuvre.

> *⅔ cup packed mint leaves (¾ cup minced)*
> *5–6 tablespoons mayonnaise*
> *5 slices Pepperidge Farm "very-thin" white bread*

Wash and dry the mint and chop fine with a large kitchen knife. (Do not use a food processor, which is likely to purée it.) Combine with enough mayonnaise to moisten.

Cut each slice of bread into 4 circles without crusts. Spread each piece with a thin layer of mayonnaise and then with some of the mint mixture. Cover with plastic wrap and refrigerate until serving.
YIELD: 20 CANAPES

COUNTRY PÂTÉ

This is a very coarse-textured pâté, made with both cubed and ground veal and pork, and without any liver.

½ pound mushrooms
2 tablespoons unsalted butter
2 eggs
½ pound lean pork, cut into
    ¼-inch cubes*
½ pound lean veal, cut into
    ¼-inch cubes*
¼ pound Canadian bacon,
    trimmed of fat and cut
    into ¼-inch cubes
¼ pound ground veal
¼ pound ground pork
¼ pound ground pork fat
⅓ cup pistachio nuts
1 garlic clove, peeled and
    pressed
¼ teaspoon dried marjoram
¼ teaspoon dried thyme
¼ teaspoon salt
Fresh-ground pepper
⅓ cup dry white wine
2 tablespoons brandy
¾ pound thin-sliced pork
    fat for larding

Wash, trim, and chop the mushrooms fine. Sauté gently in the butter until all the moisture evaporates. Remove from the heat and reserve.

Beat the eggs lightly in a large mixing bowl. Add the reserved mushrooms and all the remaining ingredients except the larding fat. Mix with a fork or your hands until combined. Sauté a spoonful of the mixture and taste for seasoning. Add more salt, if necessary.

Preheat the oven to 375°. Line a 1½-quart terrine or loaf pan with the larding fat, reserving some for the top. Pack in the pâté and cover with the remaining fat. Cover the terrine tightly with a double thickness of aluminum foil and a lid, if available. Place it inside a large pan half-filled with hot water and bake for 1¾ to 2 hours, or until the juices are a clear yellow and a meat thermometer registers 170°. Pour the water out of the large pan, place the terrine inside it, and weight the pâté by placing large, heavy cans or filled jars directly on top of the aluminum foil. Let stand until cool. Unmold, cover with plastic wrap or foil, and refrigerate. The pâté will keep for several days, well-wrapped and in the refrigerator. Do not remove the layer of fat until serving. Serve chilled or at room temperature.

YIELD: 8 SERVINGS

* The pork and veal can be diced easily if very cold.

FUSILLI D'ESTATE

A colorful summer salad made with short spiral pasta. It is light, satisfying, and easy to make.

FOR THE VINAIGRETTE

1 cup olive oil
6 tablespoons lemon juice
1 garlic clove, peeled

FOR THE SALAD

Salt
Vegetable oil
1 pound fusilli
2 pounds tomatoes, peeled and chopped coarse
2 cups small pitted black olives

½ cup chopped fresh mint leaves
Grated zest of 3 lemons
2 large or 3 small avocados
4 cups raw spinach, packed
Salt
Fresh-ground pepper

Combine the ingredients for the vinaigrette at least 1 hour before needed to allow time for the garlic to marinate.

Bring a large pot of water to a boil; add salt, a little vegetable oil, and the pasta. Cook until tender but still slightly firm. Drain well. Remove the garlic clove and toss the vinaigrette with the warm pasta. Cool to room temperature. When cool, add the tomatoes, olives, mint leaves, lemon zest, and avocados, and toss. Refrigerate. Rinse and dry the spinach and tear any large leaves into smaller pieces. Refrigerate in a separate bowl.

Just before serving, add the spinach to the pasta salad, as well as salt and pepper to taste, and toss to combine.

YIELD: 8 SERVINGS

An Elaborate Cold Dinner for Ten

CHILLED TOMATO AND PEACH SOUP

VEAL ROULADE WITH PROSCIUTTO
AND PÂTÉ STUFFING

SALSA VERDE (page 52), MUSTARD
MAYONNAISE (page 311) OR MUSTARD

SPINACH AND AVOCADO SALAD[†]

FROZEN RASPBERRY MOUSSE WITH
NUT CRUNCH

T HE less work left to do after dinner guests arrive, the better off any hostess will be. In my earlier cookbook, I tried to demonstrate that one can entertain elaborately with a completely cold (and therefore prepare-ahead) menu. For the summer section of this book, I have included a number of cold menus, particularly for fancy dinner parties when ten or twelve guests seem enough to cope with without worrying about the food.

In the following menu, everything can be prepared a day or more before serving. The appetizer is a refreshing and rather unusual chilled soup—tomato with a suggestion of fresh peaches. The main course is a boned breast of veal, rolled with layers of prosciutto and a coarse country pâté and served with either a green parsley sauce, Mustard Mayonnaise or mustard. The dessert is a fine tribute to a favorite summer fruit and can be made several days before the party. If you prefer a simpler dessert, substitute raspberries with crème fraîche or strawberries with curaçao.

Advance Preparation   The Frozen Raspberry Mousse can be made several days before serving. The Tomato and Peach Soup, the Veal Roulade, and the Salsa Verde or Mustard Mayonnaise may be made a day in advance.

CHILLED TOMATO AND PEACH SOUP

The flavor of the peaches is too subtle to be readily identified, but it creates an interesting effect.

3 pounds ripe tomatoes, cored and chopped coarse	*2 teaspoons grated fresh gingerroot*
1 large garlic clove, peeled and cut in half	*2 cups (scant) chicken stock or broth*
1 ½ tablespoons unsalted butter	*3 large peaches*
	Salt

Sauté the tomatoes gently with the garlic and butter for a few minutes. Add the grated ginger and chicken stock, cover the pan, and simmer for 20 minutes. Strain through a food mill, pressing through as much pulp as possible.

Peel the peaches by immersing in boiling water for about 20 seconds. Discard the pits, chop coarse, and purée in a food processor. Stir into the tomato mixture. Add salt to taste and chill before serving.

YIELD: APPROXIMATELY 8 CUPS OR 10 SERVINGS

VEAL ROULADE WITH PROSCIUTTO AND
PÂTÉ STUFFING

This is an elegant dish that is at its best served cold. Each slice presents a spiral-patterned mosaic of white veal, dark red prosciutto, and herb-speckled pâté. The pâté is a coarse-textured country mixture composed of ground veal and pork generously seasoned with fresh herbs and mushroom duxelles. Serve it with a garnish of lemon wedges, aspic, and watercress, and either Salsa Verde, imported mustard, or Mustard Mayonnaise on the side.

One 2¾ pound boneless breast of veal (about 5½ pounds
   before boning)

6 ounces thin-sliced prosciutto
One 14-by-20-inch plastic Brown-in-Bag cooking bag
Mustard Mayonnaise (page 311); or Salsa Verde
   (page 52*); or imported mustard

FOR THE MARINADE

¾ cup dry white wine	*Several sprigs of parsley*
2 tablespoons brandy	*2 tablespoons fresh tarragon*
3 tablespoons olive oil	*1 tablespoon fresh rosemary*
1 garlic clove, peeled and	*or thyme*
pressed	

* Prepare double the quantity of this recipe.

FOR THE PÂTÉ

¾ pound mushrooms	*1 garlic clove, peeled and*
2 tablespoons unsalted butter	*pressed*
2 tablespoons dry white wine	*½ cup minced fresh parsley*
2 eggs	*2 tablespoons minced fresh*
¾ pound ground veal	*tarragon*
shoulder	*1 teaspoon minced fresh*
½ pound ground pork	*rosemary or thyme*
shoulder	*3 tablespoons brandy*
2 ounces ground pork fat	*2 tablespoons lemon juice*
¼ cup pine nuts	*Fresh-ground pepper*

FOR THE GARNISH

Reserved aspic
Watercress
Lemon wedges

Put the veal in a large, shallow ceramic or glass bowl with the ingredients for the marinade. Cover loosely and marinate in the refrigerator for 12 to 24 hours, turning occasionally.

To make the pâté stuffing, clean and trim the mushrooms. Chop
fairly fine and sauté gently in the butter. Sprinkle with the wine and
continue cooking until the moisture has evaporated and the mushrooms are dry but not browned. Cool. Beat the eggs lightly in a
large mixing bowl. Add the remaining ingredients for the pâté and
the cooked mushrooms, mixing well with a fork or your hands. Do
not add salt, as the prosciutto will provide all that is necessary.

To cook the veal, remove it from the marinade, reserving the
marinade, and lay flat on the counter, cut side up. Cover the surface
with the sliced prosciutto and then spread the pâté evenly over the
prosciutto. Roll up loosely from the short end and tie at 2-inch intervals with kitchen string.

Preheat the oven to 325°. Proceed according to the directions on
the cooking bag package: Put 1 tablespoon flour in the bag and shake
to coat the inside. Place the bag in a large, shallow roasting pan; put

the veal and the marinade inside the bag. Tie the bag closed. With the point of a knife, make 6 half-inch slits along the top of the bag to allow steam to escape. Place in the center of the oven, allowing plenty of room around the sides so that as the bag inflates it will not touch the oven walls. Cook for 2 hours, or until a meat thermometer registers 170°. Remove from the oven, slash the bag open along the top, and allow the meat to cool. Degrease the cooking juices and boil to reduce slightly. Strain through a sieve lined with a damp cotton towel, and pour into a large, shallow pan. Refrigerate until set.

To serve, the veal is best when chilled or at room temperature. Slice it very thin and arrange overlapping slices on a platter. Score the aspic into half-inch dice and remove from the pan with a spatula. Set the aspic in a border around the veal. Garnish the platter with a border of watercress and lemon wedges, allowing 1 lemon wedge per serving. Offer the Salsa Verde, Mustard Mayonnaise, or mustard separately.

YIELD: 10 SERVINGS

FROZEN RASPBERRY MOUSSE
WITH NUT CRUNCH

This is a splendid dessert. It takes a while to prepare, but it can be made a few days before serving.

FOR THE NUT CRUNCH

4 tablespoons unsalted butter, softened
¼ cup sugar
1 tablespoon flour
1 cup coarse-chopped walnuts

FOR THE RASPBERRY MOUSSE

3 pints fresh raspberries
1 envelope unflavored gelatin
¼ cup cold water
3 tablespoons cassis syrup
1 cup plus 3 tablespoons
  sugar

½ cup water
4 egg whites
⅛ teaspoon cream of
  tartar
¾ cup heavy cream

To make the nut crunch, preheat the oven to 325°. Cream the butter and blend in the sugar and flour. Stir in the nuts. With the back of a spoon, press the mixture into the bottom of an ungreased 9-inch round pie plate. Bake for 25 to 30 minutes, or until dry and lightly browned. Cool on a rack. Crumble coarsely, turn onto a double thickness of paper towels, and reserve.

To make the raspberry mousse, put the raspberries in a large, heavy saucepan and bring to a boil over moderate heat, stirring. Crush the berries with the back of a spoon and boil gently for about 7 minutes, stirring occasionally. Strain through a sieve into a 4-cup measure, pressing through as much pulp as possible. You should have 2 to 2¼ cups purée. Turn into a bowl.

Soften the gelatin in ¼ cup cold water and dissolve over low heat, stirring constantly. Cool to room temperature and then stir into the raspberry purée. Stir in the cassis syrup.

Combine the sugar and ½ cup water in a small, heavy saucepan and bring to a simmer. Boil gently until the syrup reaches 230° to 234° on a candy thermometer or a little of the syrup can be formed into a soft ball when dropped in a glass of ice water. While the syrup is cooking, beat the egg whites until frothy. Add the cream of tartar and beat until firm, keeping an eye on the sugar syrup. When the syrup is cooked, pour it in a thin stream over the egg whites while beating continuously with an electric mixer. After the syrup has been absorbed, continue beating for 5 minutes, until the whites are cool and stiff. Whip the cream until it holds soft peaks.

Set the bowl of raspberry purée over a large bowl filled with ice cubes and stir until the mixture begins to thicken, but do not let it set. Fold together the egg whites, whipped cream, raspberry purée, and crumbled nut crunch. Turn into a serving bowl, cover well with plastic wrap, and freeze until firm.

YIELD: 10 SERVINGS

A Terrace Picnic Supper

SUPRÊMES OF CHICKEN IN ASPIC
WITH PROSCIUTTO AND SALSA VERDE
FILLING

TOMATO AND AVOCADO SALAD

FRENCH BREAD†

WALNUT TORTE WITH PEACHES
AND CREAM

ON evenings when the weather is perfect, it is a great luxury to eat outdoors. This does not have to involve tending a hot and smoky barbecue. You can entertain friends very agreeably with a cold meal prepared in your kitchen early in the day. The menu that follows is a rather festive meal that can be served outdoors with ease—not the sort of picnic you would carry off to the woods, but suitable for terrace, garden, or porch entertaining. The chicken entrée sounds elaborate, but is really very easy to put together. Accompanied simply by sliced tomatoes and avocados, with a basket of French bread, it is a colorful and appealing supper, requiring a minimum of plates. The walnut torte is an appropriately summery dessert.

Advance Preparation   The Suprêmes of Chicken and the Walnut Torte can be made a day before serving, but do not coat the chicken with aspic until the day of the party. Do not make the Tomato and Avocado Salad or the topping for the torte until shortly before serving.

SUPRÊMES OF CHICKEN WITH PROSCIUTTO AND SALSA VERDE FILLING

For this recipe, the suprêmes are split open to make a pocket, filled with a parsley-basil sauce and a layer of prosciutto, and coated in aspic. The aspic looks very attractive and moistens the chicken, but it is not essential and may be omitted if you haven't the time to prepare it.

3 whole chicken breasts, split, skinned, and boned
3 cups chicken broth
1 recipe Salsa Verde (page 52)
¼ pound prosciutto, sliced thin

FOR THE ASPIC

Reserved chicken stock
Approximately 1 cup
  additional chicken stock
  or broth
2 egg whites, lightly beaten
2 egg shells, crushed

1–2 tablespoons dry
  vermouth
1 envelope plus 2 teaspoons
  unflavored gelatin
Salt

FOR THE GARNISH

Fresh tarragon leaves
Pitted black olives
Parsley sprigs

Pound the chicken pieces with a mallet to flatten as much as possible without tearing them. (This will give you a larger surface on which to spread the stuffing.) Put them in a large skillet with the chicken broth and poach very gently, partially covered, for about 10 minutes, or just until cooked through. Be careful not to overcook or the chicken will dry out. Transfer to a plate to cool and reserve the cooking broth.

Meanwhile, prepare the recipe for Salsa Verde and chill thoroughly in the refrigerator to firm.

When the chicken has cooled, carefully slice each suprême across horizontally, leaving one long side hinged. Open each piece, cut side up, as you would a book. Trim any fat off the prosciutto and neatly cut pieces to fit over the inside of each flap. Use up all the prosciutto, dividing it evenly among the suprêmes. Spread about 1 tablespoon of the chilled Salsa Verde over the prosciutto on the bottom half of each suprême and press closed. Arrange them in pairs in a chevron pattern down the length of an oval platter. Garnish each with a couple of tarragon leaves and a piece of black olive cut to look like a truffle.

To prepare the aspic, degrease and measure the reserved poaching liquid. Add enough additional broth to equal 4 cups. Put in a large, wide saucepan with the beaten egg whites and crushed shells. Slowly bring to a simmer, stirring continuously with a wire whisk. Stop stirring and remove from the heat as soon as the mixture boils and the whites congeal on the surface. Carefully skim off the solidified whites with a perforated spatula or spoon. Line a large strainer with a dampened cotton or linen dish towel and place it over a deep bowl. Strain the broth through the wet towel. Add the dry vermouth, and salt to taste and measure the clarified stock. You should have about 3¾ cups. Chill ½ cup of the stock. Soften the gelatin in the chilled stock and dissolve over low heat, stirring constantly. Stir into the remaining stock. Pour a layer of aspic, ¼ to ½ inch deep, in a 7-by-12-inch pan and refrigerate to set. Stir the remaining aspic over a bowl filled with ice cubes until it is thick and on the verge of setting. Carefully spoon over the chicken breasts, coating each one completely. Refrigerate until set. When the pan of aspic is quite firm, score it into ½-inch dice. Lift out the cubes with a spatula and arrange in a border around the chicken. Garnish the edges of the platter with a few small parsley sprigs. Return to the refrigerator until serving.

YIELD: 6 SERVINGS

TOMATO AND AVOCADO SALAD

FOR THE VINAIGRETTE

¼ cup olive oil
1 tablespoon white wine vinegar
1 garlic clove, peeled and halved

3 medium-large tomatoes
1 large or 2 small avocados
¼ cup chopped fresh basil
Salt
Fresh-ground pepper

Combine the ingredients for the vinaigrette and allow the garlic to marinate for 1 hour or longer.

The salad can be prepared a few hours before serving. Immerse the tomatoes in boiling water for a few seconds so that they can be peeled easily. Core, peel, and slice. Peel and slice the avocados and arrange on a serving plate with alternate slices of tomato. Sprinkle with salt and pepper. Discard the garlic clove, whisk the dressing, and pour it over the salad. Cover with plastic wrap and refrigerate until serving.

YIELD: 6 SERVINGS

WALNUT TORTE WITH PEACHES AND CREAM

1 cup walnuts
½ cup fine, dry bread crumbs
4 egg whites
¾ cup sugar

1 teaspoon vanilla extract
2 tablespoons unsalted butter,
*   melted and cooled*

FOR THE TOPPING

1 cup heavy cream
1 tablespoon cream sherry
1 teaspoon sugar
2–3 peaches, peeled and sliced

Lightly butter an 8- or 9-inch pie plate. Preheat the oven to 350°.

Grind the walnuts to a powder in a food processor. Turn into a bowl and stir in the bread crumbs.

Beat the egg whites until they hold soft peaks. Continue beating while gradually adding the sugar. Fold in the vanilla and the nutcracker mixture. Quickly fold in the melted butter, being careful not to deflate the egg whites. Turn into the pie plate and bake for 20 to 30 minutes, or until the torte is lightly browned and a toothpick tests clean. Cool in the pan on a wire rack.

Shortly before serving, whip the cream with the sherry and sugar. Spread over the torte and arrange the peaches on top of the cream. Refrigerate until serving and serve the cake from the pie plate.

YIELD: 6 SERVINGS

An Elegant Salmon Dinner for Twelve

TOMATO-MINT SOUP

COLD SALMON WITH SCALLOP
MOUSSE STUFFING

GREEN MAYONNAISE

RICE SALAD

LEMON ICE CREAM WITH
STRAWBERRIES

A whole salmon glistening under a clear citrine aspic is a cooling and glamorous summer entrée. There is no doubt that the preparation takes time, but I always enlist my husband's aid when an aspic is involved. He stirs and strains and clarifies the broth with exemplary patience and then turns his considerable artistic talents to decorating and garnishing the fish. It always looks spectacular. In this recipe, the salmon is stuffed with a fish mousse and served with Green Mayonnaise flavored with mint and other herbs. Both mint and citrus are underlying themes throughout the meal, which begins with Tomato-Mint Soup. An herbed rice tossed in lemon vinaigrette accompanies the salmon, and dessert is a tart lemon ice cream liberally garnished with strawberries.

While it is an elaborate menu, there is nothing on it, except the Rice Salad and the strawberries, that cannot be prepared at least a day before serving.

Advance Preparation   The Lemon Ice Cream may be made several days before serving. The Tomato-Mint Soup, the Salmon, and the Green Mayonnaise may be made a day ahead, but do not coat the salmon with aspic until the day of the party. Make the Rice Salad on the same day it is served.

TOMATO-MINT SOUP

A chilled, light soup to make when vine-ripened tomatoes are at their peak.

4½ pounds tomatoes,
washed, cored, and
chopped coarse
2 teaspoons minced garlic
1½ tablespoons unsalted
butter

1 bay leaf
4 whole peppercorns
2⅔ cups chicken stock or
broth
6 tablespoons fine-minced
fresh mint leaves

In a large skillet, gently sauté the tomatoes and garlic in the butter for a few minutes. Add the bay leaf, peppercorns, and chicken stock. Cover tightly and simmer for about 30 minutes. Strain through a food mill, pressing through as much pulp as possible. Cool to room temperature. Stir in the mint leaves and chill until serving.

YIELD: 9 CUPS OR 10 TO 12 SERVINGS

COLD SALMON WITH SCALLOP MOUSSE STUFFING

The salmon is cooked with a creamy fish stuffing and then chilled and glazed with aspic. If you haven't time for the aspic coating, serve the fish as it is, garnished with chives, lemon wedges, and watercress. Either way, it should be accompanied by Green Mayonnaise.

FOR THE SCALLOP MOUSSE FILLING

½ pound bay scallops*
10 ounces fillet of sole
1 egg
½ cup plus 1 tablespoon
  heavy cream

1 ½ tablespoons minced
  fresh tarragon
1 tablespoon minced fresh
  chives

FOR THE SALMON

One 5-pound center cut of salmon, boned and butterflied
Salt
½ a lemon
½ cup dry white wine
¼ cup water

FOR THE ASPIC

6 cups fish stock, including reserved cooking liquid
3 egg whites
3 egg shells, crushed
2 tablespoons dry vermouth, or to taste
2–3 envelopes unflavored gelatin

* Do not substitute sea scallops or scallop pieces. They contain more moisture, and the mousse will be too thin.

FOR THE GARNISH

Lemon slices
Chives
Hard-boiled egg whites
Black olives
Diced aspic

Green Mayonnaise (recipe follows)

To make the scallop mousse filling, rinse the scallops and sole and dry well with paper towels. Cut the sole into small pieces. Purée them with the scallops in a food processor. Add the egg, cream, and herbs, and blend. Refrigerate for about a half hour to firm.

To cook the fish, preheat the oven to 375°. Rinse and dry the salmon, sprinkle lightly with salt, and rub the cavity with the lemon. Oil a large baking dish and lay 5 or 6 lengths of string across the bottom at 2-inch intervals. Place the salmon in the baking dish on top of the string and fill it with the chilled stuffing. Pull up the strings and tie closed, not too tightly or the stuffing will be pressed out. Pour the wine and water into the pan and cover tightly with aluminum foil. Bake in the center of the oven for 55 minutes, or just until the fish is cooked through at the thickest part of the back.

To make the aspic, strain the cooking liquid from the fish into a measuring cup. Add enough fish stock to equal 6 cups. Put the stock into a large saucepan. Lightly beat the egg whites and add, with the crushed egg shells, to the pan. Slowly bring to a simmer, stirring continuously with a wire whisk. As soon as the mixture boils and the egg whites congeal on the surface, remove from the heat. Carefully skim off the egg whites with a perforated spoon or spatula. Line a large strainer with a dampened cotton or linen dish towel. Place over a deep bowl and strain the stock through the wet towel. To the clarified stock, add 2 tablespoons dry vermouth, or to taste. Measure the stock. You should have about 5 cups. Chill 1 cup of the stock to soften the gelatin. Sprinkle 2 packets plus 1 teaspoon gelatin over the chilled stock (or about 1 packet gelatin for every pint of liquid). Dissolve over low heat, stirring constantly. Stir the dissolved gelatin into the rest of the fish stock. Pour a layer of aspic, ¼ to ½ inch deep, in a 7-by-12 pan and refrigerate for the diced aspic garnish. Pour a thin layer of liquid aspic into the bottom of a large serving platter and refrigerate until firm. Skin the fish, remove the strings, and lay it on top of the layer of aspic. Garnish the fish with lemon slices and chives and, if you like, egg white flowers with centers of black olive slices.

Stir the remaining liquid aspic over a bowl filled with ice cubes until it becomes thick and syrupy. Carefully spoon the aspic over the fish, coating it completely. Refrigerate. When the pan of aspic is firmly set, score it into ½-inch dice and arrange in a decorative border around the edges of the fish platter. Return to the refrigerator until serving.

Serve the fish with Green Mayonnaise on the side.

YIELD: 12 SERVINGS

GREEN MAYONNAISE

3 tablespoons fresh mint
   leaves
1½ tablespoons fresh
   tarragon
1½ tablespoons fresh parsley
1½ tablespoons chopped
   fresh chives
2 egg yolks

1 tablespoon plus 2
   teaspoons lemon juice
1 tablespoon Dijon
   mustard
¾ cup light olive oil
¾ cup vegetable oil
Salt

Mince the herbs in a food processor or blender. Add the egg yolks, lemon juice, and mustard to the work bowl. Combine the olive oil and vegetable oil in a 2-cup Pyrex measure. With the motor running, add the oil drop by drop and then, as the mayonnaise thickens, in a thin stream. Add salt to taste.

YIELD: ABOUT 1½ CUPS

RICE SALAD

A refreshing and appealing side dish for hot weather. The rice is combined with lemon zest, mint, and other herbs and tossed in a lemon vinaigrette.

FOR THE VINAIGRETTE

> *6 tablespoons olive oil*
> *4½ tablespoons lemon juice*
> *1 garlic clove, peeled and cut in half*

FOR THE SALAD

> *2⅔ cups uncooked rice*
> *Grated zest of 1½ large lemons*
> *¾ cup minced fresh parsley*
> *½ cup chopped fresh mint leaves*
> *¼ cup minced fresh chives*

FOR THE GARNISH

> *Watercress*

Combine the ingredients for the vinaigrette at least 1 hour before preparing the salad.

Bring a large pot of water to a boil. Add salt and the rice and boil rapidly for 15 to 17 minutes, or until the rice is tender but still firm. Drain well and rinse under hot water. Discard the garlic clove and toss the vinaigrette with the rice while it is still warm. Cool to room temperature and add the remaining ingredients. Serve chilled or at room temperature, garnished with watercress.

YIELD: 12 SERVINGS

LEMON ICE CREAM WITH STRAWBERRIES

Lemon Ice Cream is a tart and refreshing conclusion to any meal. In the winter, serve it with Gingerbread (page 83) instead of the strawberries. This recipe does not require an ice cream machine.

FOR THE ICE CREAM

*1 envelope plus 1 teaspoon
  unflavored gelatin
⅓ cup cold water
¾ cup plus 3 tablespoons
  strained, fresh lemon juice*

*Grated zest of 1 lemon
3 cups heavy cream
¾ cup milk
1½ cups sugar*

FOR THE GARNISH

*3 pints strawberries
1½ tablespoons sugar*

Soften the gelatin in the cold water and dissolve over low heat, stirring constantly. Remove from the heat and cool slightly.

With an electric mixer beat together the lemon juice and zest, the cream, milk, and sugar. Continue beating until the sugar is dissolved. Gradually add the gelatin in a thin stream, while beating. Cover the bowl with plastic wrap and freeze until firm.

Rinse and dry the strawberries. Hull and slice them into halves or quarters. Toss in a bowl with 1½ tablespoons sugar about 2 hours before serving.

Serve the ice cream in glass dessert bowls or goblets and spoon a generous amount of berries over each serving.

YIELD: 9 CUPS ICE CREAM OR 12 SERVINGS WITH THE STRAWBERRIES

A FEW BASIC
RECIPES

BEEF STOCK

---

2 beef shanks or soup bones
   (about 3 pounds)
3 large celery stalks, chopped
Several celery leaves
2 large carrots, scraped and
   chopped
2 medium-size yellow onions,
   peeled and quartered

1 cup mushrooms or stems,
   if available
Several sprigs of parsley
8 peppercorns
1 bay leaf
1 teaspoon salt
Approximately 4 quarts
   water

Place the beef, vegetables, and seasonings in a large pot, cover with water, bring to a boil, and remove the scum. Simmer, partially covered, for 3 to 4 hours, or until the broth has a good, strong flavor. Strain, pressing down on the solids to extract the juices, and cool to room temperature before refrigerating. Use within 3 or 4 days, or freeze for longer storage. Remove the layer of fat just before using.
YIELD: APPROXIMATELY 2 QUARTS

CHICKEN STOCK

One 3-to-4-pound chicken,
   including neck and giblets
2 large carrots, scraped and
   chopped
2 large celery stalks, chopped
Several celery leaves
2 medium-size yellow onions,
   peeled and quartered

Several sprigs of parsley
1 bay leaf
8 peppercorns
1 teaspoon salt
Approximately 4 quarts
   water

Wash the chicken and put it in a large pot with the vegetables, herbs, and seasonings and add water to cover. Bring to a boil and remove any scum. Simmer gently, partially covered, for 3 to 4 hours, or until the broth has a good, strong flavor and the chicken meat falls from the bones. Strain, pressing down on the solids to extract their juices. Cool to room temperature and refrigerate. Use within 3 or 4 days, or freeze for longer storage. Remove the layer of fat just before using.

YIELD: APPROXIMATELY 2 QUARTS

FISH STOCK

4 pounds fish heads and bones, well washed
1 large yellow onion, peeled and quartered
1 large carrot, scraped and chopped
1 large celery stalk, chopped
A few celery leaves
Several sprigs of fresh parsley

Several fresh tarragon leaves or ½ teaspoon dried
1 bay leaf
6 peppercorns
1 teaspoon salt
6 cups water
1 cup dry white wine

Place all the ingredients in a large pot. Bring to a boil and remove any scum. Simmer, partially covered, for 45 minutes to 1 hour. Strain, cool to room temperature, and refrigerate. Use within 3 days or freeze for longer storage.

YIELD: APPROXIMATELY 6 CUPS

MAYONNAISE

1 extra-large egg yolk
1 tablespoon plus ½ teaspoon lemon juice
1 ¾ teaspoons Dijon mustard

½ cup light olive oil
½ cup vegetable oil
Salt

Beat the egg yolk, lemon juice, and mustard together in a small mixing bowl. Combine the olive oil and vegetable oil in a 2-cup Pyrex measure. Beat the egg yolk continuously with a wire whisk while adding the oil drop by drop. After the mayonnaise becomes thick, the oil may be added in a thin stream. (Should the mayonnaise separate, begin again with another egg yolk and whisk in the curdled sauce drop by drop; then add any remaining oil.) Add salt to taste.
YIELD: ABOUT 1 CUP

MUSTARD MAYONNAISE

Prepare the recipe above for Mayonnaise, adding 3 additional tablespoons Dijon mustard and 1 teaspoon minced fresh tarragon or ¼ teaspoon dried.
YIELD: ABOUT 1¼ CUPS

PRALINE

This is a hard, clear brittle that is crushed or chopped and used to add flavor and texture to many desserts.

⅓ *cup hot water*
1 *tablespoon light honey*
1 *cup sugar*
½ *cup blanched, slivered almonds, lightly toasted, or ½*
   cup blanched, chopped hazelnuts

In a heavy saucepan, pour hot water over the honey and sugar and stir, off the heat, until dissolved. Place over heat and gradually bring to a boil. Let the mixture boil until it reaches the "hard crack" stage—300° to 305° on a candy thermometer—and is a light caramel color. Stir in the chopped nuts and pour the mixture onto a well-oiled marble slab or baking sheet. When cold, remove from the sheet and break into coarse pieces with a hammer. The praline will keep indefinitely in a closed jar.

YIELD: 1½ CUPS CHOPPED PRALINE

TOASTED SYRIAN BREAD

Known variously as "Sahara Bread," "Sandwich Pockets," and "Pita Bread," these round, flat loaves are best when buttered and toasted under the broiler. They can be served as an hors d'oeuvre, or with the meal as a crisp and light alternative to French bread. Avoid doughy varieties of this bread; the thin loaves are best.

To serve, preheat the broiler. Split the loaves in half by cutting around the edges with the point of a knife. Spread the cut side of each round with softened, unsalted butter and, if desired, sprinkle with sesame seeds. Place on a baking sheet and broil very briefly, just until they begin to brown. Watch carefully so that they don't burn.

Index

For many years Helen Hecht lived in New York City, where she pursued a career in book publishing. She now resides in Rochester, New York, and Washington, D.C., where her husband, Anthony Hecht, is Consultant in Poetry to the Library of Congress and their son, Evan, is in the sixth grade. Mrs. Hecht is also the author of Cold Cuisine: Summer Food to Prepare in Advance and Serve at Leisure *and co-author of* Gifts in Good Taste. *Her food articles have appeared in* Vogue *and* Cuisine *magazines.*